GANDHI AND TRUTH

AN APPROACH TO THE THEOLOGY OF RELIGIONS

GANDHI AND TRUTH

AN APPROACH TO THE THEOLOGY OF RELIGIONS

JOY KACHAPPILLY

AKANSHA PUBLISHING HOUSE
NEW DELHI
2005

AKANSHA PUBLISHING HOUSE
R 37-B, Vani Vihar, Uttam Nagar
New Delhi-110059
Email: ektabooks@yahoo.com
Ph. : 23263193 / 9811582579

Showroom
4649/21B, Ansari Road
Darya Ganj
New Delhi - 110 002

Gandhi and Truth: An Approach to the Theology of Religions

First Edition 2005
ISBN 81-87606-97-5

[The responsibility for the facts stated, conclusions reached etc. is entirely that of the Authors. The publisher is not responsible for them, whatsoever.]

PRINTED IN INDIA

Published by M.P. Misra for Akansha Publishing House, New Delhi and Printed at Tarun Offset Press, Delhi.

To

My

BELOVED PARENTS

who inculcated in me

a genuine love for Religion

PREFACE

The whole process of completing this book has been an enriching one. I turn to the Almighty in humble obeisance for the 'showers of blessings' I received during the course of writing it. the writing of this book has not only enabled me to revise my own understanding of religion but has also helped me to appreciate better other religious traditions. It also facilitated me to understand Mahatma Gandhi not merely as a political leader who helped India to win her independence through the principles of truth and non-violence, but more importantly as a person who contributed immensely towards inter-religious harmony. He achieved this both by his life and works. This book attempts to unravel a theology of religions that his writing implicitly contain. Today, more than ever before, we need to inculcate dialogue and fellowship among the followers of different religious traditions. Gandhi becomes a role model in this noble enterprise and everyone must become sincere worshippers of truth.

The present book is an adapted version of the doctoral thesis I submitted to the Madurai Kamaraj University, Madurai, Tamil Nadu in July 2003. It is revised for the sake of publication with the aim of making the book more-or-less reader-friendly. The original dissertation was titled: "Gandhian Concept of Truth: Epistemological and Ontological Basis for a Theology of Religions." My revision has been related more with form than content. I must remind the readers that the meanings of all the non-English words used in this book are given in the glossary. The Sanskrit terms are transliterated into the Roman script with using any symbols and are italicised. However, those Sanskrit terms that occur in the quotations follow the original text.

Many people have contributed generously towards the writing of this book. Dr. A. Pushparajan, Prof. & Head, Department of Interreligious Relations, Madurai Kamaraj University, has played a vital role in making this work see the light of day. He graciously accepted to supervise my research project, helped me to enroll for the Ph.D. Programme in the university, suggested to me various themes on which I could research, put his entire personal library and other facilities at my deposal, made necessary corrections and suggestions during the course of the research, and above all, he took keen interest together with his entire family members in making this study an enriching experience of learning.

I sincerely thank Prof. S. Vincent for patiently going through the entire book, making necessary corrections and suggesting improvements. I thank Dr. John Chelladurai, who was a guest lecturer till recently in the department of inter-religious Relations, for his generous help. I also thank Dr. S. Jeyapragasam, Prof. & Head, Department of Gandhian Studies and Ramalinga Philosophy, Dr. S. Andiappan, Reader, Department of Gandhian Studies and Ramalinga philosophy, and others in the department of their permission to make use of the department library and for their timely advice in enriching this dissertation. I thank Rev. Fr. (Dr.) Joseph Puthenpurackal, Sdb and Fr. George Plathottam, Sdb for helping me to get this dissertation published. I also thank Fr. Alex Mathew and Dr. Siby K. George for their generous services in getting the original dissertation revised for publication.

My sincere thanks goes to Rev. Fr. Dominic Jala, Sdb, my former Provincial Superior, Salesian Province of Guwahati, Assam (now Most Rev. Dominic Jala, Archbishop of Shillong, Meghalaya) for granting me the necessary permission to undertake this study. I am also indebted to him for writing the Foreword for the book. I thank Rev. Fr. Philip Barjo, sdb, the present Provincial superior for his sustained interest and encouragement. I place on record my gratitude to Rev. Fr. V.A. Cyriac, sdb, Principal, Don Bosco College, Tura and the College community for releasing me from the college for the past three years to undertake this study. I am also grateful to Rev. Fr. James Theophillus, sdb, Provincial Superior, Salesian Province of Tiruchy and the staff and students of Don Bosco ITI, Madurai for giving me a place to stay for the past three years in Madurai and for providing me woth whatever I needed during the period of this research. I thank especially Fr. Josephraj Sandanacruz, Fr. Xavier Rodriguez, Fr. Bhakiaraj Lourdu, Fr. Casimir Raj, Fr. Pappuraj, Br. Sagayaraj Madalaimuthu, Br. Daniel Pushparayar, Br. Jude Muthuselvan, Br. Anthony Chinnapparaj and Br.

Stephen Kulandaisamy for going out of their way in making my stay at madurai an inspiring experience. I gratefully remember the parish community of Lourdes Shrine, K. Pudur, Madurai, for their support and encouragement.

I thank the staff and students of Sacred of Sacred Heart Theological college, Shillong, Meghalaya, and Salesian College of Higher Education, Dimapur, Nagaland, for permitting me to make use of the library facilities of these institutions. Many of my friends have helped me by way of procuring source materials and reading through the book and making valuable suggestions. I thank in particular Sr. Rosina Susngi, Dr. (Fr.) Jose Kuruvachira, Dr. (Fr.) Edmund Gomes, Dr. (Fr.) C.J. Jose, Dr. (Fr.) M.C. Tomas, Fr. C. Kuriala, Fr. V.M. Thomas, Fr. P.D. Johnny, Fr. Johnson, Br. Abraham Vazhamplackal, Fr. V.P. Anthony, Fr. Biju Michael, Fr. Siby John, Fr. Francis Hembrom, Fr. Joby Manjakattil, Sr. Lucy Marak, Br. Binoy K., Br. Essaya Britto, Br. Jerish Abraham and Br. Linto for all their help and support.

Finally, the present book is a modest effort at understanding the thorny issues that surface in the context of religious plurality. It is an approach to the theology of religions. It is possible that one may differ and even raise objections to the idea of explaining the theology of religions in the terms of truth. The book is not in any way intended to demean the religious sensibilities of anyone. However, if it has been able to put forward some fresh perceptions in establishing a reasonably feasible relationship among the various religious traditions, then the writer assumes his efforts not to have been in vain. If this study in any way contributes to the existing pool of inter-religious dialogue and communal harmony, which is so vital in today's Indian context, then the present writer considers his attempt rewarding.

JOY KACHAPPILLY

Contents

	Preface	vii
	Abbreviations	xiii
	Glossary	xv
	Introduction	**1-38**
	Context of the Problem	1
	Religious Plurality and Emergence of Theology of Religions	2
	Theology and its Diverse Methods	6
	Statement of the Problem	13
	A Possible Solution to The Problem	20
	Methodology Adopted in Arriving at the Solution	24
	Limitations of the Study	28
1.	**The Theology of Religions: A Critical Overview**	**39-86**
	Religion, Paradigm and Model	40
	Exclusivism	41
	Inclusivism	46
	Pluralism	50
	Rise of Other Paradigms	70
	Beyond the Present Paradigms	75
	Conclusion	76
2.	**'Satya' – The Truth Of Gandhi's Conception**	**87-162**
	Influences	87
	What is Truth?	92

	Effects of Truth on Gandhi	107
	Non-Violence as Means to Realize Truth	112
	Satyagraha	120
	Truth Applied to Fields of Action	136
	Conclusion	146
3.	**'Satyo-Centrism': A Framework for the Theology of Religions**	**163-216**
	Religious Plurality: A Gandhian Perspective	164
	Towards a 'Satyo-Centred' Theology of Religions	173
	Conclusion	205
4.	**Concluding Remarks**	**217-227**
	Selected Bibliography	228
	Index	241

ABBREVIATIONS

1 Cor	The First Letter of St. Paul to the Corinthians
1 Tim	The First Letter of St. Paul to Timothy
2 Cor	The Second Letter of St. Paul to the Corinthians
Acts	The Acts of the Apostles
Br. Up.	The Brhadaranyaka Upanishad
Cf.	Confer
Ch. Up.	The Chandogya Upanishad
Eph	The Letter of St. Paul to the Ephesians
Ex.	The book of Exodus
Gita	Bhagavat Gita
GS	*Gaudium et Spes*, Pastoral Constitution on the Church in the Modern World (one of the Vatican II documents)
Heb	The Letter to the Hebrews
Jn	The Gospel according to St. John
Mk	The Gospel according to St. Mark
nn.	Numbers
Para.	Paragraph
RH	*Redemptor Hominis*, the first encyclical Letter of Pope John Paul II.
RM	*Redemptoris Missio*, Pope John Paul II's Letter on the Missionary Mandate of the Catholic Church.
Rom	The Letter of St. Paul to the Romans
RSV	Revised Standard Version
WCC	World Council of Churches

GLOSSARY

A se	To oneself
Advaita	Non-dual, literally; one of the Vedantic schools which upholds the monistic unity (non-dualism) of reality. Sankara is its chief proponent.
Ahimsa	Non-violence/non-killing, one of the five great vows of Jainism which Gandhi took as the means to attain truth
Ahura-Mazda	Same as Ormazd; the Supreme Deity and creator of the world in the Zoroastrian or ancient Persian religion
Allah	Muslim name for the One God
Allah-o-Akbar	God is Great
An Sich	In itself
Ananda	Bliss; one of the three transcendental attributes of the Ultimate
Anekantavada	Jaina metaphysical doctrine that reality has innumerable characteristics/sides
Apara vidya	Lower Knowledge
Aparigraha	Non-possession; one of the great five vows of Jainism, which Gandhi included in his list of eleven vows.
Asat	Unreal
Asteya	Non-Stealing; one of the great five vows of Jainism, which Gandhi included in his list of eleven vows.
Assumptio carnis	Taking of the flesh

Ashram	A residential work centre, founded by Gandhi, for those who were totally committed to the principles of non-violence as a creed and who have dedicated themselves for an integrated life of a *satyagrahi.*
Ashraya	Subject
Aut-aut	Either-or
Brahma satyam jagan mithya	Brahman alone is real and the world is illusory.
Brahmacharya	Chastity and abstention from self-indulgence of any kind; one of the great five vows of Jainism, which Gandhi included in his list of eleven vows
Charkha	Spinning wheel
Chaturma	A period of four months, literally; A vow of fasting or semi-fasting undertaken by the Hindus during the four months of the rains.
Chit	Consciousness; one of the three transcendental attributes of the Ultimate.
Deva	God
Devadhideva	God of gods
Devata	Goddess
Dharma	That which holds, literally; the Sanskrit root for religion. It is also one of the four Purusharthas (values) which Hinduism cherishes. The other three are artha, kama and moksha.
Dharmakaya	One of the triple bodies – trikaya - of Buddha; a concept developed by the Mahayana school of Buddhism which means a cosmic body, the ineffable absolute itself.
Dvaita	Dual, literally; one of the Vedantic schools which upholds multiple nature of Reality. Madhava is its chief propounder.
Ens ut Sic	Being as Such
Episteme	Knowledge
Esprit de corps	The feelings such as pride and loyalty shared by

	members of a group of people.
Et-et	And-and
Extra ecclesiam nulla salus	Outside the Church there is no Salvation. The maxim of the exclusivism as propounded by early Catholic theologians.
Ganesh	The elephant headed God in the Hindu pantheon, the son of Siva and Parvati, is the Lord of obstacles and is worshipped 'first among all.'
Gnosis	Knowledge
Hari	One of the Hindu names of God
Harijan	Children of God – a name coined by Narasimha Mehta for the untouchables and propagated by Gandhi
Himsa	Violence/killing
Ishvara	Lord
Karim	Al-Karim, one of the Quaranic names for Allah, the Muslim God, that focuses His generous nature
Karmayogin	One who practices karmayoga (way to liberation through the means of action)
Kerygma	Good news
Kevala	Final cognition of past, present and future or stage of omniscience.
Khadi	Cotton cloth that is woven by hand especially as recommended for use by Gandhi.
Konfesionskunde	Public confession
Krishna	The most celebrated deity of Mahabharata is said to be the eighth incarnation of Visnu.
Logos spermatikos	The germinative word; introduced by St. Justin in Christian theology. The germinative seeds of the Word, Jesus Christ (for Christians) are seen in the holiness and commitment of people's lives.
Maya	Illusion
Mission dei	Mission of God
Moksha	Salvation; liberation from the cycle of birth and death

Mukti	Liberated State
Nai Talim	Basic Education
Nam rupa	Name and form
Neti-neti	Not this, not this
Nirguna Brahman	Non-qualified Brahman
Nirmanakaya	One of the triple bodies – trikaya - of Buddha; a concept developed by the Mahayana school of Buddhism to denote which means the body that appears in living form to save people from suffering
Nirvana	Utter extinction of egoism; a state of perfect happiness and freedom in which the individual becomes absorbed into the Supreme Being
Niskamakarma	Disinterested action, literally; the Gita teaching that action should be performed without desiring for fruits
Ora et labora	Prayer and work
Organon	An instrument of acquiring knowledge; it is the earlier part of Aristotle's work on Logic. Influence of Plato is most marked in this part.
Para vidya	Higher Knowledge
Paramarthika satta	The highest reality or Brahman
Pneuma	Spirit
Pradosha	The fast undertaken by Hindus on third day of every *shukl* (moonlit fortnight) and *Krishna* (dark fortnight) starting with the beginning of night to worship God Shiva.
Pratityasamutpada	Dependent Origination; the pivotal Buddhist theory that everything depends on preceding cause - "from this that arises; from the ceasing of this that ceases."
Puja	A ceremony of worship among the Hindus
Purushartha	Values of humans, literally; the Indian axiological theory that stipulates four values for humans,

	namely, artha (material value), kama (psychological value), dharma (moral value) and moksa (spiritual value).
Rahim	Al-Rahim, one of the Quaranic names for Allah, the Muslim God, that focuses His compassionate nature
Rahman	Al-Rahman, one of the Quaranic names for Allah, the Muslim God, that focuses on the depths of divine mercy and benevolence
Ram	Eldest son of Dasaratha, the king of Ayodhya, descendent of the solar dynasty, worshipped as the seventh incarnation of Visnu.
Ramanama	A repetitive form of prayer using the name of Ram propagated by Gandhi
Ramdhun	Mass-chanting of the divine name of Lord Ram during inter-religious prayer organized by Gandhi
Ramzan	Month-long fast that precedes the Muslim festival of Idd-ul-Fitre
Religio	That which binds, literally; it is the Latin root for the word religion
Sacra doctrina	Sacred doctrine
Sadagraha	Clinging to the right/Firmness to a good cause
Saguna Brahman	Qualified Brahman
Sambhogakaya	One of the triple bodies – trikaya - of Buddha; a concept developed by the Mahayana school of Buddhism which means an enjoyment body – a body of magical transformation that the Buddha enjoys the fruit of the merit generated through eons of religious practice.
Saraswati	Wife of Brahma is the Goddess of learning and wisdom
Sarvodaya	Rise of everyone, literally. It is the Gandhian social philosophy of welfare of all
Sat	Reality; one of the three transcendental attributes of the Ultimate.

Satori	Zen notion of awakening
Satya	Truth; the prime of the *mahavrtas* or the five great vows of Jainism which Gandhi took as his guiding principle
Satyagraha	Clinging to Truth, literally; a non-violent and truth-based movement initiated by Gandhi to fight against the unjust political and social systems.
Soteria	Salvation
Sunyata	Nothingness, literally. A term used in Mahayana Buddhism the indescribable nature of reality.
Swadeshi	The spirit which restricts persons to the use of services in the neighbourhood to the exclusion of the more remote; one of the eleven vows, which Gandhi proposed to his ashramites.
Swaraj	Total independence
Syadvada	Theory of may be, literally; Jaina theory that every judgment is relative
Tal	The drum used during the inter-religious prayer organized by Gandhi
Tapas	A process of purification through self-imposed suffering and constant meditation
Theologia	Talk about God
Torah	Jewish Scripture
Varnashramadharma	Duty according to one's caste, literally; the Hindu social practice of division of labour according to the caste of one's birth.
Vedanta	End of Vedas, literally; last of the five classical systems of Indian philosophy which adheres to the Vedas. Vedanta is directly based on the final portion of the Vedas called the Upanisads.
Vishya	Predicate
Vyavaharika satta	Empirical reality
Yajna	Sacrifice
Zen	One of the Buddhist sects now popular in Japan

INTRODUCTION

Religion plays a dominant role in the life of any society although several scholars and thinkers, not long ago, had predicted a speedy demise of religions because they held that the influence of modern education, the advance of science and technology, and the march of secularisation would sweep away religions from the high ways of modernity. Their assumption was not only proved to be incorrect, but religions have established themselves to be a persistent fact of human life. Moreover, there are clear signs of religious revival everywhere. Whether it is in Judaism, or Islam, or Hinduism in India or Buddhism in Sri Lanka, or the traditional religions in Africa, dogmas are being questioned and structures are disintegrating, but the core of different religions is becoming more alive. Even in socialist states where atheistic propaganda has gone on for many decades, there are signs of religious recovery. The retrieval of religious values and their reinterpretation to meet contemporary needs sustain people in their struggle against meaninglessness and provide them with a vision of the future.[1] Yet, strangely enough, this same resurgence found among religions also contributes to interreligious conflicts that frustrate the prospect of peace and harmony in the world.

CONTEXT OF THE PROBLEM

The context of the problem that the present book attempts to address has arisen from the challenges posed by a new discipline called the theology of religions. This itself was born because of a greater awareness of religious plurality. Thus, it is important to describe first the fact of religious pluralism and the subsequent appearance of the theology of religions, and then to discuss, at least briefly, about theology – its definition, history of development and methods. All these issues form the context of this study.

RELIGIOUS PLURALITY AND EMERGENCE OF THE THEOLOGY OF RELIGIONS

Religious plurality is a fact that one needs to accept today. However, in the history of religions, one can see that religions, by and large, grew in isolation at different times and in different places. Often, they were oblivious of the presence of other religious traditions. In a religion's encounter with other religions, there are different phases of growth. As an example, one can take the history of Christianity. In the early part of the spread of this faith, the focus was wholly on preaching the Good News. Although it came face to face with various religions, cults and cultures, the early preachers of Christianity desisted from caricaturing other faiths and there were no reports of confrontations with them. But with the conversion of Emperor Constantine, Christianity entered a new phase. It became the state religion and eventually acquired a hostile and triumphalistic attitude towards other faiths and cultures.

With the advent of the colonial era, Christianity entered its third phase. Moving out of the monochrome cultures of European nation states, Christianity came into contact with the major religions of the world, especially those of the Indian sub-continent. In the early part of this phase the Christian thinkers and ideologues pictured Indian religions as citadels of darkness and error. But later a sober realism prevailed and they became self-critical. Western universities began to study these religions. In due course of time, India was accepted as the land of spirituality. This, of course, helped the Christians to move from an attitude of confrontation to a co-existential approach to other faiths. Except for the diehard evangelicals and charismatics, Christian thinkers began to realize that winning the whole globe for Christ was untenable and also unchristian. It recognized the need to deepen the mutual relationships among religions in order to strive after their spiritual ideals. In this relationship, religions must also see the all-pervasive materialistic and consumerist culture as their common enemy.

Since 1990, humans have entered into a new and unchartered territory as regards interreligious relations. The old interreligious rivalries were based on and validated by the world of nation states. The phenomena of village world and globalisation have made the nation-states almost a thing of the past. As early as 1960s, a number of experts claimed that in cities, neighbourhoods no longer existed and that even if they did, they were no longer important. The idea was that increased physical mobility and improved communication – radio, television, telephone and computer – had eroded the importance of the specific locality in which a person lived. The concept of the global village thus appeared. It means that communities were no longer defined in geographical terms, but in terms of networks of people who might be widely separated but who were linked by mutual interests of some kind.[2]

Globalisation, on the other hand, refers to a social process in which barriers between territories of nation-states are removed in and through economic exchanges, political homogenisation, technological advances and cultural influences due to a gigantic growth in the means of transportation and the means of mass media.[3] As a consequence, a new global vision is dawning upon humankind. Today, more than ever before, human beings are able to see the blueprint (though blurred) of the shared destiny of our species. These growing phenomena also affected religions and as a result, believers of one religion not only come to know about other religious traditions but are also influenced by them. However, in practice, the narrow parochial outlook among the followers of different religions still persists. Hence, religions must evolve a pattern of genuine appreciation among themselves and a new spiritual vision for humankind, or face obsolescence.

Further, time is ripe now for religions to make a common cause for social justice. In every religion, justice is seen as divine. Yet, paradoxically, all religions have been lacking in their actual commitment to justice. Religions tend to compete among themselves, or remain in a state of mutual suspicion and alienation, largely because they are not adequately engaged with the realities of human nature. When the commitment to social justice is diluted in a religion, it soon succumbs to the spirit of communalism[4]. Communalism is religion without universal justice and peace. It is the mobilization and politicisation of religious groups on the basis of powerful symbols to fight for narrow goals. Fundamentalism becomes still another cause for religious conflicts. The defence of one's identity in the area of religion often takes the form of fundamentalism. It emerges when other ideologies fail to produce a common code of conduct to guide the activities of the society. Fundamentalism is a religious attitude and differs from communalism, which is the use of religions as a political force. "This refers to the tendency to hold on to what one considers as the fundamentals of one's religion against the onslaught of opposing forces."[5] Again, the "fundamentalists claim to possess the truth. They know the true meaning of the world and of history. This truth is communicated to them by their scriptures. These are then literally interpreted."[6]

The true spiritual liberation that people are waiting for is the opening of the doors of the prisons that religions have been turned into. Religions must now enter into a new and effective alliance to resist the forces of exploitation and oppression that are now rising in our midst under the cover of globalisation. Globalisation portends to be the most gigantic instrument of exploitation ever devised by human genius for evil. The colonialism of the past is a minor rash in comparison.[7]

As a result of these appalling upheavals that confront every religion, efforts were made to understand religion from its own standpoint and to understand other religions from their own perspectives, thereby helping one another in meeting these challenges that threaten the globe. This resulted in the emergence of the disciplines of Comparative Religion and the Theology of Religions.

Comparative Religion[8], a shortened form of the comparative study of religion (or religions) became current in the late 19th century as a synonym for the science of religion. It is centered on the application of the comparative (or scientific) method to the data provided by the religions of the world, past and present. Its function consists in placing the numerous religions of the world side by side, in order that, deliberately comparing and contrasting them, it may frame a reliable estimate of their respective claims and values.

In other words, Comparative Religion is the fruit of a desire to understand other religions as the other without reducing the other to one's monistic categories. Panikkar writes: "the question arises: can we understand without reducing the phenomenon to our patterns of understanding? This new question is the outcome of the deleterious results of monistic approaches, one God, one Church, one Empire ... and so on."[9] Comparative Religion is not a comparison of religions but a self-understanding of each religion in the context of the other. He further observes: "Comparative Religion is rather an analysis of the self-understanding of different religions, and is ultimately a cross-cultural problem. For not only is the concept 'religion' not univocal but the various religions of the world have very different understandings of what is meant by that name."[10]

In fact, it must be noted that Comparative Religion in practice, in the strict sense of the term, is not possible because there is no neutral ground from where religions can be scrutinized. The reason has been clearly explicated thus:

> . . . the only strictly comparable entities are quantities, so that we can only properly compare if we succeed in bringing the data of philosophy and/or religion to quantitative parameters. Comparison demands a scale and any scale is quantitative. Comparative philosophy of Religion as such becomes a science like the Natural Sciences, which seek mathematical paradigms capable of expressing the behaviour of natural phenomena. The common scale necessary for comparison can only be found if both sides, the comparer and the compared, share a common ground where they are in agreement about applying a particular criterion as the comparandum.[11]

But the nature of such a ground in religions poses difficulties.

Further, comparative studies are concerned with speaking beings. But often we overlook the fact that if we are comparing speaking beings we must learn to listen to them. A comparative study is basically a question of communication and language. To come to an agreement or disagreement about any common issue, requires a common language. Comparative philosophy is then reduced to the problem of a common human language.[12] Since there is no possibility of a common language, it is not possible to really compare religions.

The theology of religions, a recent discipline, intends to determine the fundamental perspective, the principle of intelligibility, according to which theories can be proposed in order that the various religious traditions may relate to one another. To understand the discipline of the theology of religions better, one should distinguish it from the theology of religion. The theology of religion asks what religion is and seeks, in the light of any given faith (say, Christian, Buddhist, Islamic, etc.) to interpret the universal religious experience of human kind; it further studies the relationship between revelation and faith, faith and religion, and faith and salvation. However, owing to the nature of the human being as spirit incarnate and a person in society, religious experiences are naturally embodied in many religious traditions, each made up of its own creed, cult, and moral code, the theology of religion becomes in turn a theology of religions. It is important to keep in mind that the theology of religions was primarily a Christian experiment in understanding other religious traditions. It arose out of an attempt to study the various traditions in the context of the history of salvation and in their relationship to the mystery of Jesus Christ and the Christian Church.[13]

However, with a broader application of the term, the theology of religions can be defined as the critical reflection upon and the systematic expression of the meaning of one's religious tradition vis-à-vis other religious traditions. It consists not only of the inherited baggage of a religion but also a process of reflecting critically upon the way people of a particular religious tradition should live out their faith in relation to other religious traditions. Here one needs to take into consideration both theistic and non-theistic religions. Hence theology does not merely imply a belief in God but a belief in the existence of an Ultimate Reality to which every religious tradition adheres. Thus, Comparative Religion as well as the theology of religions while attempting to accept the meaningfulness and truth of religious plurality, tries to interpret the claims of one's own religion.

THEOLOGY AND ITS DIVERSE METHODS

Having examined how the theology of religions emerged as a result of a greater awareness of religious plurality, we now turn to discuss the history of theology and its diverse methods. Theology plays a crucial role in comprehending the beliefs, rituals, doctrines and practices of different religions. The plurality of methods invoked in theology not only helps us to understand how different theologies that exist today came about, but also will enable us to appreciate the problem of our study.

Theology, a word found in English twenty years before its use by Chaucer, comes from Latin and Greek *theologia*, which literally means talk about God. For Plato, the term theology meant narratives about the gods and theogenies. Aristotle contrasted the theologians who offer mythological explanation of the world with the philosophers or physiologists who look for the explanation of things within things themselves. On one occasion, he divided theoretical philosophy into three parts: mathematics, physics and theology, this last being identical with first philosophy or metaphysics. In the second century B.C. Panaetius of Rhodes distinguished three kinds of theology: mythological, natural/ philosophico-cosmological, and civil or political. Civil theology or political theology referred to the cult of the Caesars.

However, among Christians, the first application of the term theology to the knowledge of God in whom they believed occurred in the writings of Origen. Further, for Eusebius of Caesarea (d. 339), *theologia* no longer applied to paganism at all but designated exclusively to the knowledge of the Christian God and of Christ. He knew the distinction between theology and economy known to the Latin Middle Ages. Theology meant discourse about the inner life of God. Economy meant God's activity for our salvation, which includes Christ, Church, Sacraments and Eschatology. Thus, among the Christians too, as among the Greeks, the word theology came to mean discourse or speech about God.

Still the term theology did not receive wide acceptability in the Christian circles. It was only with the writings of Peter Abelard that the modern use of the term was established in Christian scholarship. He published a book on Christian dogma in entirety and named it *Theologia*. The book was meant to be a textbook that was to be taught in the faculty of theology. Since then, the term 'theology' had become more acceptable to Christian scholars.[14]

Anselm of Canterbury in the twelfth century introduced dialectics as a method of theology. This replaced the earlier procedure of relying almost entirely on authority wherein theology was limited by and large to expositions of and commentary upon recognized authorities. Dialectics engaged the subject matter of classical sources, contrasting opinions one with another on the basis of intrinsic coherence and illuminative power. Further, in the thirteenth century with the reintroduction of Aristotle in the West, dialectics in theology gave way to the logic of Aristotle's *Organon* and more significantly to his philosophy proper. This enabled theology to assume the status of a unitary science either in the strict deductive sense of Aristotle's *episteme* (Thomas Aquinas)[15] or in the broader sense of a salvific practical science of the love of God (Bonaventure). In either case, a realist metaphysics was the instrument of seeking to understand what faith confessed.

However, with the era of Enlightenment[16] initiated during the late eighteenth century, the understanding of theology as a unitary science was abandoned. Thenceforth theology became, as it remains even today, increasingly an aggregate of multiple, highly specialized disciplines: exegesis, church history, patristics, dogmatics, ethics or moral theology, pastoral theology, spirituality and comparative religion. Still further, in the neo-scholastic period, namely, late nineteenth and twentieth centuries, theology was seen from a metaphysical perspective. Later it gave way to existential thinking as seen in the writings of Bultmann and Rahner and subsequently theology was understood from a historical outlook as found in the writings of Pannenberg and Metz. Thus theology now no longer traces an objective dynamism from the cosmos to its Transcendent Cause but turns to the subject and the immanence of thought in an avowed anthropological emphasis; the latter in turn has tended towards a radical historicality and a focus upon praxis.

The contemporary theology by and large views itself as a reflection on religious experience, meaning not some special sphere of human engagement but a depth dimension to ordinary human experiences.[17] Thus,

> . . . theology is word about God: reflection on the presence of God in the world. If the Divine is only a transcendent incomprehensible mystery, no theology is possible. No human word can be said on the divine silence. But the Divine is also an immanent reality: God with us, God in the world. God's presence in the world is like the articulation of the divine Word from within the abysmal depth of the divine Silence. The human mind responds to this revelatory Word.[18]

In other words, theology is the response of the human word to the active presence (the articulated word of the divine) of the transcendent God (the silence of the Divine).

However, in the present context, theology is not simply an abstract and conceptual understanding but is a caring and comprehensive understanding of God's purpose for us in the world and history. According to Samuel Rayan, when Anselm defined theology as 'faith in quest of intellectual understanding,' the word 'understanding' should be construed thus:

> . . . the word 'understanding,' which this faith-love seeks, has little to do with conceptual abstractions and academic systematisation. It has, on the other hand, everything to do with God's purposes for us, for the world, for history. It is like friend's understanding of his friend, appreciating, respecting and supporting his person and his options. Or, it is like a father's understanding of his children with their needs, fears, fancies and sorrows – a caring understanding that seeks to help the children grow and mature as responsible persons. Thus theology would be faith seeking justice and equality, love and responsibility, resource-sharing and community, and peace and wholeness for our world.[19]

Further, the word 'faith' in Anselm's definition too needs to be understood in the perspective of self-surrender. Rayan says:

> . . . faith is a live, inter-personal relationship between God and us, made possible by God's gracious Self-disclosure and Self-giving. It is a relationship of living trust in which the human person joyfully surrenders and commits self and life to God in response to, and enabled by, a Divine offer and gift of love and life. It is a dialogue in which the very centre and foundations of our personhood engage with the ultimate Truth, which is life. (1 Jn 4:8, 16).[20]

One can also speak of different approaches to the present day theology in its attempts at reinterpretation. Firstly, in a world of secularised cultures, fundamental theology is being developed as a critical justification of the foundations of faith and therefore of theology. Secondly, in dealing with contemporary men and women, theologians must take them in their real situation and with their real dimension, and thus theology allies itself to a political or liberation theology.[21] The latter seeks to overcome the privatisation characteristic of bourgeois religion and establishes itself as a critic of society in the name of the suffering and the cross of Jesus Christ; in so doing it brings a message of hope and Christian eschatology. Thirdly, the ecumenical theology – a name given more specifically to a well-informed reflection on ecumenism and its purpose and methods, refers to a theological study of the World Council of Churches, or "to the subject matter of a professorship in *Konfesionskunde*: the study of the Christian churches in their history, worship, theology and life."[22] Finally, we have the wider ecumenical theology or the theology of religions in the context of religious plurality. Here each of the diversities of religions is so important that no religion can claim finality. Panikkar says that the traditional religions must "give up any pretense to monopoly of what religions stands for."[23] The concern of the present dissertation is to consider this last approach to contemporary theology, namely, the theology of religions, which attempts to solve the problem of religious pluralism.

Theologization in this approach needs to be born out of faith experience of religious encounter. It has to well up from a lived experience – lived through centuries of our faith and that of our forefathers. It has also to come out of a faith experience, "where other religions in the world are actually questions posed and possibilities offered to every other believer. Other religious traditions have become part of the theologian's existential situation."[24] In fact, in the context of religious encounter, the task of theology is to open one's religious traditions to other traditions. Roberly E. Whitson is of the opinion that the work of theology is to open one's religious tradition to another, both theologically and experimentally.[25]

Theology, thus, claims the status of a science, and this claim is supported by its publications and its place among the university disciplines. It is a science because of its specific objective and specific method. The specific object of theology is what a religion considers as the revelatory events or revealed truths. With regard to the specific method of theology, one can speak of a plurality of methods. A method, according to Bernard Lonergan, "is a normative pattern of recurrent and related operations yielding cumulative and progressive results."[26] In fact, it is the plurality of methods that gives rise to a plurality in theology. They include existential method, transcendental anthropological method, hermeneutical method, eschatological method, linguistic method, process thought method and liberation theology method. However, the discussion about these methods, which is given below, will point to the fact that the existing theologies have not really addressed the problem of religious pluralism.

The **Existential Method**[27] begins with the assumption that the Word exists in a threefold state: as revealed (Christ), as written (Scripture), and as proclaimed. Existential theology gives importance to the aspect of preaching. According to Bultmann, an existentialist theologian, the *Kerygma* must be demythologized, that is, free it from mythological framework. Then only can it confront human being with what is God's summons to authenticity of life. Paul Tillich, another advocate of existential theology, calls for a method of correlation in theology; that is, making an attempt to correlate the human existential situation with the revealed message of Christ. Thus to the existentialists, theology is concerned with the origin of faith in the existential interpretation of history which discloses to us the historical structure of our own existence.[28] In other words, the starting point of theology should be "the centre of the human consciousness of pleasure and pain, of desire and misery," and "not up there or out there."[29]

In existential method, theology is no longer fettered in narrow systematic structures. It is understood as developing the mystery of Christ from the sources, showing its unfolding through the centuries and confronting it with the actual situations of humankind, being better prepared to incorporate the indigenous life, both the ancient religious traditions and the quest of the modern generation. This theology must be more than an objective presentation of revealed truth; it must start with the existential problems of human beings and study the answers to these questions in the traditional religions and in Christian revelation. "The Christian answer must be given not merely intellectually, but must be realized personally. Theology must be connected with a system of practice, with an earnest spiritual effort in exterior and inner discipline."[30]

Theology as **Transcendental Anthropology**[31] attempts to uncover the a priori conditions for the very possibility of knowledge of God. According to this method, a real relation to God is co-posited in every act of knowledge by the subject, on the basis of an a priori, non-objective, pre-conceptual, innate but conscious pre-grasp of God as the very structure of consciousness. In this method we do not conclude with God but rather we begin with Him. This dynamism to God is not from the object known to its transcendent cause, but from the subject knowing to what constitutes the infinite horizon of its knowing. This pre-grasp of the Absolute, not as object but as horizon, is an a priori structure of human existence as such, yet it exists only as mediated a *posteriori* in the categorical apprehension of finite existents. Karl Rahner is the most influential exponent of this method.[32]

Theology is **Hermeneutics**[33] insofar as it is an interpretation, or reinterpretation of the Word of God that always surmounts every past event or scriptural account. The text thus mediates an encounter with the subject matter of the text, which comes to newness of expression through the text today. One hears in the text what were previously unheard, as new possibilities for present and future existence is opened up.[34] According to Paul Ricoeur, theology is hermeneutics, first of all, because its task is to interpret the faith in the light of today's questions so that the answers become relevant for contemporary men and women. It is hermeneutics in the second sense, because the texts of faith, theology is called to interpret, namely, scriptures and tradition, are already interpretations.[35]

The **Eschatological Method**[36] in Christian theology rests on the understanding of history as universal revelation. But since the end of history has not yet occurred, its final meaning appears only proleptically in the resurrection of Jesus of Nazareth. All our knowledge is thus provisional in the sense that it remains subject to revision in the light of subsequent events. Still, meaning is immanent in events themselves so that historical happenings bear within themselves their own interpretation. Meaning, and so truth which cannot be bracketed off as if autonomous from meaning, emerges from context; that is, it is contextual in the relationship of historical event to the consummation of history. Revelation becomes at once definitive and provisional, situating the believer between the "already" and the "not yet." At work here is a peculiar reversal of time in which the present comes to us, not out of the past, but out of the future. This ontological priority of the future means that God lies not "above," nor "within," but "ahead"; His actions in history thus assume the character of promises to which the pre-eminent Christian response is hope rather than faith. Thus one views "the world as history, history as history of the end, faith as hope and theology as eschatology."[37]

In viewing theology as **Linguistic Analysis**[38], we need to note that there has been a shift from the question of truth to that of meaning, from a concern about reality to the concern about language since 1960's, after the fading away of the so-called "God is dead" phenomenon. The ground question was no longer "Does God exist?" but "Does language about God convey any meaning whatsoever?" This shift was also prompted by logical positivism, which simply classified all speech about the divine as "non-sense," that is, devoid of meaning. Influenced by Ludwig Wittgenstein's analysis of ordinary language, theology too became a language game, a set of rules governing proper speech in matters religious. The question of truth was bracketed, that is, left in the domain of faith, something beyond public verification. Here, theology's concern is meaning and the focus of meaning is the proposition or statement; theology's function is therefore the analysis of the meaning of religious language.[39]

Theology as **Process Thought**[40] was influenced by Alfred North Whitehead's philosophy of organism. "Central to this endeavour is a conviction of the ontological primacy of becoming over being, in which God himself "becomes" in creative interaction with the world. In this neo-classical metaphysics, the ultimate category is not God but Creativity which is not itself actual otherwise than as instantiated in the God/world relation of mutual dependency."[41] The deity lures the world forward by presenting it with initial aims, which it can actualise in a self-creative process; then actualises itself by way of apprehending the actual values the world makes available to it. All values are in a process of constant perishing as regards themselves and are preserved only as absorbed into and transformed within the divine being. The attributes of God in His present state of becoming, though immeasurably greater than the perfections achieved passingly in the world, are, formally speaking, univocal with them. Language can thus refer to God in His own being. God here appears as a cosmic deity who does not create the world and is dependent upon it. The God of process theology appears less as a personal saving deity than as an explanatory principle of the universe.[42]

Liberation Theology[43] developed by Gustav Gutierrez, Juan Luis Segundo and Leonardo Boff owes much to the political theology developed in Germany especially by Jürgen Moltmann, Johann Baptist Metz and Dorothee Sölle. Though both view the relationship between theory and praxis as a dialectical one, they agree on the primacy of orthopraxis over orthodoxy. Liberation theology believes that Christian love is less something interpersonal than a social concern about justice for others. Faith is the freedom to be critical of existing society and the church is the institution that makes this socio-critical freedom possible. Its starting point is a reaction to the concrete experience of oppression – political, racial, economic, and sexual – inimical to the gospel. Thus according to Gustavo Gutierrez, theology must begin with the life situation of the people, which is the primary source of theology. "The way in which a people lives its faith and hope and puts its love to work is the most important thing in God's eyes and is also, or ought to be, the most important in discourse about God and God's saving will."[44] Thus black theology and feminist theology are further instances of liberation theology. It establishes theology as critical reflection on Christian praxis in the face of such oppression.[45]

STATEMENT OF THE PROBLEM

The forgoing analysis of history of theology and the different methods it has employed points to the fact that theological pluralism consists in a pluralism of methods, attributable to the differing philosophies utilized instrumentally by different theologians. The deepest source of theological pluralism is the awareness of the finitude of all human knowing, which in turn gives rise to plurality of knowing. The theologies that arose from the above methods were not applied to understand the existence of religious plurality as indicated in the fourth approach to contemporary theology;[46] instead, they were meant to comprehend Christian faith critically and to uphold it against the blitzkrieg of other religious traditions that they came face to face in the course of its growth. They made little reference to the fact that they are only a part of a wider phenomenon that included other religious traditions. On the contrary, they condemned the theological claims of other religions as untrue. These theologies considered that Christianity was the sole possessor of absolute truth.

This type of approach to theology repeated itself in the case of other religious traditions too. Exclusivist theologies seem to have been popular in every religious tradition bringing about hostilities and at times, even religious wars. It is important to note here that the resentments among religions arise from the fact that religion touches the most intimate aspects of human life. Religion arouses human feelings and emotions, which affect the motives and movements of people. It provides meaning for life from an ultimate perspective. Sometimes the believers of one religion were so convinced of the truth of their own particular understanding of the Ultimate that they were often biased in favour of their own system of beliefs. They were even blind to the truth and goodness found in other religions.

The followers of one religion have been so convinced of the superiority of their forms of worship or systems of belief that they have considered it their sacred duty to impart them to others. They have made organised efforts to spread their religion to the far ends of the earth. If some people refused to accept their system of beliefs and practices, the believers of that religion thought it proper to impose it on others somehow or other. Sometimes the adherents to a particular religion were so absolutely convinced of the truth-claim of their faith that they engaged in sacred wars with other religious believers in order to convert them to their own religious boundary. It seems that hatred is never so profound and irreconcilable as when its motives spring from the deepest levels of consciousness, from religious beliefs. Needless to say, such intolerant attitudes are also reflected in their theologies.

In fact, under such circumstances, theology tends to become narrow-minded dogmatism. This in turn leads to religious fanaticism, which is nothing but the pervasion of one of the most noble virtues, that of steadfastness in faith. Its psychological roots lie in vices such as arrogance, pride, and tacit envy, attitudes that are condemned in all religions as sin or as even mortal sin. Religious fanaticism, intolerance and religious hatred are destructive to the foundation of human solidarity. And yet none of the religions legitimise violence against those who think or believe differently.

But today we are moving from the past theologies of isolation, hostility and competition to a theology of partnership, dialogue, negotiation and integrity wherein we assume that there are truths that are common to all religions. In fact, according to Panikkar, the history of religions unfolds a common typology of relationship. He summarized them into five kairological moments, namely, isolation, indifference, condemnation, co-existence and mutual fecundation.[47] It is possible that such an attitude must have emerged among the various religions as a result of good will or because of historical compulsions. Historically, it was with the colonial era, that religions came face to face with one other, as discussed above.

At first, each religion viewed other religions with hostility. Religions were then understood as planks for attack and counter-attack against one another. Convinced of the superiority, one religion tried to eliminate the other. However, with the passage of time religions began to tolerate one another. Obviously, here there was no love lost between the religions; instead, indifference marked this type of relationship. Later through dialogue and understanding the viewpoints of other religions, prejudices gave way to a relationship of mutual recognition, acceptance and respect among religions. And still later, in the face of common problems and challenges that threaten the existence of humanity such as the problem of ecology, the problem of poverty, the problem of illiteracy, etc. religions joined hands and worked together to avert such dangers.

These changing attitudes may not rationally support the edifice of the theology of religions that can withstand the onslaughts of the nitty-gritty of relationships among religions. On the other hand, for interreligious relations to grow on a firm footing, the theology of religions should evolve a common epistemological and a common metaphysical foundation, which is acceptable to all religions[48]. Besides, it is obvious from the above discussion that the very scope and nature of theology need to be reassessed. For, the present enterprises in theology are due to a desire to understand one's own religious faith rationally and systematically and not to understand other religious faiths. Hence a re-interpretation of theology seems to be the only way out in reaching out to other religious traditions.

Further, the discussions in present-day theology of religions, especially the Christian theology of religions, are centred around certain typologies that first appeared in print in the writings of Alan Race.[49] These typologies include exclusivism (ecclesiocentrism), inclusivism (Christocentrism) and pluralism (theocentrism). They can be considered from two perspectives – salvation claims and truth claims.

With regard to salvation-claims, exclusivism asserts that salvation is confined to Christians, or even more narrowly, in the traditional Catholic dogma, that *extra ecclesiam nulla salus*, outside the church there is no salvation. This exclusivist position undermines the validity of other religions. Today, Christians themselves discard this position, which is no more a live option. Inclusivism acknowledges that the salvific process is taking place throughout the world, within each of the great world faiths and also outside them, but insists that wherever it occurs it is the work of Christ. Salvation, in this view, depends upon Jesus' atoning death on Calvary, though the benefits of that death are not confined to Christians but are available, in principle, to all human beings. Thus people of other world faiths can be included within the sphere of Christian salvation. However, this Christian position breathes imperialist attitude, which other religious traditions are not in a position to accept. Finally, in pluralism, salvation is to be sought in different religious traditions without having to refer to the person of Jesus. Obviously, this position is unacceptable to the Christians who hold Jesus to be the instrument of salvation.[50]

From the perspective of truth-claims, the problem of theology of religions is really the age-old problem of 'one versus many.' In fact, this problem has haunted philosophy all through its history. The entire philosophy of being is an attempt at solving this predicament. A terse description of the origin of this problem in philosophy and the possible solutions presented by some of the philosophers, it is hoped, will shed light on this dilemma in the theology of religions better.

Philosophy of being in the West can be traced back to a stroke of genius by which Parmenides realised that the common element in all reality is just being. But he could not understand how there could be a variety of beings since the diversifying element would have to be other than being, that is, non-being or mere nothing. Hence he concluded that everything is just being and the diversity perceived by our senses is an illusion – for by what principle can being be diversified? This principle would have to be other than being. But what can be other than being? Non-being simply is not; for you cannot think of what is not as being.[51]

Plato took up the challenge in his dialogue, *The Sophist*, after apparently giving up the struggle in an earlier work entitled, precisely, *Parmenides*. His answer to the difficulty was that diversity comes from the limitation of particular beings: each being is distinguished from the other by its limitation, by the fact that it is not the other. Now this limitation is a reality, it is not nothing; yet it is non-being, it is the absence of something. Plato wrote: "Being, and difference or other, traverse all things and mutually interpenetrate, so that the other partakes of being, and by reason of this participation is, and yet is not that of which it partakes, but other, and being other than being, it is clearly a necessity that non-being should be."[52] This is a brilliant insight, but Plato vitiated it by fitting it into his system of subsisting ideas, so that limitation itself became an eternal, independent reality, hence not non-being.

Aristotle did not consider the problem of the plurality of beings but the allied problem of change while trying to correct this defect. By invoking the theory of hylemorphism, he showed that there is diversity because particular beings are made up of two complementary elements, matter and form, neither of which is complete being nor pure non-being: each is an incomplete substance. Aristotle goes far but not far enough, for one has still to find a reality that is pure non-being – which alone can solve the problem of diversity.[53]

After many centuries, Thomas Aquinas arrived at a probable solution: what is or exists, does so ultimately because of the act of being, which is that by which a mere possibility actually comes to be. He wrote: "The act of existing of each and every being is proper to it and is distinct from the act of existing of every other being."[54] There is diversity because of the limitation of this act in each particular case, and this limitation is not pure non-being but a reality – it is, so to speak, a negative reality. "This non-being is not something, of course, but it is not nothing either. It is the absence of something in something; it is the reality of limitation in finite beings that mutually exclude one another by their limitations and are thus differentiated."[55]

In metaphysics, one of the principal attributes of the being as such is that every existent being is 'identical' to itself and different from all others. Aristotle defined this attribute of identity thus: "each thing is identical to itself."[56] Identity with itself means that every existent being is indubitably itself, and thus different from all others. One could not understand diversity if every existent were not identical to itself. Therefore, identity is the principle on which every diversity depends. One could even say that it is the foundation of diversity. However, identity, as the attribute of being, is very different from mathematical identity. In mathematics, when one says 2 = 2, it implies that the first 2 is mathematically identical to the second. But ontologically, as a written figure, every 2 has its own identity, because it is written at a different time from the other 2, in a different place and with different materials. Hence it is identical only to itself.[57]

Thus the problem of one and many in philosophy concerns mainly with the understanding of finite beings. But when this problem of being is transferred to theology it concerns with the Infinite Being. The important question asked is: How the one God is validly manifest in many religions? Exclusivism chose the One. Thus, the Christian exclusivists opted for the affirmation of the One and the universal God as manifest in incarnate Jesus so ardently that it negated all other religions as revelations of God. Inclusivism also chose the One. But it said that the one and the universal God that is identified with Jesus of Nazareth, is also hidden in creation and history so as to include all others into that manifested One. Pluralism clearly opted for the Many. It affirmed that the many religions with their own focal points are valid. If so the question is how to reconcile it with the One, for the theological explanations of the one transcendent vision or transformative life are all quite different and even conflicting with one another. It is all true and yet, we can say that the generic cycle of religious life despite the varieties of theologies is one and the same.

The problem of pluralism is acute because when it affirms the Many it accepts the diverse revelations as equally valid, although they may be seemingly contradicting with one another. To demonstrate, let us take the example of Christ versus the Buddha. Christ during his public ministry frequently spoke of a metaphysical Being, whom he called Father, and identified his own being with that Being. The Buddha, on the other hand, never cared to affirm any metaphysical Being either outside or within oneself. He even refrained from attributing 'self' to oneself. He advocated the theory of non-existence of soul. If, the diverse or contradicting revelations are thus equally accepted as valid in pluralism, then, it looks as if it is led to deny the One. It is precisely here the root of the problem lies - when pluralism denies the one God, it misses everything in theology. Then it is no more a theological enterprise. So the real problem for the pluralists is: how can we uphold the One while equally affirming the Many?

One may think of circumventing this problem by appealing to Kant's position, namely, by identifying the One with noumenon and the Many with phenomenon. However, it is not tenable because the noumenon, being unknowable, cannot be spoken of and the understanding of phenomenon can vary as it appears differently to different people. Again, the pluralists themselves do not understand the One as the one ultimate noumenon. For, all their concern is to affirm the acceptability of the diverse observed facts. In this approach pluralism may not even be considered as a theological position for it would be identical with the secularist position.

Granted that the subject matter of the theology of religions is one God, can we reconcile the diverse revelations (many religions) as equally valid, without in any way minimizing the One? Is it possible for One God to be manifest in different religious traditions thereby validating them all so that the followers of these religions can attain spiritual well being in their own religions and be in dialogue with believers of other religions? It is precisely this question that the present book attempts to consider.

Epistemologically put, can we locate a common launching pad for the theology of religions where all the religions can relate with one another on an equal footing and at the same time feel at home in their own territory? It is a universally observable fact that saints are found in every religion and that every religion provides all its followers with enough spiritual nourishment so that every follower of any religion has the possibility of becoming a saint in that religious tradition. It is at this juncture that the problem of consideration becomes very grave. On the one hand, one can encounter the fact of saints and even verify the spiritual wealth of every religion; on the other hand, it becomes difficult to find a common pool from where each religion draws its spiritual sustenance. Our concern is, therefore, to find a way to establish a common well-spring from where the variety of religions draw their spiritual sustenance and establish it on epistemological and metaphysical foundations[58].

A POSSIBLE SOLUTION TO THE PROBLEM

The challenges posed by the theology of religions, though vital, are not insurmountable. One must be bold enough to effect a fresh understanding of the theology of religions by moving further from the existing typologies. This is possible only if one can arrive at a common framework that would interweave the different religions and validate the variety of their truth claims. But the question is whether it is possible to propose a framework such that it is accepted by every religious tradition and be enriched by it. Such a framework has to be worked out within the existing religious ambience or from the teachings of the religious seers and savants of various traditions. The attempt of the present study is precisely to suggest the possibility of working out such a framework on the basis of the Gandhian concept of truth.

The concept of truth forms not only the core issue in philosophy but also in theology. In fact, the rival positions on many other major questions in philosophy are a reflection of different beliefs about the concept of truth. Hence philosophers from time immemorial have examined the exact nature and meaning of truth and have come out with differing theories. Here the philosopher is concerned about the nature of factual truth of a given proposition and not so much about the religious implications of truth. A factual truth concerns the way things are; a proposition states a factual truth if it states how things are in the world. The question that the philosopher asks is: what do we mean when we say of such a proposition that it is true? There are different theories that attempt to answer this question.

The correspondence theory holds that truth is the adequation of the mind to the object. In other words, the relationship between knowledge and truth is that true knowledge is one in which what is asserted or denied corresponds to what the case is. If knowledge is really knowledge, it has to be true. The theory found numerous adherents in the British empiricist tradition, from Locke in the seventeenth century to Russell and Moore in the twentieth century. Wittgenstein while speaking of his picture theory subscribes to a version of correspondence theory of truth. He wrote: "A picture represents a possible situation in logical space... A picture agrees with reality or fails to agree; it is correct or incorrect, true or false... The agreement or disagreement of its sense with reality constitutes its truth or falsity."[59] A more recent version of correspondence theory is found in the writings of J. L. Austin.

He makes use of linguistic convention to enunciate the theory. According to him there are two sorts of convention relevant to truth, descriptive and demonstrative conventions. Descriptive conventions correlate the words (=sentences) with the types of situation, thing, event, etc. to be found in the world; demonstrative conventions correlate the words (=statements) with the historic situations, etc. to be found in the world. Austin's definition of truth is this: "A statement is said to be true when the historic state of affairs to which it is correlated by the demonstrative convention (the one to which it 'refers') is of a type with which the sentence used in making it is correlated by the descriptive conventions."[60]

According to coherence theory[61], truth is interpreted as coherence between a proposition and a set of other well-established true propositions. The facts, the coherence theorist holds, are not 'out there' to be compared without our judgments or propositions, but exist in the same realm as propositions. They are really themselves prepositional in nature, and what looks to the correspondence theorist to be correspondence between proposition and fact is simply correspondence between proposition and proposition. In other words, a systematic coherence between propositions bestows truth. Coherence theory has long been associated with the rationalist tradition, since philosophers in that tradition subscribe to this notion of the intelligibility of nature. *Monadology* of Leibniz is a typical example. In the twentieth century, the logical positivist philosophers like O. Neurath and C. Hempel have also adopted the coherence theory. In their philosophy of science they held that brute facts are not available to the scientist. All he/she can achieve is an uncertain, conceptualised judgement of perception and the test of truth is whether this judgment coheres with the system of other judgements already accepted by the scientific community.

Another theory of truth, the pragmatic theory, maintains that the value or the truth of an assertion lies solely in its practical bearing upon human interests. In other words, this theory equates truth with success: a proposition is true if it works in practice, if it has a practical utility or usefulness. This thesis is of course in danger of collapsing into a tautology, if success is equated with successfully conforming to the facts. The Pragmatists certainly did not intend it that way, offering instead the striking and prima facie implausible claim that if a proposition satisfies the needs or wants of the individual it is true. According to William James, on pragmatic principles, if the hypothesis of God works satisfactorily in the widest sense of the word, it is true. He saw the truth of a theory in science, a metaphysical or religious hypothesis, a moral belief and so on as residing in their practical usefulness in satisfying the needs of the believer.[62]

In contrast to all these theories, Gandhi holds that truth is not merely factual nor propositional nor pragmatic. It is not merely a property of knowledge. It has its implication for one's living and being. Thus when a speaker says he/she is telling the truth, he/she means that his/her speech accords with the fact, as he/she has perceived it. When someone else endorses what the speaker said is true, he/she means that what the speaker said was according to the fact, as he/she too perceived it. This accordance of fact, perception or experience, and expression is truthfulness or the quality of being true. "The fact, its perception as it is, expression of that perception as experienced, and action in consonance with that perception completes the chain of truthfulness in its entirety."[63] Thus "when I perceive a fact as it is, express my perception according to the fact, and act according to my perception, I may be said to have perceived, expressed and acted according to truth."[64]

Further, truth has metaphysical connotations. Ontologically speaking, we know truth is the measure in which we know reality, not only in that which reality is immediately, but also in its profound structures, in its implicit references. This is because it is impossible for humans to think without thinking of being – that is, truth – even if this thought is partial, unilateral, and perhaps even deformed. That is why Parmenides wrote: "Thought and being are the same thing... Without *being* you will not find thought."[65] Plato made the idea correspond exactly with truth. The principle of Parmenides was applied with absolute coherence: fullness of truth is fullness of reality. Aristotle enlarged the Platonic meaning of the true by extending it to cosmic reality. In short, ontologically truth means this:

> Intelligence is the faculty of being. The *being* or *existent* in its immediate rapport with the intellect transforms itself into *truth*. Therefore, truth is a relative attribute, which loses every meaning outside its reference to the knowing subject. The more ontologically perfect an existent is, the richer its knowability is. Only nothingness has no rapport with truth, and thus with intelligence. Therefore, we can say that the foundation of truth is being. There exists as much truth in each being as it has measure of possessed being.[66]

As there are grades of knowledge, there are also grades of truth. Since the grades of truth coincide with the grades of existent beings and the human mind is not the author, but only the explorer of truth, then it is possible to climb towards the first Source of truth and identically to the Source of existence. "Just as only the *Being by nature* explains every other existent, so only the *Truth by nature* explains the origin of every truth."[67] It is worthwhile to note here that in one of his proofs to demonstrate the existence of the God, St. Augustine took recourse to the concept of truth. He proves "God from the truth intended as the universal and eternal value, the reflex of the incommutable Truth. The proof finds all its value and its vigour, identifying *reality with truth*, because, wherever the latter is conditioned, it postulates the Absolute Truth."[68]

Gandhi agreed with this sort of metaphysical implications of truth. He wrote:

> For me, truth is the sovereign principle, which includes numerous other principles. This truth is not only truthfulness in word, but truthfulness in thought also, and not only the relative truth of our conception, but the Absolute Truth, the Eternal Principle that is God. There are innumerable definitions of God, because His manifestations are innumerable. They overwhelm me with wonder and awe and for a moment stun me. But I worship God as Truth only. I have not yet found Him, but I am seeking after Him. . . . But as long as I have not realized this Absolute Truth, so long must I hold by the relative truth as I have conceived it. That relative truth must, meanwhile, be my beacon, my shield and buckler.[69]

Besides, the concept of truth has also religious implications. In fact, the concept of religious truth expresses wider aspects of human experience: reality that is permanent, immeasurable, unconcealed, effective and powerful; personal character that is sincere, good, genuine and valuable; and, knowledge that is certain, accurate, pure, clear, and convincing. Truth emerges out of the basic human experience of valuation (both as assessment and appreciation) as a necessity for human survival and well-being.

When people express religious truth, they are aware of different levels, kinds, or functions of truth. At the extremes are absolute and relative truths, or transcendent and conventional truths. The former expresses the deepest reality, the sacred, God, or 'what-is'; the latter indicates accurate information about life the importance of which is limited to specific situations and short-term goals. The assumption of all religious truth is that personal estimations of what-is or decisions of momentary value must be affirmed only insofar as they are an aspect of the transcendent or absolute truth. Such absolute truth transcends and incorporates the concerns defined by information dependent on time-space conditions; it establishes an overarching value in relation to which the information has significance and meaning.[70]

Gandhi seemed to exemplify such a view of religious truth in his writings on truth. For him, "the definition of Truth is deposited in every human heart. Truth is that which you believe to be true at this moment and that is your God. If a man worships this Relative Truth, he is sure to attain the Absolute Truth, that is, God in course of time."[71] In fact, although Gandhi considered 'God as Truth,' in the course of time as his search widened through his contact with sincere non-believers, Gandhi accepted its converse as more correct, namely, 'Truth is God.' Gandhi also equated Truth with Religion. Every religion contains Absolute Truth as seen in the lives of its saints. However, no religion is perfect in this world. It has many relative truths. Reducing the gap between Absolute Truth and Relative Truth by referring to the peaks of holiness within its own religious boundary becomes, for Gandhi, the essence of religion.

Thus Gandhi, as it will be amply highlighted in the course of this study, does not depend on any system of philosophy or theology for his understanding of God and religion. Gandhi's religion is a religion of the heart; the lowliest of creatures has a place in the heart of that religion. It is not the religion of the Temple. In his religion, there are no unbelievers. Sceptics, atheists and humanists search for Truth. And in his religion Truth is God. In fact, he converts the usual affirmation 'God is Truth' to 'Truth is God.' It is this converse that seems to give a common epistemological basis for the varied theologies of religions. Again, it is his understanding of God as Absolute Truth that may provide us with a common metaphysical point of convergence of all religions, theistic as well as atheistic. Hence, the possible solution to the problem is that Gandhian concept of truth can turn out to be a common basis for a theology of religions, both epistemologically and metaphysically.

METHODOLOGY ADOPTED IN ARRIVING AT THE SOLUTION

The study therefore will explore at length the various nuances and implications of the concept of truth as understood by Gandhi. Evolving a methodology for a study of this kind creates a great challenge. The study tries to combine the Gandhian understanding of truth with the theology of religions and to show that truth can be the rational basis for this new discipline. There are a number of theologians who are concerned about the theology of religions. However, being a new discipline at its infancy stage, not many books have been published on the subject proper, although a number of books have been written on topics that criss-cross the boundary of the theology of religions. Besides, the discipline is beset with controversies and there seems to be no agreement regarding the nature and scope of this discipline among the theologians. One needs to cull out from the writings of theologians regarding their understanding of the theology of religions in order to make an assessment of the nature and scope of the theology of religions.

The problem of methodology is compounded when one comes to deal with Gandhian writings so as to arrive at a Gandhian concept of truth. For, Gandhi's writings are too copious and yet they are fragmentary. Gandhi was neither a theologian nor a philosopher in the academic sense of the word. He has not written any systematic treatise on the problem of truth or religion. Most of his writings were occasional in character and their arguments are not always presented with a logical rigour as may be found in a professional philosophical or theological treatise. Besides this, his writings on truth are voluminous and still mostly fragmentary, scattered and contextual. They were all written either in answer to certain questions posed to him or in response to an invitation to comment on issues people wanted to be enlightened on. Sometimes Gandhi himself expressed his reactions on particular events or on a current social problem, which was of national or international importance. Given the variety of contexts and purposes of Gandhi's writings, one cannot deal with them as one would with systematic treatises on philosophy or theology. Hence one needs to employ a novel method to understand the various nuances and niceties of the concept of truth or any other Gandhian concept.

Fortunately, a novel method has been disseminated by Prof. K. J. Shah and profitably utilized by Prof. A. Pushparajan in his book *From Conversion to Fellowship: The Hindu Christian Encounter in the Gandhian Perspective.*[72] The author has taken inspiration from this book to arrive at this method. The method has several procedural points. They include:

i) Every statement uttered by Gandhi is taken seriously on the issues under consideration. In other words, besides taking into account all the inspiring and oft repeated assertions of Gandhi, even his unimpressive statements or those statements uttered by others are also seriously attended to. Great care has been taken to include even those assertions, which Gandhi must have made just once or twice. Although his writings are logical and coherent, one may also notice certain apparent contradictory statements. Even such writings are also considered. The study does not confine merely to those Gandhian ideas, which appeal to the researcher. In fact, on the contrary, even those ideas, which go against the ideas and views of the researcher, are also taken into account.

ii) Gandhi was a prolific writer and his writings are found in different journals he published, in his large quantum of correspondence and in his books like *Autobiography*, *Hind Swaraj*, *Sarvodaya*, etc. Happily, his close associates compiled all these writings under his own personal supervision and published them for the benefit of humanity. These anthologies and compilations of Gandhian writings are used in collecting his views on the topic under study. The assumption here is that these compilations will supply the main points of his views on a particular topic, objections to them as well as his answers. Whenever required, care has been taken to scrutinize the original sources, particularly his articles published in *Young India* and *Harijan*.

iii) In this study, Gandhian views on truth and religion, have been presented in a systematic and logical way. To arrive at this, the various writings of Gandhi on the topics under study are viewed together as a connected whole. The assumption is that Gandhi was really a synoptic thinker though he had not presented his thoughts in the form of a systematic treatise.

iv) After observing the underlying harmony of the varied writings of Gandhi on the notion of truth, an effort is made to draw out the unity of his thought and to formulate it in a synthesis. Although this is a protracted process, the outcome is greatly gratifying. At the end of such an arduous task one perceives how coherent and logically consistent Gandhi's thinking is on the concepts of truth and religion.

It should be further noted that Gandhi was more an activist, a *karmayogin*, than an academician in the professional sense of the term, but had a sound thinking. He was free from every form of prejudice, which often colours the views of a thinker. His honest research into the various nuances and ramifications of the concept of truth made his understanding more valuable. Besides the concept of truth, we are also interested in his understanding of religion and religious pluralism. Even his analysis of these important concepts is free from bias and in fact, his views affect the vital issues of an interreligious life situation.

This discovery is a matter of crucial importance for this study. Gandhi's thoughts are so rich and deep, touching the very essence of religion, that they can become tools or benchmarks to examine the truth-values of the different positions held in a religious controversy. Further, in the light of Gandhi's insights, it is possible to evolve a correct method of understanding religious differences and solving the interreligious controversies arising out of those differences. This also provides a sound basis, a common platform transcending all barriers and yet applicable to any boundary. And that in turn paves the way for formulating a viable metaphysical foundation for the theology of religions thereby bringing closer every religious tradition to work together in order to weed out the evils that eat into the very vitals of our society. This basis is also epistemological in as much as every one will be able to understand and resolve the different controversies that are found in religions.

It must also be stated here that the method employed in this study in order to understand the Gandhian notion of truth and to posit it as a framework for the theology of religions after an examination of his concept of religion, is neither historical nor sociological. A historical method demands a complete reference to facts and analyses how Gandhi developed the concepts of truth and religion in reference to the chronological setting of his life. The sociological method, on the other hand, explores the socio-economic and political conditions that influenced the origin and development of these concepts. It also probes into the contextual or circumstantial factors, which were responsible for their emergence. Instead, the concern and interest of this study is primarily theological and philosophical (although, the study does not really enter into a systematic philosophical treatment of these Gandhian concepts). The present study, thus, takes recourse to a conceptual analysis of the concepts of truth and religion as evolved by Gandhi and then attempts a possible link between them in such a way that truth becomes the basis for the theology of religion by taking into account the existing controversies that surround the theology of religions.

In fact, the book after examining the inadequacy of the various conflicting positions that exist in the present day theology of religions among the Christian scholars, formulates a new theory of 'satyo-centrism' based upon the Gandhian concept of truth. This new theory is shown to resolve the problem of theological pluralism regarding the core issue of uniqueness of Christ without having to reject any of the diverse theories. Keeping this as our model, we further show how the same theory of 'satyo-centrism' can be used in order to resolve rationally the problem of religious plurality. Therefore, it becomes a viable theory for a theology of religions both epistemologically and metaphysically.

LIMITATIONS OF THE STUDY

The dissertation, being inter-disciplinary, is not restricted to any one system of philosophy or theology. Thus it is not possible to discuss at length the various concepts introduced in this book. However, efforts are made to explain them briefly in the footnotes and suggest short bibliographies of books so that any one who wants can have further research on these concepts. Further, while discussing the concept of truth and its various theories, there is no elaborate discussion on the philosophy of truth. On the contrary, it is more a general treatment of issues at hand. And as such, the book is just a pointer to the epistemological and metaphysical foundations for the theology of religions. A more detailed treatment on the foundations themselves is desirable.

As regards bibliography, the wide gamut of Gandhian writings that exist today is a startling experience for anyone who wants to engage in a research on Gandhi. Likewise, though in its infancy, the theology of religions too has a number of adherents with a vast range of books written on it from different perspectives. Since the dissertation is concerned about Gandhian understanding of truth with a view to provide an epistemological and ontological foundations for the theology of religions, I have taken sufficient effort to study the relevant literature. It has not even considered necessary to peruse through all the literature that are available on either Gandhi or the theology of religions separately. However, care has been taken to examine the original writings of Gandhi, which are found in the authentic compilations undertaken by his own disciples with the consent of Gandhi himself. With regard to the theology of religions, the book has incorporated the views of many of the leading personalities on the subject and taken the views of some theologians in detail as specimen, although it is possible that the opinions of other scholars may be left out for practical reasons, though not intentionally.

Finally, a word on the arrangement of the chapters in the book is in order. The entire study has been structured under three chapters, excluding the Introduction and the Conclusion. The Introduction attempts to bring the topic under study in context by clarifying the various concepts. The first chapter entitled "The Theology of Religions: A Critical Overview" looks at the theology of religions from the present scenario of scholarship. A number of thinkers have contributed to the enrichment of this discipline and attempted to sort out the thorny issues regarding the status of different religions. John Hick who initiated the Copernican revolution in epistemology of religions, Alan Race, Raimundo Pannikar and Jacques Dupuis are among others who have attempted to understand the different typologies proposed by theologians for possible relationships among religions. After highlighting their contribution, the chapter pinpoints a basic problem about them: they all get stuck with Western moorings. It is at this point that we need to look to other religious traditions of the East for more plausible and comprehensive explanations to the problem of religious pluralism. Gandhian concept of truth seems to be a better point of reference in understanding the existence of different religious traditions than any other models so far proposed.

With this finding, then, we proceed to chapter two, 'Satya' – The Truth of Gandhi's Conception." The concept of truth in Gandhi is loaded with innumerable nuances and ramifications. Hence there is a need to clarify this concept in order to offer it as a possible solution to the problem of religious pluralism. To achieve this aim, an attempt is made to cull out the different references regarding this concept from the voluminous writings of Gandhi. The chapter will in particular underscore the distinction that Gandhi made between the Absolute Truth and Relative Truth. In fact, this distinction is likely to become the philosophical basis for accepting pluralism in religions.

With the perspective of Truth evolved in the previous chapter, the third chapter, 'Satyo-centrism': A Framework for the Theology of Religions," proceeds to take a fresh look at the epistemology and ontology of theology of religions and proposes a possible new paradigm for the theology of religions. The different typologies being inadequate, there is a need to proffer a new paradigm. This model is found in the concept of truth that Gandhi speaks of. It will also attempt to show that the 'satyo-centric' model is adequate in understanding and explaining the plurality of religions. Gandhian understanding of Religion and religious plurality will also be deliberated upon to arrive at a possible solution to the problem. The Concluding Remarks bring out the various consequences in effecting 'satyo-centrism' in the theology of religions.

NOTES

1. Cf. Stanley J. Samartha, "The Lordship of Jesus and Religious Pluralism," *Christ's Lordship & Religious Pluralism*, eds. Gerald H. Anderson & Thomas F. Stranksy (New York, Maryknoll: Orbis Books, 1981), pp. 20-21.
2. For further readings on the concept of 'global village,' cf. Peter Marsh, ed., "Human Behaviour," *The Marshal Cavendish Encyclopaedia of Personal Relationships*, vol. 12 (New York: Marshall Cavendish Corporation, 1990), pp. 1424-1431.
3. Although ideologically globalization has brought about a sense of 'shrinking space, shrinking time and disappearing boundary' whereby enabling the humans to live like a family and making the world into a global village, but as it unfolded itself in the present day, globalization has become nothing but a new form of economic, social and cultural colonialism. For further readings, cf. Amartya Sen, "Globalisation," *The Guardian*, 27 April 2000; M. Walters, *Globalisation* (1995; London and New York: Routledge, 2001); Jan Aart Scholte, *Globalisation: A Critical Introduction* (New York: Palgrave, 2000); Joe Arun, "Taming the Global Demagogue.1: A spirituality for Globalisation," *Vidyajyoti*, 66 (2002) 6, pp. 419-425; Joe Arun, "Taming the Global Demagogue.II: A spirituality for Globalisation," *Vidyajyoti*, 66 (2002) 7, pp. 526-537; James Petras, "Globalization: A socialist Perspective," *Economic and Political Weekly*, 8 (February 1999), pp. 20-26.
4. The term communalism literally means 'belonging to a group of people or used by a group of people rather than one single person.' It also means, especially in the Indian context, 'based on racial or religious divisions within a larger social group and considered as political threat to the existence of the polity, economy, culture and religious harmony.' Here communalism is an ideology which has three basic elements. First, it is the belief that people who follow the same religion have

common secular interests, that is, common political, economic, social and cultural interests. The second element of communal ideology rests on the notion that in a multi-religious society like India, the secular interests of the followers of one religion are dissimilar and divergent from the interests of the followers of another religion. The third stage of communalism is reached when the interests of the followers of different religions or of different communities are seen to be mutually incompatible, antagonistic and hostile. It is in the latter sense that the term is used here. For further readings, cf. Bipin Chandra, *Communalism in Modern India* (New Delhi: 1984); Bipin Chandra, Mridula Mukherjee, Aditya Mukherjee, K.N. Panikkar and Sucheta Mahajan, *India's Struggle for Independence* (New Delhi: Penguin Books, 1989), pp. 398-442; Afaque Khan, *Gandhian Approach to Communalism: A Critical Study* (Delhi: Ajanta Publications, 1986); S. Arulsamy, ed., *Communalism in India: A Challenge to Theologizing* (Bangalore: Claretian Publications, 1988); Sita Ram Sharma, *Anatomy of Communalism: Historical Perspectives on Communalism*, vols. 6 (New Delhi: Aph Publishing Corporation, 1998); Peter Heehs, *Nationalism, Terrorism, Communalism in Modern Indian History* (Delhi: Oxford University Press, 1998); K.N. Panikkar, *The Concerned Indian's Guide to Communalism* (New Delhi: Viking, 1999).

5. Michael Amaladoss, *Making Harmony: Living in a Pluralist World*, (Delhi: Indian Society for Promoting Christian Knowledge; Chennai: Institute of Dialogue with Cultures and Religions, 2003), p. 15. Henceforth, Amaladoss, Making Harmony. For readings on how religious fundamentalism adversely affects religious, social, political and economic fabric of a country, cf. Nani Palkhivala, *We the People* (Bombay: Strand Book Stall, 1984); Ramesh Thapar, "A Call to Arms," *The Illustrated Weekly of India*, December 7-13, 1986, pp. 8-17.

6. Amaladoss, *Making Harmony*, p. 17.

7. Cf. Swami Agnivesh, "The Church and Other Religions – A Hindu Perspective," *Yesu Krist Jayanti 2000: Towards a New Society*, ed. Paul Puthanagaday (Bangalore: National Committee for Yesu Krist Jayanti 2000, 2001), pp. 349-355.

8. For further readings, cf. Louis Henry Jordan, *Comparative Religion: Its Genesis and Growth* (Edinburgh: 1905); Louis Henry Jordan, *Comparative Religion: Its Adjuncts and Allies* (London: 1951); Eric J. Sharpe, *Comparative Religion: A History* (London: 1975); Wilfred Cantwell Smith, *The Meaning and End of Religion* (London: SPCK, 1992); Joachim Wach, *The Comparative Study of Religions* (New York: Columbia University Press, 1958); Seshariri K.L. Rao, *Mahatma Gandhi and Comparative Religion* (Delhi: Motilal Banarsidass, 1978).

9. Raimundo Panikkar, "Hermeneutics of Comparative Religion: Paradigms and Models," *Journal of Dharma*, 5 (January – March 1980) 1, p. 44. Henceforth, Panikkar, "Hermeneutics of Comparative Religion."

10 Panikkar, "Hermeneutics of Comparative Religion," pp. 40-41.

11. Panikkar, "Hermeneutics of Comparative Religion," pp. 40-41.

12. Cf. Panikkar, "Hermeneutics of Comparative Religion," p. 43.

13. Cf. Jacques Dupuis, *Toward a Christian Theology of Religious Pluralism* (Anand: Gujarat Sahitya Prakash, 2001), pp. 7-8. Henceforth, Dupuis, Toward a Christian Theology of Religious Pluralism.

14. Cf. Yves Congar, "Christian Theology," *The Encyclopedia of Religion*, trans. Mathew J. O'Connell, ed. Mircea Eliade, vol. 14 (New York: Macmillan Publishing Company, 1987), pp. 455-456. Henceforth, Congar, "Christian Theology."

15. St. Thomas Aquinas contributed to the growth of theology especially with his monumental work *Summa Theologia.*

16. Enlightenment is a late 18th century international movement in thought with important social and political ramifications. The Enlightenment is at once a style, an attitude, a temper-critical, secular, empirical, and practical. It is also characterized by core beliefs in human rationality, in what it took to be nature, and in the nature feelings of humankind. Four of its most prominent exemplars are Hume, Thomas Jefferson, Kant and Voltaire. Some of the aspects of the belief in human rationality are (i) human beings are free to the extent that their actions are carried out for a reason; (ii) human rationality is universal, requiring only education for its development; and, (iii) the true forms of all things could be discovered by human rationality whether of the universe (Newton's laws), of the mind (associationist psychology), of good government (the US Constitution), of a happy life or of beautiful architecture. For further readings, cf. Carl J. Friedrich, *The Philosophy of Kant* (New York: The Modern Library, 1977), pp. 132-139.

17. Cf. William J. Hill, "Theology," *The New Dictionary of Theology*, eds. Joseph A. Kamonchak, Mary Collins and Dermot A. Lane (Bangalore: Theological Publications of India, 1994), pp. 1011-1012. Henceforth, Hill, "Theology."

18. Sebastian Painadeth, "Theologising As Doing-Mission – Inter-religious Hermeneutics in Theology," Third Millennium: *Indian Journal of Evangelisation*, 4 (October-December, 2001), p. 6. Henceforth, Painadeth, "Theologising As Doing Mission."

19. Samuel Rayan, "Theologian As Disciple – Disciple As Theologian," Third Millennium: *Indian Journal of Evangelisation,* 4 (October-December, 2001), p. 103. Henceforth, Rayan, "Theologian As Disciple."
20. Rayan, "Theologian As Disciple," p. 102.
21. Liberation Theology is also considered as a method in theology. It is discussed in the latter part of this section.
22. Congar, "Christian Theology," pp. 461-462.
23. Raimundo Panikkar, "Have 'Religions' the Monopoly on Religion?", *Journal of Ecumenical Studies,* 11 (1974), p. 517.
24. Lucien Richard, *What are they Saying about Christ and World Religions* (New York: Paulist Press, 1981), pp. 2-3. Henceforth, Richard, What are they Saying.
25. Cf. Roberly E. Witson, The Coming Convergence of World Religions (New York: Newman, 1971), p. 3.
26. Bernard Lonergan, *Method in Theology* (London: Darton, Longman and Todd, 1975), p. 4. Henceforth, Lonergan, Method in Theology. For further readings on methods in theology, cf. Avery Dulles, *The Craft of Theology: From Symbol to System* (New York: The Crossroad Publishing Company, 1995), pp. 41-53; Roger Haight, *Dynamics of Theology* (New York: Paulist Press, 1990), pp. 169-189.
27. In fact, existentialism began as a philosophical movement is a revolt against rationalism, with its stress on reason alone, for its failure to progress beyond the obvious, its lack of engagement with people, and its ignoring of their real needs. It revolted against romanticism on the grounds of its self-deceptive escape from the horrors of life in the here and now, and its unjustifiable optimism about people. It rejects various existing systems and built a philosophy based on certain themes such as anxiety, being and existence, intentionality, absurdity, choice and the individual, etc. Existentialism influenced the theology of Barth, Bultmann, Tillich and Macquarrie. This approach stressed the existential moment in hermeneutics and preaching, in which humanity is summoned to respond to the call of God to live an authentic life. Jesus is the perfect example of an authentic existence. Existentialist philosophy asks the fundamental human questions of existence. Theology's task is to provide the answers. For further readings, cf. J. Macquarrie, An Existentialist Theology (London: SCM Press Ltd., 1960); D.E. Roberts, Existentialism and Religious Belief (New York: 1957).
28. Cf. Hill, "Theology," p. 1021.
29. A.M. Mundadan, *Paths of Indian Theology* (Bangalore: Dharmaram Publications, 1998), p. 2.

30. J. Neuner, "The Place of World Religions in Theology," *The Clergy Monthly*, 32, (March, 1968) 3, p. 108.

31. This method is based on the biblical anthropology enunciated both in the Old Testament and New Testament. For further readings on biblical anthropology, cf. G.C. Berkouwer, *Man: The Image of God* (Michigan: Eerdman's Publishing, 1975); H.W. Wolff, *The Anthropology of the OT* (London: SCM Press Ltd., 1973); Louis Berkhof, *Systematic Theology* (Edinburgh: The Banner of Truth Trust, 1976).

32. Cf. Hill, "Theology," pp. 1022-1023.

33. Hermeneutics is the art or theory of interpretation, as well as a type of theology or philosophy that starts with the questions of interpretations. Originally concerned more narrowly with interpreting sacred texts, the term acquired a much broader significance in its historical development and finally became both theological and philosophical positions in twentieth century German thought. There are two positions in hermeneutics: the first one follows Dilthey and sees interpretation as a method for the historical and human sciences, the second follows Heidegger and sees it as an ontological event, an interaction between interpreter and text that is part of the history of what it understood. For further readings, cf. D.Z. Phillips, *Religion and the Hermeneutics of Contemplation* (Cambridge: Cambridge University press, 2001); Kurt Mueller-Vollner, ed., *The Hermeneutics Reader* (New York: The Continuum Publishing Company, 1989).

34. Cf. Hill, "Theology," pp. 1022-1023.

35. Cf. Joseph Putti, *Theology as Hermeneutics* (Bangalore: Kristu Jyoti Publication, 1991), pp. 211-212.

36. The method finds its basis on the Christian doctrine of last things – death, life after death, heaven, hell, etc. For further readings on eschatology, cf. G.C. Berkouwer, *The Return of Christ* (Michigan: 1972); R. Bultmann, *History and Eschatology* (Edinburgh: 1957); O. Cullmann, *Salvation in History* (London: SCM Press Ltd., 1967); G. E. Ladd, *The Presence of the Future* (Michigan: 1974); H. Küng, *Eternal Life?* (New York: Crossroads Publishing Company, 1991).

37. J.B. Metz, "Le Eglise et la monde," *Theologie d'aujourd'hui et de demain*, 1967, p. 140; as cited by Hill, "Theology," p. 1024.

38. Theological method of linguistic analysis follows an approach in philosophy that holds that a careful study of how language is actually used, taught and developed in everyday discourse can illuminate, and even transform or dissolve, time-honoured philosophical problems. Its most influential exponents have been Wittgenstein, J.L. Austin and Gilbert Ryle. For further readings, cf. George Pitcher, *The Philosophy*

of Wittgenstein, Eastern Economy Edition (New Delhi: Prentice-Hall of India Private Limited, 1985); Gilbert Ryle, *The Concept of Mind* (Harmondsworth, Middlesex: Penguin Books Ltd., 1986).

39. Cf. Hill, "Theology," pp. 1024-1025.

40. Process Theology is the theological system that has been developed on the basis of the philosophy of Alfred North Whitehead and Charles Harthshorne. The name itself derives from the central tenet of both of these philosophers that reality is a process of becoming, and not a static universe of objects. From this, a unique concept of both God and human being is derived, and from that in turn a complete theology. For further readings, cf. J. Cobb and D.R. Griffin, *Process Theology: An Introductory Exposition* (Philadelphia: The Westminster Press, 1976); D.R. Griffin, *A Process Christology* (Philadelphia: 1973); C. Harthshorne, *Man's Vision of God and the Logic of Theism* (Chicago: 1941); A.N. Whitehead, *Process and Reality* (New York: The Free Press, 1979).

41. Hill, "Theology," pp. 1024-1025.

42. Cf. Hill, "Theology," pp. 1024-1025.

43. Liberation Theology, initiated in the Latin American countries, argues that theology must start with the view from below with the sufferings of the excluded and oppressed. The domain of this theology is the concrete social situation and the method is the reflection on the praxis. For further readings, cf. L. and C. Boff, *Liberation Theology: From Confrontation to Dialogue* (New York: 1986); E.A. Núñez, *Liberation Theology* (Chicago: 1985); Enrique Dussel, *History and Theology of Liberation: A Latin American Perspective* (Maryknoll, New York: Orbis, 1976); Gustavo Gutierrez, *A Theology of Liberation* (Maryknoll, New York: Orbis Books, 1973); Alfredo Fierro, *The Militant Gospel* (Maryknoll, New York: Orbis Books, 1975); Hugo Assmann, *Theology for a Nomad Church* (Maryknoll, New York: Orbis Books, 1975).

44. Gustavo Gutierrez, *A Theology of Liberation* (Maryknoll, New York: Orbis Books, 1973), pp. xxviii-xxix.

45. Cf. Hill, "Theology," p. 1026.

46. This is discussed in the preceding section of this chapter. Cf. p. 9.

47. Cf. Panikkar, "Hermeneutics of Comparative Religion," pp. 38- 39.

48. In fact, there are theologians who acknowledge the fact that the theology of religions does not have an epistemological status. The International Theological Commission, for example, in its document Christianity and the World Religions, writes: "theology of religions does not yet have a clearly defined epistemological status." International Theological

Commission, *Christianity and the World Religions*, Vatican City: 1996, no.4; as cited by Michael L. Fitzgerald and Felix A. Machado, "Emerging Christian Theology of Religions," Pro Dialogo, 3 (2002) 3, p. 318. Henceforth, Fitzgerald, "Emerging Christian Theology of Religions."

49. Cf. Alan Race, *Christians and Religious Pluralism*, 2nd ed. (London: SCM Press and Maryknoll, New York, 1983), 1994. The three typologies of exclusivism, inclusivism and pluralism will be discussed at length in the next chapter in order to bring out their inadequacies in the theology of religions.

50. Cf. John Hick, *The Rainbow of Faiths: Critical Dialogues on Religious Pluralism* (London: SCM Press, 1995), pp. 18-23. Henceforth, Hick, The Rainbow of Faiths.

51 Cf. Jacques Maritain, *Preface to Metaphysics* (London: Sheed and Ward, 1939), p. 56.

52. The Sophist, 259 a., in Plato, *The Works of Plato*, trans. Jowet, ed. I. Edman (New York: Modern Library, 1928).

53. Cf. Parmananda R. Divarkar, *The Act of Being: A Centenary Tribute to Thomas Aquinas* (Bombay: The Newman Institute, 1973), pp. 71-72. Henceforth, Divarkar, The Act of Being.

54. Thomas Aquinas, *Disputations: The Power of God*, VII, 3; as cited by Divarkar, The Act of Being, p. 98.

55. Divarkar, The Act of Being, p. 109.

56. Aristotle, *Commentary to the Physics*, book 5, lecture 3, no. 667; as cited by Luigi Bogliolo, *Metaphysics*, trans. Myroslaw A. Cizdyn (Bangalore: Theological Publications of India, 1987), p. 19. Henceforth, Bogliolo, Metaphysics.

57. Cf. Bogliolo, Metaphysics, p. 19.

58. The present book presupposes the fact that there can be one theology of religions common to every religious tradition. However, this assumption has been questioned in some quarters. Thus, for example, in the document *Christianity and the World Religions*, the International Theological Commission attempts to answer the questions: Can there really exist a theology of religions which is acceptable to all? Is a universal theology of religions possible? The document says that "if theology is *fides quarens intellectum* it is not clear how one can abandon the dogmatic principle or reflect theologically, if one dispenses with one's own resources of truth." (International Theological Commission, *Christianity and the World Religions*, Vatican City: 1996, nn. 6 and 7). In other words, "if by definition theology is making sense of reality in the light of a particular faith, then there cannot be a theology of

religions which can become acceptable to the persons who live outside that particular faith." Fitzgerald, "Emerging Christian Theology of Religions," p. 318. However, not everyone is going to accept the definition of theology given by the Commission. Besides, if its line of reasoning is taken further, then it can be argued that since individuals belonging to similar faith traditions can have conception of God which is different from the conceptions of God others have, theology will also vary from individual to individual belonging to the same faith tradition. Hence, such arguments, I guess, are very naïve. Further, it is felt that there are certain common elements that we can pinpoint in every religion such as a belief in the existence of a Supreme Reality, adherence to a set of moral code that bind the followers of a particular religion, a belief in the existence after one's death, etc. although variations persist due to differences in cultural, environmental and other factors. In fact, some scholars are now speaking of a possibility of a trans-religious understanding of God. Cf. A. Pushparajan, "Gandhi's Contributions to a Trans-religious Understanding of God," *Shepherd's Voice*, 1 (October- December 2002), 4, pp. 344-366. Hence, our contention here is that there is a possibility of having a theology of religions common to all religions. We are exploring the philosophical basis for this science in this dissertation.

59. Ludwig Wittgenstein, *Tractatus logico-philosophicus*, eds. D.F. Pears and B.F. McGuinness (London: Routledge and Kegan Paul, 1961), 2.202-2.222. For further readings on Correspondence theory of truth, cf. D.J. O'Connor, *The Correspondence Theory of Truth* (London: Hutchinson, 1975); J.L. Mackie, *Truth Probability and Paradox: Studies in Philosophical Logic* (Oxford: Clarendon Press, 1973), pp. 17-58.

60. J. L. Austin, "Truth," *Truth*, ed. George Pitcher (New Jersey: Prentice Hall, Englewood Cliffs, 1964), p. 22.

61. For further readings on Coherence theory, cf. Nicholas Rescher, *The Coherence Theory of Truth* (Oxford: Clarendon Press, 1973); Keither Lehrer, Knowledge (Oxford: Clarendon Press, 1978), pp. 45-47.

62. Cf. William James, *Pragmatism* (New York: McKay, 1907), p. 299. For further readings on Pragmatic theory of truth, cf. David McKay, *The Meaning of Truth* (New York: David McKay, Inc., 1909); Charles Morris, *The Pragmatic Movement in American Philosophy* (New York: George Braziller, 1970); William Alston, "Pragmatism and the Theory of Signs in Pierce," *Philosophy and Phenomenological Research*, 17 (1956-57), 79-88.

63. R.R. Diwakar, *Saga of Satyagraha*, 2nd ed. (New Delhi: Gandhi Peace Foundation, 1969), p. 18. Henceforth, Diwakar, Saga of Satyagraha.

64. Diwakar, *Saga of Satyagraha*, p. 18.

65. Diels, fragment 5 & 8; as cited by Bogliolo, Metaphysics, p. 25; Emphasis in the original.
66. Bogliolo, Metaphysics, p. 25; Emphasis in the original.
67. Bogliolo, Metaphysics, p. 27; Emphasis in the original.
68. Bogliolo, Metaphysics, p. 25; Emphasis in the original.
69. M.K. Gandhi, *An Autobiography* (*The Story of my experiments with truth*), trans. Mahadev Desai, reprint, 1996 (Ahmedabad: Navajivan Publishing House, 1927), p. xi. Henceforth, Gandhi, Autobiography. 1976 reprint of the same book is also used. Henceforth, Gandhi, An Autobiography, reprint 1976.
70. Cf. Frederick J. Streng, "Truth" *The Encyclopaedia of Religion*, ed. Mircea Eliade, vol. 15 (New York: Macmillan Publishing Company, 1987), p. 63.
71. Mahadev Desai, The Diary of Mahadev Desai (Ahmedabad: Navajivan Karalaya, 1953), p. 120.
72. Cf. A. Pushparajan, *From Conversion to Fellowship: The Hindu-Christian Encounter in the Gandhian Perspective*, Dialogue Series No. 6 (Allahabad: St. Paul's Publications, 1990), pp. 25-28. Henceforth, Pushparajan, From Conversion to Fellowship.

1

THE THEOLOGY OF RELIGIONS: A CRITICAL OVERVIEW

The theology of religions is a recent science. It arose from a Christian effort to wrestle with the problem of understanding the existence of other religious traditions. Most of the Christians were brought up in a mono-religio-cultural ambience of Europe and hence, in the process of their encounter with other religions, they were unable to come to terms with the vibrant and deep-rooted faith of the followers of other traditions as it contradicted their hegemonistic views on Christianity. This resulted in an *impasse* in the theology of religions.

This stand off consisted in whether or not to recognize squarely the fact that distinct religious communities actually propose definite aims for human life and to grant legitimacy to such claims from the viewpoint of their faith. To put it differently, can one belong physically to one's religious habitat and practise one's faith in the theological mould proposed by one's religion and yet psychologically feel for the truth claims of other religious traditions which centre around an understanding of God, which is incompatible with one's own? Christian theologians have come up with possible ways of understanding such relationships. This chapter begins with a brief clarification of some concepts and then proceeds to critically evaluate the various solutions presented by the different thinkers in solving the impasse in the theology of religions.

RELIGION, PARADIGM AND MODEL

An understanding of the distinction among the three major concepts, namely, religion, paradigm and model becomes imperative because the theology of religions is concerned mainly with three models which have undergone further shifts. The distinction between paradigm and religion is one of content and form, image and frame or text and context. The term paradigm[1], understood in the sense in which Thomas Kuhn used it in his book *The Structure of Scientific Revolutions,* means total constellation, the conscious-unconscious "total constellation of convictions, values, and patterns of behaviour"[2] that obviously shape religion but not just religion. "Insofar as religion is a particularly large fact within this total constellation and represents a very specific (transcendentally grounded and with immanent consequences) theoretical-practical system of coordinates, it is more than a paradigm, more concentrated than a paradigm."[3]

The distinction between a model[4] and a paradigm, on the other hand, can be succinctly explained thus: "Models" are descriptive; they call attention to aspects of some reality without claiming to define the reality in any adequate and distinctive manner. Consequently, models do not exclude each other; on the contrary, they must be viewed as complementing each other and need to be combined in order to yield a comprehensive view of the reality concerned."[5] The opposite is the case where paradigms are concerned.

Now, the theology of religions has undergone a double paradigm shift, from ecclesiocentrism through Christocentrism to theocentrism, that is, from exclusivism through inclusivism to pluralism. According to the ecclesiocentric view, salvation was deemed available to people only through the Church community which explicitly professed faith in Jesus Christ. The underlying implication in replacing Christocentrism with theocentrism is that it is no longer possible to refer universal salvation to Jesus Christ, whether or not faith in Him be explicitly professed in the Church. Jesus Christ is no longer to be seen as the constitutive Saviour for all humankind whose saving power is operative beyond the boundaries of the Christian Church. Rejected here are not only the notions of obligatory belonging to the Church for salvation but also the universal mediatorship of Jesus Christ in the order of salvation.[6]

Theologians involved in the theology of religions have defended these typologies. Paul Knitter, for example, argues in favour of the typology in the theology of religions – exclusivism, inclusivism and pluralism – saying that "these three classifications represent in broad lines the differing presuppositions and approaches within recent Christian efforts to make sense of the many religions."[7] Knitter adds the caveat that theological models are only illuminating so long as they are treated as a 'workable framework' and leave room for expansion and modification. Alan Race, another thinker, is of the opinion that the three broad typological approaches in the theology of religions are useful. He says that many of those who distance themselves from it nearly always illustrate one of its categories in their positive proposals.[8]

It is in line with these theologians that an effort is made in this chapter to critically examine the three typologies that are in vogue in the theology of religions. However, realising their inadequacies in effecting a solution to the problems in the theology of religions, theologians have come forth with further models. After discussing these models, which are shown to be deficient, the present chapter endeavours to go beyond these models and suggests possibilities of taking recourse to categories other than Western in order to help in understanding and solving the problems in the theology of religions.

EXCLUSIVISM

Exclusivism was a dominant position during the patristic period in Christianity's approach to other religions.[9] However, the major turning point in Christianity's relation with other religions coincided with the establishment of Christian faith as the official religion of the Roman Empire in the fourth century. From being victims of persecutions, Christians eventually destroyed the Roman Empire's pagan temples, fostered a culture of contempt for the Jews, and later went to war with Muslims. The attitudes and beliefs that spawned this behaviour derived from both Christianity's sense of its own religious absoluteness and the Hellenistic (later Western) sense of its own cultural superiority and universal destiny.[10]

In the Christian context, exclusivism can be understood as the position which accepts as the basis for its view of other religions the following four propositions: (a) Jesus Christ is the unique Incarnation of God, fully God and fully man; (b) only through the person and work of Jesus Christ is there the possibility of salvation; (c) the Bible is God's unique revelation recorded, and thus is true and authoritative; and (d), where the claims of Scripture are incompatible with those of other faiths, the latter are to be rejected as false.[11]

In other words, exclusivism avers that the Christian revelation is the only bona fide revelation while other revelations are not. To quote Alan Race, "Exclusivism is the view that only in Christian faith can the authentic truth of God's offer of transcendent vision and human transformation in the world be found . . . "[12] It accepts that what is at stake is not a comparison of religious benefits, fruits or experiences but a theological judgment. "It is simply that those who 'organize life outside the covenant community of Jesus Christ' are not recipients of divine grace. 'Christian faith' and 'the rest' are different species."[13]

Exclusivism is also known as ecclesiocentrism because it held that outside the Church there is no salvation. It believes that any recognition of the truth or saving power of other religions or religious figures is an insult to God; it denigrates what God has done in Jesus. Therefore, it becomes imperative on the part of every Christian to engage actively in the mission of winning people for Christ. Every possible means should be employed in this process. Even dialogue becomes an instrument in working for the conversion of peoples. There is to be one religion.[14]

The word, 'exclusivism', however, has negative connotations. In fact, it has undesirable nuances of narrow-mindedness, arrogance, insensitivity to others, self-righteousness, bigotry, and so on. Hence this model of understanding religions has been criticised for various reasons. Alan Race is of the opinion that one can notice two main principles at work in exclusivism. "First, there is an appeal to the theological notion of revelation – 'God has given'; and second, there is the confessional clinging to the 'structure and content of Gospel faith itself.'"[15] However, these two principles cannot stand the scrutiny of reason.

In the first principle, revelation is spoken of as something static. But Charlesworth says that revelation is essentially a voluntary act. In fact, an "authentic religion is the gratuitous human response to a gratuitous revelation of the divine."[16] This implies that human response to revelation cannot be one of passive reception. In the voluntary act of its recognition, revelation is experienced as a gift and creatively appropriated, moulded and interpreted through human religious imagination. Hence the exclusivist claim of a neat revelation cannot be entertained.

The second principle poses a twin dilemma in understanding the biblical story in itself and in relation to other religions. Exclusivism appeals "to the 'structure and content of Gospel faith itself' with its background in the 'biblical story' as a whole."[17] But this requires that we need to interpret the biblical literature in respect of 'other religions' besides interpreting the Bible as a single 'biblical story culminating with Jesus Christ.' These can cause problems from both exegetical and theological perspectives. Exegetically, the problem is within, namely, that even today, there are people who do not accept Jesus as the culmination of the biblical story. Theologically, the problem is from without, namely, how to recognize and relate this uniqueness with other uniquenesses.

Gavin D'Costa raised another question against exclusivism. He is of the opinion that exclusivism is very inflexible and its either-or position is impossible in matters of salvation. In his book *Theology and Religious Pluralism,* D'Costa wrote:

> Exclusivism stands in diametrically opposite corner but is equally rigid, it too being based on dialectic of either-or. It is untenable from a biblical and theological point of view and actually involves intrinsic contradictions. An exclusive emphasis on merely one of the pairs of crucial axioms that ought to govern a Christian theology of religions leads to insoluble theological problems. [18]

A major factor contributing to the undermining of an exclusivist approach to other religions is the unprecedented exposure people in the West have today to adherents of other faiths.

> For those led to believe that morally Christianity is vastly superior to other religions, and that only those who acknowledge the lordship of Jesus Christ can exemplify saintly virtues, it is a rude shock indeed to be confronted with outstanding religious figures from other traditions. How are we to account for the towering figure of Mohandas Gandhi? If Hinduism is false, how is it that Gandhi could live such a morally exemplary life as a Hindu? . . . .[19]

The growing acceptance – even within Christian circles - of the doctrine of soteriological universalism, according to which all persons, regardless of religious affiliation, will in the end enjoy God's salvation, is still another factor that negates Christian exclusivism. It is argued that if God is indeed a God of love, He is morally obligated to provide all persons with equal opportunity to respond to Him. Maintaining that salvation is necessarily linked to personal response to the person and work of Jesus Christ is said to be incompatible with God's goodness and love, since it allegedly cuts off from the possibility of salvation those who through no fault of their own have never heard of the gospel of Jesus.[20]

Exclusivism is irreconcilable with the growing concept of interdependent global family. It is frequently assumed that there is something necessarily arrogant and intolerant about holding that one religion is true, and that those differing from it are false. Similarly, it is often claimed that exclusivism must be rejected because it has such reprehensible effects upon the relations between various cultures and religious traditions. Since we are today members of an increasingly interdependent global community, and all face common threats of nuclear annihilation, famine, and overpopulation, we must at all costs strive for harmony and peaceful cooperation among various cultures and traditions. Maintaining that one particular religion is uniquely true and that the followers of other faiths embrace false beliefs is, it is said, somehow unable to get along with this shared vision.[21]

Further, Christian exclusivism is undermined by what we might call the pragmatic view of religion[22], which minimises the questions of truth and falsity and emphasizes instead what religion does for its adherents. For many people, the purpose of religion is simply to help people cope with in the complex and bewildering world. One looks to religion in times of major crisis such as serious illness or death to provide peace, solace, and encouragement. It is simply something to help us to attain inner peace and tranquillity in a complex and uncertain world. Thus to look to religion to answer ultimate metaphysical questions about the nature of humankind and its relation to God is to misunderstand the nature and role of religion. It follows, then, that different religions should be evaluated on the basis of how effective they are in providing the desired solace and tranquillity and not in terms of truth claims.[23]

Still another factor that contributed to the rejection of exclusivism is what Lesslie Newbigin and others have referred to as the tendency today to make a sharp distinction between the public realm of facts and the private world of values, opinions, and preferences. Truth is held to belong to the public realm of facts – pre-eminently in the physical sciences – and not to the private world of values and preferences. Since religion is said to be limited to this private world of values and preferences, questions of truth and falsity are inappropriate in religious matters. Hence the very idea of exclusivism does not arise.[24]

Lesslie Newbigin points out the implications of the dichotomy between the public domain of fact and the private realm of values and the banishment of religion to the latter.

> In contrast to traditional societies, modern Western society leaves its members free, within very wide limits, to adopt and hold their own views about what is good and desirable, about what kind of life is to be admired, about what code of ethics should govern one's private life. As a natural extension of this, with the growing presence of large numbers of Muslims, Sikhs, Hindus, and Buddhists in areas formerly designated as Christendom, it is assumed by a large number of Christians that the principle of pluralism applies here also. The rival truth-claims of the different religions are not felt to call for argument and resolution; they are simply part of the mosaic – or perhaps one should say kaleidoscope - of different values that make up the whole pattern.[25]

The growing impact of relativism[26] also contributed to the decline of exclusivism. Roger Trigg has observed that historically epistemological and moral relativism have always been attractive options when people who had previously led settled and complacent lives are suddenly confronted with new and different ideas and practices.[27] In his recent provocative work *The Closing of the American Mind*, Allan Bloom provides an incisive analysis of the impact of relativism on American higher education. He states: "There is one thing a professor can be absolutely certain of: almost every student entering the university believes, or says he believes, that truth is relative."[28] Thus, "tolerance and openness – radical openness to anything and everything – are prized as the greatest of virtues, and frequently the implication is that critically evaluating or rejecting as false the beliefs of others is incompatible with this spirit of tolerance."[29] Obviously under such growing impact of relativism, many challenge Christianity's claim to possess absolute, unchanging and universally valid truth about God and humankind.

Biblical scepticism is another factor that explodes the theory of exclusivism. The biblical scepticism, characteristic of much of twentieth-century higher criticism of the New Testament[30], casts suspicion on any attempt to justify theological positions merely by appealing to what the New Testament record portrays Jesus as saying and doing.

> No longer can one justify Christian exclusivism simply by referring to texts such as Jn 14: 6 or Acts 4: 12. For many biblical scholars claim that we cannot conclude that Jesus actually said what is attributed to him in Jn 14: 6 and deny that Peter's statement in Act 4: 12 can be interpreted as supporting the idea that salvation is available only through Christ.[31]

The demise of exclusivism can also be traced to the pervasive influence of skepticism[32] about religion during the twentieth century. The roots of modern scepticism, in fact, go back at least to philosophers such as Hume and Kant. However, within the twentieth century, the legacy of logical positivism, as well as the fideistic themes of the later Wittgenstein, has also contributed to the widespread suspicion of claims to knowledge in religious matters. "It [skepticism] is pervasive throughout the academic world and cannot help but be felt by students who enter the university. Much of contemporary academia – including theology – is inundated with an epistemological scepticism which regards any claim to religious truth as problematic and which views with incredulity those who hold that God has revealed himself definitively in one religious tradition."[33]

From the above discussion it is sufficiently clear that exclusivism cannot be held as a feasible model in understanding the legitimate existence of other religions. One needs to rise above the exclusivistic limits and search for other models in the pursuit of a viable theology of religions.

INCLUSIVISM

Justin the Martyr (ca. 100-165) seems to have introduced in Christianity an inclusivistic approach to other religious traditions. He developed a doctrine of the divine Logos, according to which every human being possesses a seed (sperma) of the Logos. Thus, even pagan philosophers such as Plato and Socrates had a seminal element of the Logos (*Logos spermatikos*), and it was due to the Logos that they were able to discern the truth they so persuasively taught. He wrote: "Christ is the Word [Logos] of whom all man partakes. Those who lived by reason [Logos] are Christians, even though they have been considered atheists: such as, among the Greeks, Socrates, Heraclitus, and others like them; and among foreigners, Abraham, Elias, Ananias."[34]

By the third century, most of the Church Fathers acknowledged the positive religious value not only of Judaism and the Greek philosophers but also of Indian sages, even if they simultaneously considered the Christian revelation to surpass all of them. Clement of Alexandria, for example, in the third century noted the positive spirituality of "some of them called Sarmanae, and the others Brahmins . . . Some, too, of the Indians obey the precepts of Buddha; whom, on account of his extraordinary sanctity, they have raised to divine honour."[35]

Inclusivism claims to balance the two theological axioms, namely, the affirmation that Christian salvation has been made effective in the world through its embodiment in the person of Jesus Christ (particularity) and the belief in the universal will of God to save all peoples (universality). It "accepts that elements of religious value and truth springing from God's universal presence in creation and history are necessarily embodied in tradition. Therefore other traditions *per se* can be vehicles of Christian saving grace."[36]

Inclusivism or Christocentrism recognises truth in other religions but sees them in relation to the decisive truth in Christianity. Therefore, it holds that Jesus is constitutive of salvation; that is, God's offer of truth and saving grace has been brought about, or made possible, by the historical life, death, and resurrection of Jesus. Therefore, whatever truth or presence of the spirit is found in other faiths is in some way "anonymously Christian"[37] – Christian without a name – caused by and directed towards the fulfilment in Jesus and His community. Jesus is seen as the representative of God's saving love and truth. He does not cause God's love, for love is part of the fabric of God's being, but He does embody and manifest, and thus represent God's saving love as fully as is possible in the human condition.[38]

Thus inclusivism considers one's understanding of truth as so decisive and normative that other religious truths are to be gauged only in the light of one's own and be fulfilled by one's own. So dialogue here is just a means for understanding other truths and judging them in the light of one's own and to fulfil them by one's own.

For the inclusivists, this is what Christ is for Christians – the decisive truth by which they live their lives and the guiding norm by which

> they step into the arena of other truths. To deny this is to deny the way we function as human beings. All religions want to include other religions in their own understanding of truth. This is what gives dialogue its substance, excitement and value. To remove normative, decisive, final claims for truth is to rob dialogue of its muscle and to fill it with hot, innocuous air.[39]

In the Indian context, Dr. Radhakrishnan held an inclusivist approach towards religions. He said: "The different religions have now come together, and ... they must develop a spirit of comprehension which will ... bind them together as varied expressions of a single truth."[40]

From the Christian perspective, Gavin D'Costa held that inclusivism alone is the right theory. He recalled two basic axioms of traditional Christian faith: the universal salvific will of God and the necessary mediation of Jesus Christ. He showed that contrasting attitudes toward these two axioms account for the three basic positions of exclusivism, inclusivism and pluralism. While exclusivism relies on the second axiom, neglecting the first, and pluralism on the first, to the detriment of the second, inclusivism alone succeeds in accounting for and holding both at once.[41] Here Gavin may be right in holding inclusivism as a viable theory. This is because it explains the doubts[42] he has raised. Again these doubts were raised just because he considered the two truths as axioms. If somebody else considers something else as axioms, then the so-called axioms of Gavin would not raise any kind of questions. In other words, this kind of sophistication that Gavin is raising is least relevant to another person who holds other truths as axioms. Hence Gavin's attempt at comparing the different models is unjustified.

The inclusivists give a philosophical justification in upholding inclusivism. They say:

> We do not experience truth in general, or in the abstract; it is always delivered to us and made attractive and persuasive for us, through some concrete mediation or form. It is through a particular manifestation of truth that we know the truth. Therefore, this particular expression is decisive or normative for us. We cannot but encounter and evaluate all other claims for truth through the particular decisive form in which we have been convinced of truth or goodness in the first place.[43]

This position is untenable, as it will lead to multiple decisive truths, given the existence of multiple communities of faith. But it is contradiction in terms for something to be multiple as well as decisive.

The magisterium in the Catholic Church recognised the operative presence of the spirit in other religions, although the official position of the Church is inclusivism[44]. According to Jacques Dupuis, the singular contribution of Pope John Paul II to the theology of religions consists in the emphasis with which he affirms the operative presence of the Spirit of God in the religious life of non-Christians and the religious traditions to which they belong. In his first encyclical letter, *Redemptor Hominis* (4 March 1979), the Pope saw in the "firm belief" of non-Christians an "effect of the Spirit of truth."[45] In fact, the internal logic for the official Catholic pronouncements on dialogue derives from inclusivism, whereby the values inherent in other traditions, although prized in themselves for those who follow them, nevertheless remain 'unfulfilled' in the light of the incarnation of Christ. But this, according to Alan Race, undercuts the assumptions and aspirations of dialogue itself.[46]

The Jewish, Muslim and Buddhist representative theologians and philosophers also articulated the ambiguous position of the Christian Church, namely, openness versus absoluteness (inclusivism). On the one hand, they applauded the openness of the Pope when he speaks dialogically – the basis for which might be human rights and respect for common humanity, or a sense of transcendental spirit at the heart of all human cultures, or the need for collaboration to combat the distortions of materialism. Yet, on the other hand, they expressed grave disappointment when he continues to express Christian absolutism in his theology of religions. The mutuality inherent in dialogical relationships is eclipsed when it comes to theological reflection.[47]

Inclusivism is criticised on various grounds. It fails to identify the grace that is found outside Christianity with Christ. In order to demonstrate how it is that the grace of Christ is experienced without knowing or naming it as such from within the historical life of other faith-traditions, some theological linkage between Christian faith and other traditions needs to be specified. In the past, the notion of 'fulfilment' provided the conceptual assurance of this linkage. But this is given up in the context of Jewish-Christian encounters. Alan Race is of the opinion that such a linkage is not forthcoming from the inclusivist theologians.[48]

Another problem with inclusivism concerns about the meaning, which can be attached to the notion of Christ's 'Sacrifice' extending to other religions. How can a historical event-cum-belief – the death and resurrection of Jesus – be effective retroactively before the life of Jesus himself? How can it extend to the Buddhist tradition, which began five hundred years before the birth of Christianity? One way to circumvent this difficulty is to point not to the origins of salvation in the historical Jesus but to the climactic expression of his universal effectiveness through the presence of the logos, which He is said to embody and exhibit in quintessential measure. But this undermines the historical normativity of Christ.[49]

In order to thwart the problems of inclusivism that arose due to its link with the figure of Christ, some theologians proposed a Kingdom-centered or Spirit-centered inclusivism.[50] But these moves do not really resolve the central difficulty. Dupuis said:

> While the believers of other religious faiths perceive God's call through their own traditions and respond to it in the sincere practice of these traditions, they become in all truth – even without being formally conscious of it – active members of the Kingdom. In the final analysis, then, a theology of religions following the Kingdom-centered model cannot bypass or avoid the Christocentric perspective.[51]

It can be concluded that there is a good reason why both Exclusivism and Inclusivism are not always capable of being distinguished succinctly from one another.

> In so far as exclusivist thinking has a universalist aspect (recognizing the general divine presence throughout creation) and therefore leans towards inclusivist thinking, and in so far as inclusivist thinking bases its universal emphasis (recognizing other faith-traditions as vehicles of salvation) on Christian absolutism and therefore leans towards exclusivist thinking, Exclusivism and Inclusivism are two sides of the same coin. They are distinguished mainly by their attitudes towards other faith-traditions as valid vehicles of . . . 'transcendent vision and human transformation.'[52]

PLURALISM

Pluralism is another model introduced as an alternative to both exclusivm and inclusivism. It is the very idea of growth in religions that promoted theologians to speak of this model. In fact, John Hick says that the biggest step in the development of interreligious relations is to accept the very idea of development. Christianity, like other religions, has liked to think of itself as unchanging truth flowing down the centuries. But in fact it has, like every other religion, been a continuous history of change.[53] Further, in Asia, religious plurality is an accepted fact. V. F. Vineeth writes: "it is a reality into which we are born, in which we are brought up and with which we continue to live. Encounter with other religions is not a matter of surprise, but a mode of living for us. It helps us to develop in our hearts a vision of God, as a loving Father, whose children we all are, irrespective of our different religions."[54]

The most influential exponent of theological pluralism, which believes that religion, like any other aspect of the human species, could be shown to be in the process of development, is the German liberal theologian Ernst Troeltsch. "As a historian of religion, Troeltsch sees religion as a series of separate complexes and more particularly sees Christianity as a historical phenomenon, which must be set in its own context and not treated, as a unique supernatural entity, which owes nothing to the culture out of which it has been formed."[55] In fact, in recognizing this reality of religious and historical pluralism, he felt painfully how it clashed with what he had learnt about the nature of Christianity.

Pluralism as a theory of religion accepts all religions on equal footing without ascribing any special status to any one religion including Christianity. However, it should be borne in mind that pluralism does not imply undermining of one's beliefs. It only accepts other possible saviours for others. Therefore,

> . . . the theocentric pluralists have no intention of undermining the faith-commitment of Christians, nor the integral demands which such a commitment makes on the person. At stake, however, is the universal significance and constitutive role which Christianity attributes to it. The contention is that a person's faith in Jesus Christ implies that one has encountered God's self-gift and communication of life in the human person of Jesus of Nazareth – not, however, that this historical person is the obligatory way for all human beings in whatever circumstances of place and time. In other words, to believe in Jesus Christ is to believe that I am saved through him, not that he is the Saviour of the world. Jesus is the way for Christians, but other ways make him unnecessary for others.[56]

On the contrary, what religious pluralism implies is that beyond the varieties of forms of religions, there is the reality of God, the ultimate incomprehensible one, to whom we move with forms of religious worships and patterns. It does not mean that many religions worship and believe in the same God and that therefore religious differences and philosophical and theological clashes between different religions in their reflective-systematic dimensions are irrelevant.[57]

This follows that pluralism in its vedantic sense is not accepted. For, Vivekananda, a follower of Advaita Vedanta, recognised a type of pluralism when he spoke of the image of a circle with different radii as an explanation of the unity-in-diversity of the religions. Variety is to be expected; but the goal of the religions remains the same: that "they are true manifestations of the same truth, and that they all lead to the same conclusions as the *advaita* has reached."[58] But for the pluralists, variety is only in the philosophical and theological realm but basically the same God is worshipped.

Further, pluralism does not mean equality of all religions in every respect. Instead, it only means equality of rights. Giving up finality is not the same as accepting without question every dimension, belief and value of any religion in the dialogue. Paul Knitter says: "Pluralists do not mean that all religions, in their nature as religions and their present condition, are equally valid in all they teach or do, or really say the same thing. Rather, pluralists are stating that in order to have a real dialogue, all the religious participants have to have equal rights."[59]

Pluralism also implies the denial of constitutive universal mediatorship of Jesus Christ, and acceptance of the equal validity of all religions. It refers to the substitution of many "ways" or saving figures leading to God-the-Center, in place of the one, universal, constitutive mediation of Jesus Christ. The various religions, Christianity included, represent as many ways leading to God, all of which, differences notwithstanding, have the same validity and equal value. Hence pluralism endeavours to renounce claims to uniqueness. The reasoning of the pluralists is as follows: "If Christianity sincerely seeks a dialogue with the other religious traditions – which it can only seek on a footing of equality – it must first of all renounce any claim to uniqueness for the person and work of Jesus Christ as a universal constitutive element of salvation."[60]

Religious pluralism as a theory of religious plurality is not only a rational act but also a theological act. In other words, religious pluralism is to be accepted not only by reason but also by faith. This entails an acceptance of the fact of other religions and an understanding of other religions from the perspective of each one's religious experience, but not separated from the perspective of one's own faith. This obviously does not exclude an evaluative judgment. To the Christian, this theological act of religious pluralism requires to place one's Christ experience vis-à-vis his experience of religious pluralism as a given fact. In other words, to the Christian, religious pluralism means that he must be committed to Christ and open to all religions. It also demands one to be humble and deeply prayerful in one's religious assertions. It also asks one to approach other religions with deep respect, wondering at the mysterious way God guides His people all over the world.[61]

Schillebeeckx was able to appreciate the plurality of religions when he asserted: "The multiplicity of religions is not an evil which needs to be removed, but rather a wealth which is to be welcomed and enjoyed by all."[62] Elsewhere he observed: "logically and practically, multiplicity now takes priority over unity . . . the multiplicity of religions is not an evil which needs to be removed, but rather a wealth which is to be welcomed and enjoyed by all."[63] He considered the problem of pluralism not merely as factual. "In my view," says Schillebeeckx, "the question for us is whether the pluralism of religions is a matter of fact or a matter of principle."[64]

Theologians in India seem to favour pluralism. The statement issued by the Thirteenth Annual Meeting of the Indian Theological Association (28-31 December 1989), under the title "Towards an Indian Christian Theology of Religious Pluralism" said:

> The religions of the world are expressions of the human openness to God. They are signs of God's presence in the world. Every religion is unique and through this uniqueness, religions enrich one another. In their specificity, they manifest different faces of the supreme Mystery, which is never exhausted. In their diversity, they enable us to experience the richness of the One more profoundly. When religions encounter one another in dialogue, they build up a community in which differences become complementarities and divergences are changed into pointers to communion. (32).[65]

Positively, religious pluralism seems to have its roots in the depth of the Divine Mystery itself and in the manifold ways in which human cultures have responded to that mystery. "Far from being a hindrance that must be overcome, or else a fact of life to be tolerated, religious pluralism needs to be welcomed, with thankfulness, as a sign of the superabundant riches of the Divine Mystery, which overflows to humankind, and as an outstanding opportunity for mutual enrichment, "cross-fertilization," and "transformation" between the traditions themselves."[66]

In the context of religious pluralism, what is more important is not merely the existence of religions but their persistence in providing the adherents with a transcendental vision and a possibility for transforming human life. It is this reason that compels one to accept religious pluralism. Hence any other religious tradition is to be perceived from within one's own tradition and from one's own commitment. A type of cross-fertilization must take place where the spiritual wisdom and experience of another's religion affects one's own religious outlook.[67]

The Contributing Factors of Pluralism

Alan Race speaks about a number of factors that have contributed to the modern Christian response to other faith-traditions. They include religious studies, friendships, mission, dialogue, critical thinking, toleration, secular ethos and interdependent world. A brief account of these factors will give a better understanding of religious pluralism.

Religious Study in the recent times, according to Alan Race, is a multidisciplinary endeavour wherein religions are studied without faith conviction on the part of the student. "It employs numerous methodological specialisms, including historical, phenomenological, psychological, sociological and anthropological approaches, among others. The upshot of this mushrooming of perspectives and knowledge is that we know more about the world's multiplicity of religious life than ever before."[68] Formerly, religious studies were governed only by one methodology, namely, the light of one's own faith. But today religious studies follow various methodologies. It is precisely these differing modes of study that deepen one's knowledge regarding religious plurality.

Friedrich Heiler, the celebrated German historian of religion, outlines the results of the new studies undertaken in religion. He claims that while removing mutual suspicion, the new religious studies bring in open-mindedness and collaboration. He contends: "A new era will dawn upon mankind when the religions will rise to true tolerance and cooperation on behalf of mankind (sic). To assist in preparing the way for this era is one of the finest hopes of the scientific study of religions."[69]

It is possible to sum up the scholarly goals of scientific study of religions thus: They include: a) clarifying terms and correcting misconceptions about particular faith-traditions and their historical developments; (b) offering scholarly challenges to assumptions and processes governing encounters between individuals and faith-communities and (c) assisting the intellectual critique of models that seek to honour both the 'strangeness' and the 'resonance' between traditions.

A second factor that contributed to today's recognition of religious plurality is personal friendships beyond one's religious boundary. In fact, friendships between people of different traditions trespass the boundaries of religious commitment. In friendship, people learn how a religion informs other persons as a way of life rather than simply as a giving set of beliefs, ritual or moral prescriptions. "Through friendship, self-sufficiency in religion is turned inside out, suggesting that religious identity is not only a function of one's own stories, traditions and practices, but is also evolving to become dependent on the broader context of interfaith relationships."[70]

The friendship that existed between Charlie F. Andrews and a fellow Muslim from Delhi Munshi Zaaka Ullah is an illustration of genuine interreligious friendship. Speaking about their friendship, Nazir Ahmed, a Muslim scholar said: "Their love for each other was pure and disinterested. Both of them had penetrated deep down into the fundamental truth of religion itself, apart from creeds and dogmas. Their mutual affection, which was so profound and sincere, was really love for the sake of God. It did not depend on man."[71]

Another factor that made religious pluralism possible is the changed outlook on the concept of mission in the contemporary missiology. Earlier mission understood as implanting churches across the globe. Missionary activity has often been accused of playing a role, however that role be, in the destruction of non-Western cultures, the political and economic subjugation of colonized peoples, and the denigration of non-Christian religious commitments. But today mission is understood differently. David Bosch, the celebrated missiologist said: "The *missio dei* is God's activity which embraces both the church and the world, and in which the church may be privileged to participate."[72]

Formerly, mission meant destroying other cultures because they were diabolic and implanting the Western Church and its culture. But today it is understood in terms of sharing of God's mission and hence mutual enrichment. The roots of these changing perceptions of mission in relation to the world religions stem also from experiential encounter. Most missionaries travelled from Europe convinced of the superiority of the Christian message and its power for salvation. But their experience brought them face to face with a different reality.[73]

One more factor that opened up new vistas in religious pluralism is dialogue. Dialogue involves the critical sharing of experiences, insights and values through commitment to mutuality in the search for truth. It is most clearly a process, a bringing together of different voices without prescribing necessarily to a particular outcome. Dialogue is, as Wesley Ariarajah affirms, "an attempt to help people to understand and accept the other in their 'otherness.'"[74] In this sense, it shows a tendency towards valuing plurality and this explains its adoption by the interfaith movement.

Reinterpretation of exclusive biblical texts is an additional factor for the recent change in Christian approach to other religions. Critical thinking implies that our notions from the past regarding religions need to be revised. Often it is the scriptures that need to be critically studied. Thus for example, the so-called exclusivist texts found in the Bible should be studied in their context. The texts become misleading when taken out of their first-century context. Thus commenting on Jn 14: 6 which says, "I am the way, the truth, and the life; no one comes to the Father but by me," John Fenton, a British New Testament Scholar said:

> What seems to have happened is that awareness of what they had received through faith in Christ and baptism in his name led Christians to make claims for Jesus that were total: all that they had was his gift; in this context, that was all they could say, and they could not be expected to say less. To ask whether those who are faithful to another religion, either before the birth of Christ or after, are in communion with God and partake of his Spirit, is to raise an entirely different question, and to move into a context that calls for other considerations.[75]

In other words, Jn 14: 6 is the outcome of the experience of totality of the disciples and not the outcome of a comparative study, which was entirely out of the question.

The recent revivalism in other religions demands one to go beyond tolerance and accept religious plurality. "Toleration implies 'putting up' with the one who is 'other', provided that this 'other' does not interfere in the internal affairs of 'my' community and tradition."[76] But this minimalist view has become unrealistic in the face of the strain that the sheer variety of religious traditions and groupings jostling for equal recognition in the civic sun, places on tolerance. Hence there is a need to go beyond tolerance.

Formerly, the imperialist British in India (East India Company), for example, tolerated local faiths by not interfering with their rituals, temple worship, etc. This was merely out of pure survival concerns and not out of any acceptance of the validity of local religions and a subsequent love for them. But today, the British even in the United Kingdom are moving towards recognition of Hinduism as a religion in the context of the presence of a large group of Hindus residing in that country.

Secular ethos is still one more factor for acceptance of religious plurality. This is because a tolerant spirit allows in principle the faith-communities to be treated on an equal basis in a society determined largely by a secular ethos. For, in a secular society, every individual voice will be given equal respect and a hearing. That means a spirit of tolerance will not hold good. We need to move far beyond tolerance, which necessarily implies that an attitude of superiority of self as against inferiority of others be given up.

Many of the problems that the world faces do not respect national boundaries. They are global problems. Thus the threats of population increase, poverty, ecological degradation, disease, militarisation in league with a flourishing arms trade, and political instability affect every nation. Under such problems of planetary scale, people speak of an interdependent world. Some theologians have tried to identify the spiritual resources for tackling these global crises. But such resources will have to be derived from a sense of shared values and beliefs found in different religions. The problems that ignore boundaries require to be answered by a religious approach, which is equally impatient with boundaries. Hence interreligious approach is a must in today's context.

The emergence of global ethics demands religious plurality as well as social and cultural pluralism. Bruce Grelle, a scholar of comparative religious ethics, said: "The inter-faith movement is one of the few places in contemporary society where it is possible to employ a moral language of universal interests and the common good while recognising and even celebrating the irreducible plurality of religious, social, and cultural life."[77]

Theologians on Pluralism: Panikkar

In his theology of religions, Raimundo Panikkar introduced different models of understanding the phenomenon of religion. Each of these models advocated pluralism. The Rainbow model implies that

> ... the different religious traditions of mankind are like the almost infinite number of colours that appear once the simply white light of reality falls on the prism of human experience; it diffracts into innumerable traditions, doctrines and religions, through culture, geography and many other factors. Through any particular colour, namely, religion, one can reach the source of the white light. Provided there is not total darkness, any follower of a human tradition can reach his or her fullness, salvation. Just as the mixing of two colours may give rise to another, so the meeting of two religious traditions may give birth to a new one. In fact, most of today's religions are the result of such mutual combinations.[78]

This model not only validates each religion but also accounts for the fact of religious pluralism. Each religion is valid in so far as it has the same source (Reality) and it removes darkness (sin, ignorance, etc.) and leads one to fullness (salvation, mukti, etc.).

In the linguistic model, each religion like languages is complete in its own way and yet there is a need for further growth. Explaining the model, Panikkar wrote:

> Each religion in the linguistic model, like any language, is complete in its own way and capable of expressing everything it feels the need to express. When the need to express something new arises, the means to express it is found. New needs emerge since no particular language can exhaust the range of human experience or possibilities. Religion as language must thus be open to growth and evolution and be capable of change and redefinition as the occasion calls. Constituting a word in itself, each language gives and takes from its neighbours, exercising a mutual and reciprocal influence. However, and this is an important point, each language only takes

> as much as it can assimilate. Before a totally foreign word can be introduced, there must be receptivity and a readiness to accept, or the word cannot even be received. In short, there must already be something within the language capable of accepting, understanding, adapting or refuting the particular word, sentence, or vision of the world, which is introduced by the impact of the other. The same, of course, applies to religion.[79]

The geometrical model establishes that deformation of religions is essential and is also valid so long as it is linked to the primordial position. Panikkar wrote:

> In the geometrical or topological model, deformation, not defraction, is the cause of the different forms and shapes of religions. Geometrically speaking, topological deformations are the different homeomorphic correspondence of one primordial position. Different sets of symbols express that reality according to the topological situation of any given body. This means that each religion is a dimension of the other although they appear different and even mutually irreconcilable unless a topological invariant is found. The invariant may be the theory of families of religions, or the hypothesis that all the various human ways come from a fundamental experience transformed according to laws, which have to be discovered. Or again, it might be that all religions are actually different until the topological transformations have been constructed.[80]

Further, Panikkar by using a familiar image, explains his understanding of diversity among religions. "It is not simply that there are different ways leading to the peak, but that the summit itself would collapse if all the paths disappeared. The peak is in a certain sense the result of the slopes leading to it.... It is not that this reality (the ultimate mystery) has many names as if there were a reality outside the name. This reality is the many names and each name is a new aspect."[81] The differences of naming the One Reality are so vital that their disappearance would mean the disappearance of the Reality itself. Therefore, for Panikkar, the names are not apart from the Reality but are constitutive of the Reality.

Thus, Panikkar insisted on the importance of diversity among religions. Differences, for him, make a vital difference. Each interpretation, each name for the fundamental religious fact, both enriches and qualifies that Mystery which is neither purely transcendent nor purely immanent. Panikkar affirms that the mystery within all religions is both more than and yet has its being within the diverse experiences and beliefs of the religions.[82]

Anto Karokaran, while making a critical evaluation of Raimundo Pankkar's contribution to the theology of religions, said: "The basic intuition and central thought permeating Panikkar's entire theology and practice of religion is: pluralism is grounded in the nature of man and reality. According to him reality is to be understood more as relational than as subsisting in itself."[83]

Theologians on Pluralism: John Hick

John Hick begins his epistemology of religions with a Copernican Revolution. He wrote:

> The traditional dogma has been that Christianity is the centre of the universe of faiths, with all the other religions seen as revolving at various removes around the revelation in Christ and being graded according to their nearness to or distance from it. But during the last hundred years or so we have been making new observations and have realized that there is deep devotion to God, true sainthood, and deep spiritual life within these other religions; and so we have created our epicycles of theory, such as the notions of anonymous Christianity and of implicit faith. But would it not be more realistic now to make the shift from Christianity at the centre to God at the centre, and to see both our own and the other great world religions as revolving around the same divine reality?[84]

Speaking about this Copernican Revolution in theology in his *God and the Universe of Faiths*, John Hick wrote:

> It involves an equally radical transformation in our conception of the universe of faiths and the place of our religion within it . . . (It demands) a paradigm shift from a Christianity-centered or Jesus-centered to a God-centered model of the universe of faiths. One then sees the great world religions as different human responses to the one divine Reality, embodying different perceptions which have been formed in different historical and cultural circumstances.[85]

Further, in proposing a 'new map for the universe of faiths,' John Hick offers another alternative to theocentrism, namely, Reality centeredness. In describing this map, he speaks repeatedly about the one Spirit, the one Divine Reality or Absolute, the one Logos behind all the religions. Although religions may conceive this one Reality either theistically (as personally) or nontheistically (non-personal), Hick implies that such differences are only historical, cultural, or psychological adaptations.[86] In fact, when he explains his new map more technically, Hick makes it clear that for him the differences between the religions are not incidental or insignificant. In affirming the one "ultimate reality" behind all the religions, he concludes not that every religious expression is therefore true, but that every religious expression is therefore relative.[87]

The distinction that Hick draws between the Real *an sich* and the Real as humanly thought-and-experienced becomes the starting point of his pluralistic hypothesis in religions.[88] This distinction is found in every religious tradition. Thus Hindu thought distinguished between *nirguna* Brahman, Brahman without attributes and *saguna* Brahman, Brahman with attributes. In Mahayana Buddhism there is the distinction between, on the one hand, the ultimate *Dharmakaya* and, on the other hand, this diversified into the heavenly Buddhas constituting the *Sambhogakaya* and, again these incarnate in the *Nirmanakaya*. The Taoist scripture, the *Tao Te Ching*, begins by affirming that the "Tao that can be expressed is not the eternal Tao"[89] Jewish thinker Maimonides distinguished between "the essence and the manifestation of God."[90] In Islam it is proclaimed that Allah transcends human experience and yet is manifested to human awareness. This is seen in the Quranic phrase, "The eyes attain Him not, but He attain the eyes."[91] Paul Tillich spoke of the "God above the God of theism."[92] Gordon Kaufman distinguished between the "real God" and the "available God," the former being an "utterly unknowable X" and the latter "essentially a mental or imaginative construction"[93]

In making this distinction, Hick held that religious experience is never a direct experience of the Real *an sich* but is always experience of one of the personae/impersonae. He says that there is no direct, unmediated experience of the Real. But this contention is objected on the ground that religions believe in mysticism in its varying forms. *Advaita Vedanta*, for example, distinguishes between two levels of knowledge – *apara vidya*, lower knowledge about the phenomenal reality (*vyavaharika satta*) and *para vidya*, or higher knowledge of Brahman (*pararthika satta*). The higher knowledge is direct, unmediated, intuitive knowledge of the actual nature of Brahman. Similarly, the Zen notion of *satori*, awakening, is held to be an immediate, direct, unmediated apprehension of ultimate reality transcending all duality and dichotomies.[94]

Incidentally, John Hick himself was aware of the claims of Zen and Advaita Vedanta to a direct perception of ultimate reality. Nevertheless, he argued that even in these cases there is no direct, unmediated awareness of reality and suggested to the contrary that "that which is being directly experienced is not the Real an sich but the Real manifested respectively as *Sunyata* and Brahman."[95] In other words, Hick maintained that even mystical experience involves interpretive activity and thus does not provide privileged, direct access to ultimate reality.

Besides, in developing the pluralistic thesis, John Hick depends heavily on one of Kant's most basic epistemological insights, namely that the mind actively interprets sensory information in terms of concepts, so that the environment as we consciously perceive and inhabit is our familiar three-dimensional world of objects interacting in space. John Hick wrote:

> I do not however propose to enter into questions of Kantian exegesis: for to do so could only divert attention from the application of the basic Kantian insight to an area to which he himself did not apply it, namely the epistemology of religion. For Kant's broad theme, recognising the mind's own positive contribution to the character of its perceived environment, has been massively confirmed as an empirical thesis by modern work in cognitive and social psychology and in the sociology of knowledge. In applying it to the epistemology of religion we are therefore employing a well consolidated development of contemporary understanding.[96]

It is interesting to note that the Kantian basic epistemological insights have been already stated long before by St. Thomas Aquinas, although without any thought of the kind of application to the epistemology of religion, when he wrote that "Things known are in the knower according to the mode of the knower."[97] Hick applied this basic epistemological principle to faith considered as prepositional belief, concluding that although God *a se* is simple and undifferentiated, God can only be known by human beings through complex propositions. Based on this insight, Hick argued that in relation to the divine the 'mode of the knower' differs within different religio-cultural systems so that the Real is thought-and-experienced in a wide variety of ways.

Even a near contemporary of Thomas Aquinas, a Muslim thinker al Junaid, drew a similar conclusion in a metaphor which he applied to the plurality of forms of awareness of God: "The colour of the water is the same as that of its container."[98] Although the Thomist maxim, that things known are in the knower according to the mode of the knower, says in principle all that is needed as the starting point for a pluralistic epistemology of religion, Hick says that Kant's thesis is particularly helpful because he went on to distinguish explicitly between an entity as it is in itself and as it appears in perception. For the realisation that the world, as we consciously perceive it, is partly our own construction leading directly to a differentiation between the world *an sich*, unperceived by anyone, and the world as it appears to, that is, as it is perceived by us.[99]

Thus in exploring the pluralistic hypothesis, Hick accepted that

> . . . the great world faiths embody different perceptions and conceptions of, and correspondingly different responses to, the Real from within the major variant ways of being human; and that within each of them the transformation of human existence from self-centredness to Reality-centeredness is taking place. These traditions are accordingly to be regarded as alternative soteriological 'spaces' within which, or 'ways' along which, men and women can find salvation/liberation/ultimate fulfilment.[100]

Further Hick claimed that the major religions could be regarded as different responses to the same religious ultimate:

> . . . we always perceive the transcendent through the lens of a particular religious culture with its distinctive set of concepts, myths, historical exemplars and devotional or meditational techniques. And it is this inexpungible human contribution to religious awareness that accounts for the fascinating variations of religious thought, experience, and practice around the globe and down through the centuries, in all their rational and irrational, profound and shallow, impressive and absurd, morally admirable and morally reprehensible features.[101]

The different conceptions of the religious ultimate in the major religious traditions are said to be culturally and historically conditioned human responses to the one divine reality. John Hick wrote:

> The basic hypothesis which suggests itself is that the different streams of religious experiences represent diverse awarenesses of the same transcendent reality, which is perceived in characteristically different ways by different human mentalities, formed by and forming different cultural histories . . . One then sees the great world religions as different human responses to the one divine Reality, embodying different perceptions which have been formed in different historical and cultural circumstances.[102]

However, Hick acknowledges that only recently the West perceived the fact that the other world religions have produced equally great saints, mystics and thinkers, and have been sources of spiritual and moral life and orderly frameworks of social existence, for many millions of men and women through centuries. To dismiss them as inferior now seems dangerously reminiscent of the traditional arrogance of the whites towards the black and brown majority of humankind. Therefore, the one time cultural and religious superiority is no longer tenable.[103]

This implies that pluralism is arrived not only through reason but also inductively through observation of the range of human religious experiences. These experiences show that the great world faiths embody different perceptions and conceptions of, and correspondingly different responses to, the Real or the Ultimate from within the major variant cultural ways of being human. Such a theory, according to John Hick, "will do justice to both the fascinating differences between the religious traditions and to their basic complementarity as different human responses to the one limitless divine Reality."[104] This complementarity is connected with the fact that the great world religious traditions are fundamentally alike in exhibiting a soteriological structure or in terms of Alan Race, generic religious behaviour expressed as attainment, realisation, transformation, etc.

Although there is a move towards religions coming closer, Hick is of the view that such phenomenon does not imply wishing away differences among religions but they only wash away the hostile implications of their differences. Thus as the "growing world ecumenism" spreads, however, "the common commitment of faith in a higher reality which demands brotherhood on earth"[105] will become more important than differences in doctrine and ritual. As these differences become less significant, there will be a transformation of the individual religions. Perhaps "one day such names as Christianity, Buddhism, Islam, Hinduism will no longer describe the then current configuration of men's religious experience and belief."[106] Certainly "the sense of belonging to rival ideological communities"[107] will diminish.

One of the advantages of pluralism according to John Hick is that it removes misunderstandings of the past and helps in enriching the religions now. Hence Hick wrote: "The effect of an acceptance of pluralism will not only be to end mutual misrepresentation and communal conflict, but will bring a positive mutual enrichment. Those who accept the pluralist vision are free with good conscience to benefit from the immense spiritual values and insights of other traditions."[108]

Objections to Pluralism

In his book *Theology and Religious Pluralism*, Gavin D'Costa shows that despite its apparent liberalism, the pluralistic theory with its emphasis on theocentrism imposed on the encounter of religions a divine model that corresponds exclusively to the God of the so-called monotheistic religions. It is not universal and commits the same mistake of exclusivism.[109]

To demolish pluralistic thesis, D'Costa speaks with particular force against Hick's Kantian distinction between the noumenal Real *an sich* and the phenomenal 'images' of the Real known and experienced within the specific religious traditions of global human history in varied forms.

> This is the centrepiece of Hick's hypothesis and the main give-way of Hick's capitulation to secular modernity, as far as D'Costa is concerned. It amounts to a form of exclusive intolerance, the very opposite of its intention: Hick's Enlightenment exclusivism stems from his Kantian epistemology and establishes his ontological agnosticism.[110]

However, Alan Race is of the opinion that D'Costa while raising genuine issues, has polemically overplayed his hand. In fact, Hick has repeatedly said, as seen in the preceding section, that he is using only one strand of Kan't giant *corpus,* applying it to the problems of interpreting religious plurality.

> One may accept the validity of the challenge posed by the postmodern critique of Enlightenment – that the dream of formulating an all-embracing form of universal reason has been mistaken – without thereby dismissing many of the Enlightenment's valid

insights. Similarly, one need not accept the whole of Kant's philosophy in order to see the truth of some of his proposals. Hick does not in fact repeat Kant's religious epistemology, as D'Costa seems to think, but borrows from his central insights concerning the active role of the human mind in perceiving and conceptually structuring our experience of reality. Applying this to religious experience, Hick is then able to account for the significant variations between the religious traditions concerning their basic outlooks and developed theologies and philosophies, while retaining a 'hidden common ground' in the transcendent Real.[111]

From the philosophical angle, pluralism is criticised on the ground that it is dependent on Enlightenment philosophy, which affirmed a totalising universality of reason and thereby played the role of grand narrative and became absolutist. Secondly, pluralistic approach is secularistic because it emphasised the ethical universal principles as against a cultic God.

In answer to the first objection of D'Costa against pluralism, namely, that it is a form of Enlightenment grand narrative, Alan Race said:

> The critique of Enlightenment reason has demonstrated that Enlightenment reason is itself as much a tradition-specific product as any other intellectual movement or religion. Therefore the 'grand narrative' of the Enlightenment can be seen for what it is: one narrative among others. D'Costa views Pluralism as a form of Enlightenment 'grand narrative' in religious guise, and as such fails when measured against the post-modern critique of the Enlightenment.[112]

In other words, the role of totalising universality is not really there.

Further, pluralism rejects the noumenal differences among religious phenomena but accepts real differences among the religious traditions. Hence Alan Race wrote:

> Pluralism does not erect another grand narrative, so much as follow through the consequences of philosophical observations about how knowledge comes to human consciousness and then applies this in the realm of (plural) religious consciousness. So the differences between the names given to 'That Which' is conceived of as ultimate in the different religious traditions are differences between different phenomenal manifestations of the one noumenal Ultimate Reality.

> They are not differences between different names for the same directly accessible ultimate referent.[113]

For, what Kant's philosophy observed about the knowledge conditions in human consciousness, pluralism accepts and applies to religious consciousness.

Regarding the second objection, it must be borne in mind that Hick's understanding of pluralism is not secularistic. It does not affirm ethical agnosticism; instead, it is a religiously motivated doctrine. In fact, he accepts the basic cognitive character of his Christian conviction and experience that, in turn, is confirmed by the moral and spiritual fruits it yields. He then applies the same ground rules to other traditions arguing inductively to formulate the hypothesis of an ultimate divine reality which is being differently conceived, and therefore differently experienced, from within the different religio-cultural ways of being human. Hick further explains: "This is an hypothesis offered to explain, from a religious as distinguished from a naturalistic point of view, the facts described by the historians of religions."[114] Thus Hick's position does not play the role of a grand narrative.[115]

Again, pluralism is not a form of secularism although it accepts the human conditions related to religious beliefs, traditions, symbolic patterns, and so on. On the contrary, it concerns with something sacred and affirms different centres rather than the one universal plan of salvation. In fact, Alan Race wrote: "In terms of the tension between the particularity and universality of Ultimate Reality in its Christian form, pluralism recognizes that the affirmation of universality is not the evocation of a generalized sense of divine presence in creation and history but turns out to be an affirmation of a series of differently centred and organized religious particularities, each with their own validity."[116] In this tension between universal and the particular, if one chooses to affirm one universal plan of salvation and one divine presence in creation and history, then that would be inclusivism. Instead, pluralism views universality not in the usual sense of hidden divinity in creation and history but in the generic cycle of religious life.

Specialists from Religious Studies background raise a question against pluralism. They feel that the tendency of pluralism is towards assuming similarities where in fact great divergence exists. The phrase 'transcendent vision and human transformation' pre-empts what we are to think of the religions prior to their actual encounter. Religions display different views of what is 'Transcendent' and recommend different ways of 'human transformation.' But Alan Race is of the opinion that despite divergence of views, a generic cycle of religious life is a legitimate inference to make based on observation and experience.[117]

Given the pluralists' stand that the different particular religions with their respective centres and radii are to be considered as valid, they may easily be criticised on the ground that they cannot really affirm anything about universality. If at all they do their stand on universality will be purely an assumption. However, pluralists do speak about universality because of the real generic cycle of religious life.

Politically, pluralist theology, critics say, is nothing but a handmaid of Western imperialism that seeks to mould the unity of our one world for its economic-political interests through the phenomenon known as globalisation. Alan Race says that such a criticism makes all intellectual activities including interreligious dialogue into a form of political discourse and this is unwarranted. However, the criticism is valid if we can show that the pluralist theology is incapable of developing criteria for discrimination between different values and beliefs. But such criteria are seen in the concept of 'global ethic' proposed by theologians like Alan Race.[118]

From the Christian theological point of view, pluralism is criticised on the ground that if someone is committed to God's love as revealed in Christ one cannot accept God's love in other ways. In further explaining this objection, Christoph Schwöbel wrote: "From the perspective of Christian faith there is no escape from the universality of God's presence in the particularity of religions. The particular constitution of this conviction, however, excludes the theological possibility of talking about a plurality of revelations in the religions."[119] He insists that we only know about the universal presence of Ultimate Reality by virtue of Christ. Of course, if revelation is defined as a Christian term then there will obviously be no revelation outside the Christian appreciation of it.

This objection can be answered by a counter question: just because one is committed to the love of God as manifested in Christ, does it mean that one should deny the references of God's love present in the scriptures, theologies and practices of other religions? In fact, the scriptures, theologies and practices of other religious traditions are full of references to God's love. It is odd to believe that it is permissible for a Christian to recognize the love that is bound to exist elsewhere only in terms of its Christian definition.

However, the real problem of religious pluralism lies in the central question of the meaning of revelation. It is

> . . . the dynamic tension in religious apprehension between, on the one hand, the particular experience of transcendent vision that has been generated initially under specific cultural and local circumstances, and on the other hand, the universal power and presence of transcendent vision that is accepted as the prior ground of its local manifestation. There is a theological tension between the two: the apprehension of divine universal presence derives from the power of particular experience and the particularity of experience serves a universal purpose. Negotiating this theological tension becomes . . . complex[120]

in the context of pluralism.

One way of circumventing this theological tension is to accept religions not in terms of their truth claims but in terms of the transformative purpose. Hence the pluralists accept that the religions, when conceived merely as systems of beliefs, are bound to exhibit conflicting beliefs at conceptual levels.

> However, as contexts of 'transcendent vision and human transformation' the religions are not primarily systems of philosophical and theological rationality, although of course they do involve themselves in extensive reflective processes and are shaped in large measure by them. But if the issue of plurality is approached from the perspective of the *transformative* purpose for which the religions exist, then a different possibility in the theology of religions becomes available.[121]

Another solution to the problem of pluralism lies in going beyond the forms and cherishing the essence of religions. This is because one can make a fundamental distinction between the essence (esoteric) and form (exoteric) of religion and not distinction among the religions.

> For everyone who understands truth primarily by reference to its givennes in a specific religion lives on the exoteric level; those who penetrate behind the forms to the essence and sense the primordial oneness of all religions live on the higher esoteric level. All forms are relatively false; the essence alone is true. It will eventually be discovered that what binds the religions together is

> far deeper and far more primordial than that which separates, for on the vertical axis all religions alike misrepresent the essence of things even while representing it.[122]

Further one should not be judgmental towards other forms of religions but consider them with love. This is because "a truth which in the first instance is a truth for us (in our cultural or historical context) is nevertheless still truth and life. . . .If all of us in every group seek to develop what is highest and deepest, then we may hope to meet one another. . . . In our earthly experience, the divine life is not one but many. To apprehend the one in the many – this is however, the special character of love."[123]

Finally, it is satisfying to note that John Hick initiated a Copernican Revolution in the theology of religions. However, his shift from ecclesiocentric to theocentric position is itself Christian. Perhaps his shift is not enough, although it is a plausible one. If Kantian distinction is to be taken seriously, then to say 'God-centeredness' itself may not be wholly in agreement with the Real in itself. Perhaps, one has to look for other models.

RISE OF OTHER PARADIGMS

The inadequacy of the above models in answering the various problems posed by the existence of different religious traditions, gave rise to new models in the theology of religions. One of the main objections raised against the the theocentric paradigm was its uncritical assumption of a concept of the Absolute Reality akin to the monotheistic and prophetic religions of the Western Hemisphere, one totally alien to the mystical traditions of the East. This situation forced the protagonists of theocentric pluralism to propose further models that, as it will be shown, just amount to a little more than new variations of theocentrism itself.[124]

Paul Knitter suggested soteriocentrism. He observed that all religions propose a message of salvation or human liberation. However different be the way in which such attainment is conceived and pursued, all religions share the same potential of becoming ways of salvation for their followers. The criterion according to which they need to be evaluated is the measure in which, rather than being sources of enslavement and oppression, they actually contribute to the liberation of people. In specifically Christian parlance this means that all religions are destined to be visible signs of the presence in the world of the Reign of God; all can and ought to contribute on different counts to the growth of God's reign among persons and peoples.[125]

The *soteria* that Knitter advocated calls for the global responsibility and shared commitment of the different religious traditions for "eco-human well-being"[126] and not merely the state of other-worldly existence after one's death. Therefore, the concept of salvation will include the liberative praxis that every religion speaks of.

Similarly, Paul Knitter proposed a regnocentric model. Here the theology of religions is no longer centred on the Christ-event but on the Reign of God, which builds itself up through history and is destined to reach its fulfilment in the eschatological time. The focus is no longer on the past but on the future; God and His Reign are the goal of history toward which all religions, Christianity included, tend together as to their common destiny.[127]

The Reign of God model has the merit of affirming that the followers of other religious traditions are already members of the Reign of God in history and that together with Christians they are destined to meet in God at the end of time. Nevertheless, quite apart from the fact that it continues to refer to a concept of God proper to the monotheistic religions, it does not, nor it can, for traditional Christian faith, represent a paradigm shift from the Christological to the regnocentric model. However, in the context of dialogue, the Reign of God model has the advantage of showing how Christians and the members of other religious traditions are co-pilgrims in history, heading as they do together toward God's eschatological fullness. Hence regnocentric model, it seems, guarantees cooperation of Christians with other religious traditions.[128]

Theologians further introduced other models such as logocentrism and pneumatocentrism. In both logocentric and pneumatocentric models, the *Logos* and the *Pneuma*, the Word and the Breath of God, whom Saint Irenaeus saw as the "two hands of God"[129] conjointly doing His work, tend to be severed from the Christ-event, to be viewed as autonomous and independent agents, transcending the historical and the particular, whose distinct action constitutes alternative economies of divine salvation.

In the logocentric model, it is remarked that the revealed message itself witnesses to Christ's universal action through world history; the post-biblical tradition of the early apologist does likewise, as observed previously. The conclusion is being drawn that in every event and in all circumstances it is the Word of God who saves, not precisely the Word-of-God-made-flesh, that is, Jesus Christ. "He who reveals, who saves and transforms is the Word himself"[130] 'The Christ' is a title; a title does not save. As for Jesus, He is "he in whom Christians recognize the Word, as seen, heard and touched by human senses."[131] Since for the Christians, Jesus is the Logos who saves, this model is not different from Christocentric model.

Jacques Dupuis explains this reduction to Christocentrism by taking recourse to the Johannine Prologue. After John's Prologue (Jn 1:1-4) one must affirm a universal presence of the Logos before his incarnation in Jesus Christ.

> He is the "true Light that enlightens every human being." (Jn 1:9). This anticipated presence and action of the Logos do not, however, prevent the New Testament from seeing in the Word incarnate, of whom the Prologue of the Johannine Gospel also speaks (1:1-4), the universal Saviour of humankind. Christianity has traditionally understood this to mean that the anticipated action of the Word of God is related to the event of Jesus Christ in which God's plan for human kind comes to a climax. The Word-to-be-incarnate and the Word incarnate are one indivisible reality. Jesus Christ, the incarnate Word, remains at the centre of God's plan of salvation and of its unfolding in history.[132]

Hence one can say that both Logocentrism and Christocentrism are not mutually opposed; they call to each other in a unique dispensation.

However, the whole approach as well as the formulation of the prologue, as given by Jacques Dupuis seems to be lopsided. To think that John was first aware of the logos and its varied presences everywhere in history and then finally coming to know that this Jesus was the climax of those presences of the logos is wrong. On the contrary, first he was faced with the particular man called Jesus and His singularity in terms of life transformation as well as societal transformation. Then in the course of his life when he came across the Greek concept of logos only did he realise the identity of the particular with the logos, the universal. It is this recognition that is formulated in the prologue and not its opposite. In one word, John's prologue was existential (from particular to universal) and not theoretical (from universal to particular).

In order to avoid the pitfalls of Christocentric perspectives in logocentrism, there is a need for a theology of religions to be built on a pneumatocentric model. Unlike the economy of Christ-event, unavoidably limited by the particularity of history, the economy of the Spirit knows no bounds of space and time. Free of all constraints, the Spirit "blows where it wills" (Jn 3:8). It was Paul Knitter who initiated this model. He wrote: "A pneumatological theology of religions could dislodge the Christian debate from its confining categories of 'inclusivism' or exclusivism' or 'pluralism'."[133]

It is held that the Spirit of God has been universally present throughout human history and remains active today outside the boundaries of the Christian fold. He it is who inspires people belonging to other religious traditions the obedience of saving faith, and enriches the traditions themselves with the word spoken by God to their adherents. Hence the proponents of pneumatocentrism say that while Christians secure salvation through the economy of God's Son incarnate in Jesus Christ, others receive it through the immediate autonomous action of the Spirit of God.

> The "hypostatic independence" or personal distinction between God's "two hands" is warrant for the two distinct channels through which God's savaging presence reaches out to people in distinct economies of salvation. In short, the Holy Spirit being God's necessary "point of entry" into the life of human beings and of peoples, his immediate action – which bypasses the punctual event of Jesus Christ – opens up the way for a distinct model of a Christian theology of religions, one no longer Christocentric but pneumatocentric.[134]

It is true that this model bypasses the Christocentric problems that vitiated the acceptability of other models. However, the basic question would be regarding the function of Christ if the Spirit was already working. In other words, the question is why at all, Christ needs to be born as Jesus. In fact, it can be shown that pneumatocentrism is parallel to Christocentrism. It is certain that the Holy Spirit is God's 'point of entry' wherever and whenever God reveals and communicates Himself to people. One needs to affirm clearly the universal action of the Spirit throughout human history, either before or after the historical event, Jesus Christ. But Christian faith has it that the action of the Spirit and that of Jesus Christ, though distinct, are nevertheless complementary and inseparable. Pneumatocentrism and Christocentrism cannot, therefore, be construed as two distinct economies of salvation, one parallel to the other. They constitute two inseparable aspects, or complementary elements, within a unique economy of salvation.[135]

Walter Kasper attempts to overcome this issue of parallel understanding by speaking of a pneumatologically oriented Christology. He wrote:

> A Christology in a pneumatological perspective is . . . what best enables us to combine the uniqueness and the universality of Jesus Christ. It can show how the Spirit who is operative in Christ in his fullness is at work in varying degrees everywhere in the history of humankind, and also how Jesus Christ is the goal and head of all humanity.[136]

One can raise at least two objections to the approach taken by Walter Kasper. The first objection is that if the Spirit's action is to be taken as full in Christ, does it mean that it was partial before the coming of Christ? Secondly, all these attempts are doomed to fail because theologians seem to take the problem merely at the conceptual level while the problem of revelation is one of life and existence.

Further it is held that if the Spirit was present and active in history before the Jesus event, He was so in view of, and in relation to, the historical event, which stands at the centre of the history of salvation. The specific function of the Spirit consists in allowing persons to become sharers, whether before or after the event, of the paschal mystery of Jesus Christ's death and resurrection (GS 22). Thus through the power of the Spirit, the Christ-event is being actuated through all times; it is present and active in every generation. In all cases the immediate influence of the Spirit gives expression to the operative presence of God's saving action, which has come to a climax in Jesus Christ.[137]

The problem is not at all addressed by saying that the Spirit worked in view or in relation to Christ. This will only add to the existing problem: if the Spirit was working in view of Christ-event, was it as a precursor or was not his work sufficient? If granted so, then the equality of persons in Trinity would be at stake.

Above all, the basic problem arises because one considers that there could be and there is only one way of looking at the history of salvation. To think that the history of salvation is to be understood only in the Christian perspective is presumptuous. It is true that from God's point of view, there is only one history. But from the human point of view, one can ask why one should not realistically accept the different understandings of history of salvation depending upon the different racial and cultural histories. If one thinks that there will be different histories of races, yet only one understanding of salvation history for the whole of humanity, it is wrong. It is based upon the former dichotomous understanding of body versus spirit and that the temporal deals with body and salvation deals with the spirit (soul). But this distinction is itself questioned today. If the present day holistic understanding of the human being is accepted, then the salvation history of human beings cannot be dichotomised from the temporal history of people. This means that depending upon the variety of histories of different races, their understanding of salvation histories will also be varied and many. If plurality of understanding the salvation histories is accepted, one need not be bogged down by the Jewish understanding of the history of salvation as the only one salvation history. Even within Jewish history, Jesus-event is disputed as its climax. Thus one cannot take this as the centre of human history.

To conclude, this model, as all other models, evades the crucial problems of Christian faith, namely, the uniqueness of Jesus versus the faith other religions. It does not solve them. The crucial problem in Christian faith is how to understand the universality of God's salvation in the very limited and particular revelation of Jesus. Therefore, it becomes imperative to rise above these Western models and go beyond them.

BEYOND THE PRESENT PARADIGMS

Although new models were initiated in order to thwart the criticism that the existing models did not care to take account of the Eastern religions, it is clearly shown above that even the new models failed to address the crucial issues. In fact, they could very well be reduced to the existing three models. It is in this context that M. Barnes argues that an escape must be negotiated from the rigid patterning of the threefold paradigm. The answer is not to be found in shifting from a Christocentric to a theocentric position. It lies beyond pluralism. Under the influence of interfaith encounter, the theology of religions is in fact shifting "from a pluralist to a post-modern mode."[138] This requires that theologians learn to be ""systematic without being systemic." While holding on to their religious identity, they must engage in a "theology of dialogue," not merely build a "theology for dialogue."[139]

The crux of the problem in today's theology of religions is that the problematic of shifting paradigms around which the discussion revolves implies an either-or (*aut-aut*) mode of contradiction, little congenial to the Eastern frame of mind, which thinks in terms of and-and (*et-et*). Jacques Dupuis is of the view that the Western problematic must be abandoned if one should hope to build a theology of religions founded not on mutual contradictions and confrontation but on harmony, convergence, and unity.[140]

In other words, implication in eschewing the Western problematic in the theology of religions seems to be that one needs to understand the theology of religions differently. Only then shall one be able to discover the specificity and singularity of each religious tradition, as well as the positive significance of the plurality of those traditions.[141] Thus the problem in the theology of religions lies in the content dimension.

Hence, Aloysius Pieris, an Asian theologian, expresses his disaffection with the Western approach to the theology of religions. He wrote: "I have found myself gradually appropriating a trend in Asia, which adopts a paradigm wherein the three categories mentioned above [of exclusivism, inclusivism, and pluralism] do not make sense."[142] This new paradigm is a praxis oriented approach which will recognize the "magisterium of the poor"[143] and will teach a theology of liberation that is located in the basic human community and that affirms Jesus as God's "defence pact with the oppressed."[144]

CONCLUSION

From the above analysis it is amply clear that there is a need not only to go beyond the three models but also beyond the other models which were suggested in order to circumvent the problems created by them. It is a fact that for most part, three perspectives incompatible among themselves have dominated the recent debate on the theology of religions. The argument evolved around the possibility of, or the need for changing paradigms from ecclesiocentrism to Christocentrism, and beyond to theocentrism. The other models are only substitutes for the theocentric paradigm. However, these categories within which the debate is thus being framed betray a Western way of thinking which can yield no satisfactory answer to the problem.[145] None of these models have drawn a convincing framework from where every religion can acquire legitimate existence without having to be inferior to any. The issue of uniqueness still haunts them so much that they fail to proffer a satisfactory explanation. It is very clear that these models have not addressed the issue of a common epistemological and metaphysical foundation. Instead, they have continued to emphasise their standpoint from the same epistemological and metaphysical foundation so that any legitimate and rational relationships among religions become impossible.

It is under these constraining circumstances that the present writer is compelled to search for an alternative from a non-Western background. The 'satyo-centric' model evolved from by M.K. Gandhi seems to be a viable alternative in understanding religious plurality. The difference between this model and other models discussed above is that Gandhi evolved his understanding of truth not merely from his intellectual acumen as many other scholars did, but through a consistent living of this truth in every aspect of his life. In this way, this model is not purely a speculative proposal. It has an exemplar in the very person of Gandhi himself. Therefore, the next chapter will discuss how Gandhi developed this concept of truth both in his life and in his writings.

NOTES

1. Thomas S. Kuhn initiated the term 'paradigm' in philosophy of science, where it meant, a central overall way of regarding phenomena, within which a scientist normally works. The paradigm may dictate what type of explanation will be found acceptable, but in periods of crisis a science may exchange paradigms. However, in its usual employment in the present context, the term is both ambiguous and vague. For further readings, cf. Thomas S. Kuhn, *The Structure of Scientific Revolutions* (Chicago: Chicago University Press, 1962).
2. Thomas S. Kuhn, *The Structure of Scientific Revolutions* (Chicago: Chicago University Press, 1962); as cited by Hans Küng, *Theology for the Third Millennium: An Ecumenical View*, trans. Peter Heinegg (New York: Doubleday, 1988), pp. 210-212. Henceforth, Küng, Theology for the Third Millennium.
3. Küng, Theology for the Third Millennium, pp. 210-212.
4. By a model is not meant a description of reality or a hypothesis about reality. It is simply an intelligible, interlocking set of terms and relations that it may be well to have about when it comes to describing reality or to forming hypothesis. Model is something worth keeping in mind

when one confronts a situation or tackles a job. Cf. Lonergan, Method in Theology, p. xii.

5. Dupuis, Toward a Christian Theology of Religious Pluralism, p. 181.
6. Cf. Dupuis, Toward a Christian Theology of Religious Pluralism, pp. 183-184.
7. Paul Knitter, *One Earth, Many Religions: Multifaith Dialogue and Global Responsibility* (Maryknoll: Orbis Press, 1995), p. 26. Henceforth, Knitter, One Earth, Many Religions.
8 Cf. Alan Race, *Interfaith Encounter: The Twin Tracks of Theology and Dialogue* (London: SCM Press, 2001), P. x. Henceforth, Race, Interfaith Encounter.
9. This model is similar to one of the four positions that Hans Küng speaks of with regard to the question of what is true religion, namely, that only one single religion is true and all other religions are untrue. This was the traditional Catholic position prepared in the early Christian centuries by Origen, Cyprian and Augustine. This position is defined in the Fourth Lateran Council (1215) as "*Extra Ecclesiam nulla salus*," which means, "Outside the Church there is no salvation." For further readings, cf. Küng, Theology for the Third Millennium, p. 231.
10. Cf. Küng, Theology for the Third Millennium, P. 1.
11. Cf. Harold A. Netland, *Dissonant Voices: Religious Pluralism and the Question of Truth* (Grand Rapids, Michigan: William B. Eerdmans Publishing Company, 1991), P. 34. Henceforth, Netland, Dissonant Voices.
12. Race, Interfaith Encounter, P. 23.
13. Race, Interfaith Encounter, p. 23.
14. Cf. Knitter, One Earth, Many Religions, P. 26.
15. Race, Interfaith Encounter, P. 23.
16. Max Charlesworth, *Religious Inventions: Four Essays* (Cambridge University Press, 1997), p. 10; as cited by Race, Interfaith Encounter, P. 23.
17. Race, Interfaith Encounter, p. 24.
18. Gavin D'Costa, *Theology and Religious Pluralism: The Challenge of Other Religions* (Oxford: Basil Blackwell, 1986), p. 136. Henceforth, D'Costa, Theology and Religious Pluralism.
19. Netland, Dissonant Voices, p. 28.
20. Cf. Netland, Dissonant Voices, p. 33.
21. Cf. Netland, Dissonant Voices, pp. 33-34.

22. From a philosophical point of view, pragmatism as a theory of truth and religion is untenable for a number of reasons. However, the scope of this paper does not permit a detailed discussion.

23. Cf. Netland, Dissonant Voices, p. 32.

24. Cf. Lesslie Newbigin, *Foolishness to the Greeks: The Gospel and Western Culture* (Grand Rapids: Eerdmans, 1986), p. 16. Henceforth, Newbigin, Foolishness to the Greeks.

25. Newbigin, Foolishness to the Greeks, p. 16.

26. Relativism as a philosophical theory denies that there are certain kinds of universal truths. There are two main types, cognitive and ethical. Cognitive relativism holds that there are no universal truths about the world. Some of the exponents of this version of relativism are Protagoras, Goodman, Putnam and Rorty. Ethical relativism is the theory that there are no universally valid moral principles; all moral principles are valid relative to culture or individual choice. However, relativism is unacceptable for several reasons. The scope of this paper does not permit a detailed discussion. For further readings, cf. J.A. Passmore, *A Hundred Years of Philosophy* (London: Penguin Books, 1968); G. V. Hinshaw, "Epistemological Relativism and the Sociology of Knowledge," *Philosophy of Sciences*, 15 (1948), 4-10.

27. Cf. Roger Trigg, "Religion and the Threat of Relativism," *Religious Studies* 19 (1983), p. 297.

28. Allan Bloom, *The Closing of the American Mind* (New York: Simon & Schuster, 1987), p. 25.

29. Netland, Dissonant Voices, p. 30.

30. Biblical scholars applied the principles of literary criticism to study the content of New Testament and historical criticism to study the New Testament as a historical document. In the 20th century, scholars took several new directions in this regard. They included abandoning of the liberal quest of the historical Jesus, birth of form criticism introduced by K.L. Schmidt and M. Dibelius, demythologization of the New Testament by Rudolf Bultmann, emergence of catholic critical scholarship, redaction criticism, etc. For further readings, cf. John S. Kselman and Ronald D. Witherup, "Modern New Testament Criticism," *The New Jerome Biblical Commentary*, eds. Raymond E. Brown, Joseph A. Fitzmyer and Roland E. Murphy (Bangalore: Theological Publication in India, 1999), pp. 1130-1145.

31. Netland, Dissonant Voices, p. 29.

32. The philosophical theory of skepticism refuses to grant that there is any valid knowledge; it doubts that a claim or statement is true. It cannot withstand the scrutiny of reason for several reasons. The scope

of this paper does not permit a detailed discussion. For further readings, cf. Keith Lehrer, "Why Not Scepticism?" Philosophical Forum, ii (1971), 283-298; Peter Unger, "A Defense of Skepticism," *Philosophical Review*, lxxx (1971), 198-219.

33. Netland, Dissonant Voices, p. 29.
34. Justin Martyr, "The First Apology," para. 46 in *Writings of Saint Justin Martyr*, trans. Thomas B. Falls (New York: Christian Heritage, Inco., 1948), p. 83; as cited by Netland, Dissonant Voices, p. 12.
35. Stromata I, 15; as cited by A. Roberts and J. Donalson, eds., *The Ante-Nicene Fathers*, vol. 2 (Grand Rapids, Michigan: Eerdmans, 1979), p. 316.
36. Race, Interfaith Encounter, p. 26.
37. Karl Rahner held that there is a hidden, unknown operative presence of the mystery of Christ in other religious traditions. He designated it as anonymous Christianity. This theme is treated by Karl Rahner in several essays contained in his Theological Investigations. Cf. Karl Rahner, *Theological Investigations*, 23 vols. (London: Darton, Longman & Todd, 1961-1992); Joseph H. Wong, "Anonymous Christians: Karl Rahner's Pneuma-Christocentrism and East-West Dialogue," *Theological Studies*, 55 (1994), 609-637; Gavin D'Costa, "Karl Rahner's Anonymous Christian: A Reppraisal," *Modern Theology*, 1 (1985), 131-148,
38. Cf. Knitter, One Earth, Many Religions, pp. 27-28.
39. Knitter, One Earth, Many Religions, p. 28.
40. S. Radhakrishnan, *Eastern Religions and Western Thought*, 2nd ed. (London: Oxford University Press, 1940), p. 308.
41. Cf. D'Costa, Theology and Religious Pluralism, p. 136.
42. This point will be discussed at length in the conclusion. Cf. pp. 219-221.
43. Knitter, One Earth, Many Religions, P. 28.
44. The position of the Catholic Church regarding the scope of the theology of religions and the status of other religious traditions is succinctly explained in the article "Emerging Christian Theology of Religions," written by Archbishop Michael L. Fitzgerald and Fr. Felix A. Machado of the Pontifical Council for Interreligious Dialogue and published in *Pro Dialogo*, the official bulletin of the Council. (*Pro Dialogo*, 3 (2002) 3, 313-324). For the Catholic Church, "the question to be resolved for a Christian theology of religions is not whether other religions are parallel ways of salvation but rather how they are "participatory" in the 'Way', namely Christ, the Saviour of all." (Fitzgerald, "Emerging Christian Theology of Religions," p. 320). She

believes in the possibility of salvation for all people but the question that the theology of religions should answer is: Can other religious traditions qualify as 'ways of salvation'? Do religions mediate salvation to their members? For the Christians, the article claims, the question of mediation is fundamental as Jesus Christ is believed to be "the sole mediator between God and the human person." Therefore, "one must not simply talk of all religions as "globally salvific."" (Fitzgerald, "Emerging Christian Theology of Religions," p. 322). This according to the article it would be "an epistemological error and a methodological faux pas." (Fitzgerald, "Emerging Christian Theology of Religions," p. 322). Other religions, instead, "contain in themselves values which can be related to the mystery of Christ and therefore can contribute to the rich heritage of the mystery of the Church." (Fitzgerald, "Emerging Christian Theology of Religions," p. 323).

45. RH 6, text in Acta Apostolicae Sedis 71 (1979) 257-347; as cited by Dupuis, Toward a Christian Theology of Religious Pluralism, pp. 173-174.
46. Cf. Race, Interfaith Encounter, p. 108.
47. Cf. Byron L. Sherwin and Harold Kasimow, eds., *John Paul II and Inter-religious Dialogue* (Maryknoll: Orbis Press, 1999), p. 217.
48. Cf. Race, Interfaith Encounter, pp. 26-27.
49. Cf. Race, Interfaith Encounter, pp. 26-27.
50. These models will be discussed later in this chapter. Cf. pp. 71-75
51. Jacques Dupuis, Toward a Christian Theology of Religious Pluralism, Maryknoll: Orbis Press, 1997, p. 328; as cited by Race, Interfaith Encounter, pp. 28-29.
52. Race, Interfaith Encounter, p. 37.
53. Cf. John Hick, *The Second Christianity* (London: XPress Ltd., 1994), p. 91. Henceforth, Hick, The Second Christianity.
54. V.F. Vineeth, "Committed to Christ & Open to all Religion: Theology as a Story of My Life," *Third Millennium: Indian Journal of Evangelisation*, 4 (October-December 2001), p. 24. Henceforth, Vineeth, "Committed to Christ."
55. Michael Barnes, Religions in Conversation: Christian Identity and Religious Pluralism (London: SPCK, 1989), pp. 15-16.
56. Dupuis, Toward a Christian Theology of Religious Pluralism, p. 190.
57. Cf. Race, Interfaith Encounter, p. 29.
58. Anandanand Rambachan, "Swami Vivekananda: A Hindu Model for Inter-religious Dialogue," *Inter-Religious Dialogue: Voices from a New Frontier*, ed. M. Darrol Bryant and Frank Flinn (New York: Paragon House, 1989), p. 18; Emphasis in the original.

59. Paul F. Knitter, "Between a Rock and a Hard Place: Pluralistic Theology Faces the Ecclesial and Academic Communities," *Journal of Theology* (Summer, 1997), p. 80.

60. Dupuis, Toward a Christian Theology of Religious Pluralism, p. 186.

61. Cf. Vineeth, "Committed to Christ," pp. 25-32.

62. Edward Schillebeeckx, *Church: The Human Story of God* (London: SCM Press, 1990), p. 167. Henceforth, Schillebeeckx, Church.

63. Schillebeeckx, Church, p. 166.

64. Schillebeeckx, Church, p. 164.

65. K. Pathil, ed., *Religious Pluralism: An Indian Christian Perspective* (Delhi: ISPCK, 1991), pp. 347-348. Henceforth, Pathil, Religious Pluralism.

66. Raimundo Panikkar, *The Intrareligious Dialogue* (New York: Paulist Press, 1978); John Cobb, *Beyond Dialogue: Toward a Mutual Transformation of Christianity and Buddhism* (Philadelphia: Fortress Press, 1982); as cited by Dupuis, Toward a Christian Theology of Religious Pluralism, p. 198.

67. Cf. Richard, What are they Saying, p. 3.

68. Race, Interfaith Encounter, p.2.

69. F. Whaling, ed., *Contemporary Approaches to the Study of Religion*, vol. 1 (Mouton: 1985), p. 182; as cited by Race, Interfaith Encounter, p.5.

70. Race, Interfaith Encounter, p.7.

71. Daniel O'Connor, *Relations in Religion* (Bangalore: Allied Publishers, 1994), p. 7.

72. David Bosch, *Transforming Mission: Paradigm Shifts in theology of Mission* (Maryknoll: Orbis Books, 1991), p. 48.

73. For further readings on how the concepts of mission and evangelization should be understood today in the light of biblical scholarship and the present context, cf. Joseph Pathrapankal, ""Making Disciples" (Mt. 28:18-19) in the Early Church and its Contemporary Challenges," *Third Millennium*, 5 (October- December, 2002) 4, 6-25.

74. S. Wesley Ariarajah, *Not Without My Neighbour: Issues in Interfaith Relations* (Geneva: WCC Publications, 1999), p. 14.

75. John Fenton, *Finding the Way through John* (London: Cassell Mowbray, 1995), p. 95.

76. Race, Interfaith Encounter, p. 14.

77. Bruce Grelle, "Scholarship and Citizenship: Comparative Religious Ethicists as Public Intellectuals," *Explorations in Global Ethics:*

Comparative Religious Ethics and Inter-religious Dialogue, eds. Sumner B. Twiss and Bruce Grelle (Boulder, Colorado: Westview Press, 1998), p. 56; as cited by Race, Interfaith Encounter, p. 17.

78. Panikkar, "Hermeneutics of Comparative Religion," pp. 46-47.
79. Panikkar, "Hermeneutics of Comparative Religion," pp. 46-47.
80. Panikkar, "Hermeneutics of Comparative Religion," pp. 47-48.
81. Raimundo Panikkar, *The Unknown Christ of Hinduism*, rev. ed. (Maryknoll, New York: Orbis, 1981), pp. 23-24. Henceforth, Panikkar, The Unknown Christ of Hinduism.
82. Cf. Panikkar, The Unknown Christ of Hinduism, p. 23.
83. Anto Karokaran, "Raymond Panikkar's Theology of Religions: A Critique," *Vidyajyoti*, 58 (October 1994) 10, p. 664. Henceforth, Karokaran, "Raymond Panikkar's Theology of Religions."
84. Hick, The Second Christianity, p. 82.
85. John Hick, *God and the Universe of Faiths* (New York: St. Martin's press, 1973), p. 131. Henceforth, Hick, God and the Universe of Faiths.
86. Cf. Hick, God and the Universe of Faiths, p. 131.
87. Cf. John Hick, "Pluralism and the Reality of the Transcendent," *Christian Century*, 98 (1981) 46-47; as cited by Paul F. Knitter, *No Other Name? A Critical Survey of Christian Attitudes Toward the World Religions* (London: SCM Press Ltd., 1985), p. 148. Henceforth, Knitter, No Other Name.
88. Cf. John Hick, An Interpretation of Religion: Human Response to Transcendent (London: Macmillan Press Ltd., 1989), P. 236. Henceforth, Hick, An Interpretation of Religion.
89. *Tao Te Ching*, trans. Ch'u Ta-Kao (London and Boston: Mandala Books, 1982), p. 17.
90. Moses Maimonides, *Guide to the Perplexed* (12th century), trans. M. Friedlander, 2nd ed., book 1 (London: Routledge & Kegan Paul, 1940), chapter 54.
91. *Qur'an*, trans. Zafrulla Khan (London and Dublin: Curzon Press), 6:103.
92. Paul Tillich, *The Courage to Be* (New Haven: Yale University Press, 1952), p. 189.
93. Gordon Kaufmann, *God the Problem* (Cambridge, MA: Harvard University Press, 1972), pp. 85-86.
94. Cf. Netland, Dissonant Voices, p. 224.
95. Hick, An Interpretation of Religion, p. 294.
96. Hick, An Interpretation of Religion, p. 236.

97. Thomas Aquinas, *Summa Theologica*, Part II/II. Q. 1, art. 2; as cited by Hick, An Interpretation of Religion, p. 236.
98. R. A. Nicholson, Mystics of Islam (London and Boston: Routledge & Kegan Paul, 1963), p. 88.
99. Cf. Hick, An Interpretation of Religion, p. 236.
100. Hick, An Interpretation of Religion, p. 240.
101. Hick, An Interpretation of Religion, p. 16.
102. John Hick, God Has Many Names (Philadelphia: Westminster, 1982), p. 83. Henceforth, Hick, God Has Many Names.
103. Cf. Hick, The Second Christianity, p. 78.
104. Hick, The Second Christianity, p. 86.
105. Hick, God and the Universe, p. 146.
106. Hick, God and the Universe, pp. 146-147.
107. Hick, God and the Universe, p. 147.
108. Hick, The Second Christianity, p. 90.
109. Cf. D'Costa, Theology and Religious Pluralism, p. 136.
110. Race, Interfaith Encounter, p. 113.
111. Race, Interfaith Encounter, p. 113.
112. Race, Interfaith Encounter, pp. 112-113.
113. Race, Interfaith Encounter, p. 35.
114. Hick, The Rainbow of Faiths, p. 50
115. Cf. Race, Interfaith Encounter, pp. 113-114.
116. Race, Interfaith Encounter, p. 33.
117. Cf. Race, Interfaith Encounter, pp. 33-34.
118. Cf. Race, Interfaith Encounter, pp. 111-112. In fact, in chapter seven of his book, *Interfaith Encounter: The Twin Tracks of Theology and Dialogue*, Alan Race discusses about a possible formulation of a global ethics.
119. Christoph Schwöbel, "Particularity, Universality, and the Religions," *Christian Uniqueness Reconsidered: The Myth of a Pluralistic theology of Religions*, ed. Gavin D'Costa (Maryknoll: Orbis Books, 1990), p. 39.
120. Race, Interfaith Encounter, pp. 21-22.
121. Race, Interfaith Encounter, p. 31; Emphasis in the original.
122. Paul Varo Martinson, *A Theology of world Religions: Interpreting God, self and world in Semitic, Indian and Chinese Thought* (Minneapolis: Augsburg Publishing House, 1987), p. 207.

123. Ernest Troelstch, *Christian Thought: Its History and Application*, ed. F. Von Hugel (New York: Living Age Books, 1957), p. 63.

124. Cf. Dupuis, Toward a Christian Theology of Religious Pluralism, p. 193.

125. Cf. John Hick & Paul Knitter, eds., "Towards a Liberation Theology of Religions," *The Myth of Christian Uniqueness: Towards a Pluralistic Theology of Religions* (Maryknoll, NY: Orbis Books, 1987), pp. 178-200.

126. Knitter, One Earth, Many Religions, p. 118.

127. Cf. Paul Knitter, "Catholic Theology of Religions at the Crossroads," *Christianity among World Religions. Concilium 183/1*, 99-107; as cited by Dupuis, *Toward a Christian Theology of Religious Pluralism*, p. 194.

128. Cf. Dupuis, Toward a Christian Theology of Religious Pluralism, pp. 195-196.

129. St. Irenaeus, *Contra Haereses*, IV, 7, 4; SC 100: 462-65; as cited by Dupuis, Toward a Christian Theology of Religious Pluralism, p. 195.

130. Aloysius Pieris, "Inculturation in Asia: A Theological Reflection on an Experience," In Jahrbuch für kontextuelle Theologien (Frankfurt: Verlag fur Interkulturelle Kommunikation, 1994), p. 60. Henceforth, Pieris, "Inculturation in Asia."

131. Pieris, "Inculturation in Asia," p. 60.

132. Dupuis, Toward a Christian Theology of Religious Pluralism, p. 196.

133. Paul Knitter, "New Pentecost?" in *Current Dialogue* 19 (1991), p. 35.

134. Dupuis, Toward a Christian Theology of Religious Pluralism, pp. 196-197.

135. Cf. Dupuis, Toward a Christian Theology of Religious Pluralism, p. 197.

136. Walter Kasper, *Jesus the Christ* (London: Burns and Oates, 1976), pp. 267-268.

137. Cf. Dupuis, Toward a Christian Theology of Religious Pluralism, p. 197.

138. M. Barnes, "Theology of Religions in the Post-modern World," *The Month*, 28: 270-274, (1994), 325-330; as cited by Dupuis, Toward a Christian Theology of Religious Pluralism, p. 200.

139. David Tracy, *Dialogue with the Other: The Inter-religious Dialogue* (Louvain: Peeters Press, 1990); as cited by Dupuis, Toward a Christian Theology of Religious Pluralism, p. 197.

140. Cf. Dupuis, Toward a Christian Theology of Religious Pluralism, p. 198.

141. Cf. Dupuis, Toward a Christian Theology of Religious Pluralism, p. 198.

142. Aloysius Pieris, "An Asian Paradigm: Inter-religious Dialogue and Theology of Religions," *The Month* 26, (1993), p 130. Henceforth, Pieris, "An Asian Paradigm."

143. Pieris, "An Asian Paradigm," p. 130.

144. Pieris, "An Asian Paradigm," p. 130.

145. Cf. Dupuis, *Toward a Christian Theology of Religious Pluralism*, p. 198.

2

'SATYA' – THE TRUTH OF GANDHI'S CONCEPTION

The life of Gandhi was rooted in India's religious tradition with its emphasis on a passionate search for truth, a profound reverence for life, the ideal of non-attachment and the readiness to sacrifice all for the knowledge of God. He lived his whole life in the perpetual quest of truth. It is from his life-pursuit that Gandhi evolved his concept of truth. He was not an academic thinker in the strict sense. So it becomes necessary to study his life and activities to grasp his understanding of truth. It is there that one can discover the emergence of 'satyo-centrism' as the sole sustainer of his very being. This chapter, therefore, intends to examine the concept of truth as understood and lived by Gandhi. It will highlight the various nuances and shades of meaning that Gandhi gave to this all-important concept that became very crucial to his understanding of religions.

INFLUENCES

In his pursuit of truth, Gandhi was influenced by different persons, events and traditions that he came in contact with. The young Gandhi was influenced by his father Karamchand Gandhi who was truthful, brave and generous. "He was incorruptible and had earned a name for strict impartiality."[1] In fact, Gandhi said that but for the love he bore to his father he might not have come to pledge himself to truth. "It became an instinct with him to speak the truth, not because he realized the significance of truthfulness then, but because he felt that he must do so for the love of his father."[2]

On the other hand, the strong impression his mother made on Gandhi was one of saintliness. "She was deeply religious."[3] She spent her time in prayer, visiting temples and in fasting. She would take the hardest vows and keep them unflinchingly. For example, she would eat one meal a day during *chaturmas;* she would take food only on alternate days on some occasions; and, she would have her food only after seeing the sun. These were some of the fasts she used to observe, sometimes even simultaneously. Her observance of those fasts was so rigorous that if at the height of the rainy season, the sun was not visible for two or three days together, she would deprive herself of the meal rather than breaking her fast. These rigorous religious practices of his mother had touched the tender heart of Gandhi so deeply that it gave him in his later days tenacious strength to observe fasts for social causes.[4]

Young Gandhi saw a play named *Harishchandra.*[5] It captivated his gentle spirit. He could never be tired of seeing it. To follow truth and to undergo all the ordeals Harishchandra went through for the sake of truth was the one ideal that Gandhi wanted to emulate. "Why should not all be truthful like Harishchandra?"[6] was the question he asked himself day and night.

Gandhi was allowed to leave for England to qualify as a lawyer in 1888, only after he took an oath before his mother that he would never touch wine, woman and meat. Despite many provocations and temptations, Gandhi was able to keep the vows because of his firm conviction that a vow is a vow and it cannot be broken at any cost.[7] On all such occasions of trial, Gandhi believed that God saved him and these trials, in turn, deepened his commitment to lead a truthful life.

On his return from England after qualifying for the Bar, Gandhi was influenced by the life of a certain jewellery merchant by name Raychandbhai. The merchant had a prodigious memory. Although a businessman, he had a great desire to see God face to face. He was a real seeker after Truth. Gandhi wrote: "I saw him absorbed in godly pursuits in the midst of business . . . I never saw him lose his state of equipoise . . . His words went straight home to me . . . In my moments of spiritual crisis, he was my refuge."[8] The influence of Raychandbhai must have been profound on young Gandhi. For, as he admitted later, he discovered truth to be the foundation of all morality and this belief was implanted in him at the early part of his life. He was convinced that "morality is the basis of things, and that truth is the substance of all morality. Truth became my sole objective. It began to grow in magnitude every day, and my definition of it also has been ever widening."[9]

Leo Tolstoy contributed a great role in shaping Gandhi's understanding of truth. His teachings penetrated the very core and matrix of his being. They presented, in modern garb, some of the great truths proclaimed by India's ancient seers.

> It was not Tolstoy's writings alone, but the example of his life – his passion for truth and ceaseless striving after perfection, that enthroned him in Gandhiji's heart and led him later to describe himself as "a humble follower of that great leader whom I have long looked upon as one of my guides." In him he found a kindred spirit – a single-minded seeker after truth; an aristocrat turned peasant and shoemaker in pursuit of the meaning of life, who dedicated his wealth and talents and genius to the service of humanity while he himself strove to live by his body labour.[10]

In fact, one can notice a similarity between them in their search for truth. Tolstoy's "worship of Truth, by causing him to question the very existence of God who meant everything to him, thus led him back to what Gandhiji later called "God that is truth and Truth which is God."[11] Tolstoy held that there is a need to recognize and profess relative truth. He is of the opinion that God does not require from humans what is unreasonable and impossible. "He demands of us only what is reasonable and possible . . . to recognize and profess the truth, revealed to us, which it is always in our power to do."[12]

According to Tolstoy, truth will impel human beings in either case, irrespective of their recognition or non-recognition of it – like steam in a locomotive, if they willingly cooperate with it; like a slave-driver, lash in hand, if they resist. "Not only does truth point out the direction a man's life *should* take, but it opens the only road he *can* take. Hence, all men will invariably, free or not, follow the road of truth; - some willingly, doing the work they have set themselves to do; others involuntarily, by submitting in spite of themselves to the law of life. It is in the power of choice that a man's freedom lies."[13]

Tolstoy advocated that the searcher after truth can discover different levels of truth. For he held that humans are not static but ever growing, ever evolving beings by virtue of their inborn faculty of recognizing truth, which in its turn determines their future lines of action. As human beings advance in life they have a fuller and still fuller glimpse of truth. "Some truths are so familiar to him that they have become the unconscious springs of action; others are only dimly revealed to him; again others, though still unfamiliar, are revealed to him so plainly that they force themselves upon his attention, and inevitably, in one way or another, he is obliged to consider them. He cannot ignore them, but must either recognize them or repudiate them."[14]

Gandhi's faith in the infallibility of Truth was also deeply rooted in his own Hindu tradition. Through a long history there was known in Hinduism the act of Truth. Frequently it had fictional and magical connotations. "There is nothing that cannot be accomplished by the Truth. A person could perform an act of truth, by referring to some virtue or freedom from evil in his life, and command or demand that a desire or need of his be fulfilled on this account."[15] As Zimmer said: " . . . Truth (sat-ya: is-ness) must be rooted in the heart. The Act of Truth has to build out from there. And consequently, though dharma, the fulfilment of one's inherited role in life, is the traditional basis of this Hindu feat of virtue, nevertheless, a heart-felt truth of any order has its force."[16] So it will be seen that Gandhi's insistence on truth force is not unrelated to the ancient tenets of Hinduism.

Vedantic philosophy of Shankara played a key role in Gandhi's understanding of the concept of truth. Answering the criticism of Tagore on his emphasis on *charkha*, Gandhi wrote an article entitled "Sir Rabindranath". Here he gave one of the most succinct statements of his metaphysical position. Gandhi wrote:

> The idea of sameness or oneness was carried by Shankara to its utmost logical and natural limit and he explained that there was only one truth, one God – *Brahman* – and all form, *nam, rupa* was illusion or illusory, evanescent. We need not debate whether what we see is unreal; and whether the real behind the unreality is what we do not see. Let both be equally real if you will. All I say is that there is a sameness, identity or oneness behind the multiplicity and variety. And so do I hold that behind a variety of occupations there is an indispensable sameness also of occupation.[17]

The sameness of substance behind the multiplicity of forms was a paramount presupposition to which Gandhiji tenaciously clung. There is no dichotomy of the real and the unreal, the nounmenon and the phenomenon, as Kant held. The relative was not antithetical to the absolute. It was the way the absolute was manifested and could be comprehended. Philosophers, using logic, posed the problem in terms of 'either-or,' that is, 'either this or that.' Gandhiji posited in its place 'this as also that'.

Gandhi strengthened his Vedantic position further by subscribing to the Jaina theory of *anekantavada* or *syadvada*. Reality, according to *anekantavada* or 'manyness' of Truth or Reality, has a complex structure. Every proposition is true, but only from a particular standpoint. Since the same thing may be regarded from different aspects or standpoints, what is true from one standpoint may not be true from another. For instance, to a passenger on a running train the trees are moving in a direction opposite to that of the train but a person standing outside finds them stationary. Lukewarm water is cold in relation to hot and hot in relation to cold water. "Truth being relative to our standpoints, to occupy one standpoint is not to deny other standpoints. . . . Reality to be comprehended must be examined from all the various aspects, and an integrated view taken of the whole."[18]

In subscribing to *anekantavada*, Gandhi was able to accept the truth of the contradictory theories like *Advaita* and *Dvaita* and different viewpoints like those of his critics. Hence in answer to a friend's question, Gandhi wrote:

> I am Advaitist and yet I can support Dvaitism (dualism). The world is changing every moment, and is therefore unreal. It has no permanent existence. But though it is constantly changing, it has something about it, which persists, and it is therefore to that extent real. I have therefore no objection to calling it real and unreal, and thus being called an Anekantavadi or a Syadvadi. But my Syadvada is not the Syadvada of the learned, it is peculiarly my own . . . It has been my experience that I am always true from my point of view, and am often wrong from the point of view of my honest critics. I know that we are both right from our respective points of view. And this knowledge saves me from attributing motives to my opponents or critics.[19]

Perhaps, this led Gandhi to enunciate the doctrine of absolute truth and relative truth, which in turn, enabled him to apply this concept in a creative and unique way in the different dimensions of life in such a way that he became a true worshipper of truth. The next part of this chapter will examine this dimension.

WHAT IS TRUTH?

'What is truth?' (Cf. Jn 18: 38). Perhaps the question, which was asked by 'jesting Pilate', still remains unanswered. Jesus when confronted asserted that he was the truth. (Cf. Jn 14: 6). Gandhi on his part has tried to answer that question as adequately and satisfactorily as is possible for a human being by experimenting with truth all the time. "His sole endeavour has been to answer that question in his life and if necessary by his life. He did so both in his life and by his life."[20] Gandhi also effected a distinction between Absolute Truth and Relative Truth, and equated the former with God while the latter he understood in terms of inner voice. This distinction is of utmost importance in understanding his views on religion. This section attempts to highlight the various salient features of this all-important distinction that Gandhi made.

For Gandhi, the concept of truth was an all-inclusive concept embracing every aspect of his life. He wrote: "The more I search after Truth the more I feel it is all-inclusive. Truth is not covered by non-violence. But I often experience that non-violence is included in truth. What a pure heart feels at a particular time is truth; by remaining firm on that, undiluted Truth can be attained."[21] However, one can understand this concept by appealing to the distinction that Gandhi himself makes between Absolute Truth and Relative Truth. This distinction is important for the present thesis, as it is basic for understanding the Gandhian concept of religion. Gandhi made a similar distinction between religions and Religion that underlie the various religions and came to the conclusion that all religions like relative truths are imperfect. The implications of this distinction are discussed in the next chapter. Therefore, a thorough understanding of Gandhi's distinction between Absolute Truth and Relative Truth is of paramount significance.

Absolute Truth

In its absolute sense, Gandhi equated Truth with God. He wrote: "The word *Satya* (Truth) is derived from *Sat*, which means 'being'. Nothing is or exists in reality except Truth. That is why *Sat* or Truth is perhaps the most important name of God. In fact it is more appropriate to say that Truth is God, than to say that God is Truth."[22] Contemplating on this subject deeply, Gandhi concluded that *Sat* or *Satya* is the only correct and fully significant name for God. Hence Truth becomes the basis of all rules in life. The sole justification for our existence on earth, according to Gandhi, is devotion to Truth. All our activities and even the very breath of our life should be centred on Truth. Without Truth it is impossible to observe any principles or rules in life.

Gandhi held that Truth is nothing but God. He asserted: "Truth is God – nothing else, nothing less.... The nearest word answering to Truth in Sanskrit is *Sat*. *Sat* means 'being'. God alone is *Sat*. He alone is; nothing and no one else is. Everything else is illusion. *Satya* means *Sat*. Truth alone is in the world, nothing else is."[23] Further speaking of truth, Gandhi said that for humans it is a relative term. It is because Absolute Truth is God. He further said: "whatever we understand by God is implied in Truth . . . It alone really sustains us. For a time many other things may sustain us, but this alone sustains us for all time."[24]

The ancient seers of India spoke about the mighty-ness and unanalysableness of Truth, which is understood as God. So Gandhi wrote: "The seers have described God as '*Neti*,' '*Neti*' ('Not this', 'Not this'). Truth will elude you. The sum total of all that is true is Truth. But you can't sum all that is true.... There are things that can't be analysed. God who can be analysed by my poor intellect won't satisfy me. Therefore I do not try to analyse Him. I go behind the relative to the absolute and I get my peace of mind." [25] A Vedic concept that can explain the concept of Truth is *Rta*. The Vedic seers spoke of *Satya* as the knowledge of truth while *Rta* as the action according to truth. Hence they insisted that both *Satya* and *Rta* must go together.[26]

The concept of *Sat* has its mention in the various sacred books of Hinduism. The whole Chapter 7 of the *Chandogya Upanishads*, for example, is a discussion and meditation on *Sat*. We read: "In the beginning, dear boy, this was Being alone, one only, without a second. Some say that, in the beginning, this was Non-being alone, one only, without a second. From that Non-being arose Being" (*Ch. Up*. VI, 2.1).[27] Again we read: "That Being which is this subtle essence (cause), even That all this world has for its self. That is the true. That is the Atman. That thou art, O Svetaketu" (*Ch. Up*. VI. 8.7).[28] Or, in the *Brhadaranyka Upanishad* we read: "As a spider moves along the thread (it produces), or as from a fire little sparks scatter, just so from this

Self issue all organs, all words, all gods, and livings beings. Its secret name is the Truth of truth. The vital force is truth, and it is the Truth of that" (*Br. Up*. II.1.20).[29] Most of the commentators translate *Sat* as the Reality or the Supreme reality. Deriving from the root *as* = to be, *sat* means existence. The word *satya* (Truth) is thus linked to the Reality, the existence. This reality is the root of all; the inner self of all the immanent reality.[30] The same *Upanishad* also speaks of truth in terms of *dharma*. According to the *Ramayana*, *dharma* is truth or the basis of truth. In Advaita Vedanta *Sat* implies permanent existence, the sole, eternal, effulgent and ever free reality. Dr. K.L. Seshagiri Rao, sums up the Hindu perspective of Truth thus: "Brahman is the whole Truth. It is immanent and transcendent, dynamic and static, personal and impersonal. These qualities appear to be incompatible to our limited minds, but in Brahman all paradoxes are resolved and incompatibilities are reconciled."[31]

Likewise, in the Holy Bible, there is the concept of 'Self-existent' or 'I am.' The Old Testament formula of the divine self-identification is 'I am Who I am' (Ex. 3, 14). Jesus appropriates this name of God in number of instances especially in the gospel of St. John. "Yes, if you do not believe that *I am He* you will die in your sins" (Jn 8, 24); "When you have lifted up the Son of Man, then you will know that *I am He*" (Jn 8, 28); "I tell you most solemnly before Abraham ever was, *I Am*." (Jn 8, 58).[32] The use of 'I am Who I am' or 'I am He' or 'I am' bring out the Christian conception of the transcendence of a God for whom humans can never find a worthy name. Having read the sacred books of both Hinduism and Christianity, it was quite natural that Gandhi was influenced by them when he spoke of truth in terms of *Sat* or Self-existent.

Further, the meaning of Truth as the ultimate *Sat* is not unfamiliar to the Western world but it understood quite differently from the way Gandhi conceived Absolute Truth. "The West distinguished reality as it is and reality as it presents itself to our minds: the 'given' and that which is found by trial and error. We think of truth at times in its ultimate sense, as in "You will know the truth, and the truth will make you free" (Jn 8:31, RSV). The more common usage is 'the agreement of opinion with fact.'"[33]

Gandhi also gives reasons for equating God with Truth. He says that when he was young he was told to repeat what in Hindu scriptures are known as one thousand names of God. But these names are by no means exhaustive. God has as many names as there are creatures. Hence we consider Him as nameless. Likewise, God has many forms and we call Him formless. In Islam too God has many names. But he feels that deep down in him he used to say that "though God may be Love, God is Truth, above all. If it is possible for the human tongue to give the fullest description of God, I have come to the conclusion that for myself, God is Truth."[34]

Gandhi linked Truth with God and endowed it with all the attributes which one usually grants to God. In fact, speaking about Truth Gandhi said:

> It is That which alone is, which constitutes the stuff of which all things are made, which subsists by virtue of its own power, which is not supported by anything else but supports everything that exists. Truth alone is eternal; everything else is momentary. It need not assume shape or form. It is pure intelligence as well as pure bliss. We call It *Ishvara* because everything is regulated by its will. It and the law It promulgates are one. Therefore it is not a blind law. It governs the entire universe.[35]

Another reason for Gandhi equating Truth with God is that seeing God through Truth is a less hazardous path and promises the ultimate knowledge of God. Gandhi wrote:

> We lose all interest in seeing or hearing about miracles. Seeing God is difficult to understand; but seeing Truth presents no such difficulty. Seeing Truth is indeed a hard task, but as we approach nearer and nearer to truth, we catch a glimpse of the God of Truth, so that we hope to have a full view of His in good time and our faith also burns brighter and brighter.[36]

Further Gandhi held that he had known God only as Truth. "There was a time," wrote Gandhi, "when I had doubts about the existence of God, but I never doubted the existence of Truth. This Truth is not something material but pure intelligence. It rules over the universe; therefore it is *Ishvara* (the Lord) . . . This is for me almost a matter of experience."[37] Still further, Gandhi was of the opinion that Truth is God not because God is without form, in fact even Truth is without form, but because "Truth is the only comprehensive attribute of God. Other attributes are only partial expressions of the reality that is God."[38]

Writing to Mr. P. G. Mathew, Gandhi explained the meaning of 'God is Truth.' He said: "In 'God is Truth' *is* certainly does not mean 'equal to' nor does it merely mean, 'is truthful'. Truth is not a mere attribute of God, but He is That. He is nothing if He is not That. Truth in Sanskrit means *Sat*. *Sat* means *Is*. Therefore Truth is implied in *Is*. God is, nothing else is. Therefore the more truthful we are, the nearer we are to God. We *are* only to the extent that we are truthful."[39] In this way Gandhi makes efforts at understanding truth in its epistemological and ontological sense in the course of his action in the field of human relationships.

The nature of the concept of Truth that Gandhi equated with God is similar to the Scholastic philosophical concept of Transcendental Category of Truth. *Ens ut Sic* (Being as such), according to them, was the most primary, the simplest and the most comprehensive attribute. Although Gandhi did not have any academic training in philosophy, what he arrived at by his personal search seems to be corroborated by academicians as very correct and accurate.

In the course of time, Gandhi went a step further and effected a shift from 'God is Truth' to 'Truth is God.' Speaking about this shift, Gandhi wrote:

> For the last few years I have been saying that 'Truth is God' instead of 'God is Truth.' The former statement is more consonant with facts, for in this world there is nothing besides Truth. Truth here should be understood in a wide sense. It is full of intelligence. God as Truth and His Law are not different but one and the same; therefore it also is full of intelligence. Indeed it is all the same whether we say that the universe is a function of truth or that it is a function of Law. This Truth is charged with infinite power. In the language of the Gita, (chapter 10), the universe is sustained by a fraction of it. Therefore if you replace the word God by the word Truth wherever it occurs, you will have some idea of what I mean.[40]

It is interesting to take note of the growth that took place in Gandhi's understanding of the concept of Truth. Early in his public comments on the concept of truth, Gandhi had identified God with Truth. In 1925, in a talk with Christian missionaries in Darjeeling, Gandhi had said that for him God and Truth are convertible terms.[41] The following year in an address at Wardha he declared: " . . . to me Truth is God and there is no way to find Truth except the way of non-violence."[42] But in 1931, when asked by a group of conscientious objectors in Switzerland why he regarded God as Truth, Gandhi explained how he had come to believe that the phrase 'God is Love' was inadequate. Hence he concluded that God is Truth. He then added that he had found it necessary to go a step further and say that Truth is God. "You will see the fine distinction between the two statements, 'God is Truth' and 'Truth is God'. I came to that conclusion after a continuous and relentless search after truth, which began fifty years ago. I then found that the nearest approach to truth was through love."[43]

In the same speech, Gandhi said that he preferred Truth to God because of the atrocities committed in the name of God. But he was quick to add that scientists very often commit cruelties in the name of truth. He said: "I know how in the name of truth and science inhuman cruelties are perpetrated on animals when men perform vivisection. There are a number of difficulties in the way, no matter how you describe God. But the man's mind is a limited thing, and you have to labour under limitations when you think of a being or entity that is beyond the power of man to grasp."[44]

For Gandhi, 'God is Truth' was doubtable while 'Truth is God" was undoubtable. Writing to the Ashram boys and girls on 21 March 1932, Gandhiji said: "Instead of saying 'God is Truth' I now say 'Truth is God' . . . There was a time when I doubted the existence of God. Even at that time I did not doubt the existence of Truth. This Truth is not a material quality; it is pure consciousness. Since it orders the whole universe it is God."[45]

This fine distinction that Gandhi makes between 'God is Truth' and 'Truth is God' has been taken by some commentators to be of substantial significance. R.R. Diwakar is of the opinion that in effecting this shift, Gandhi had several reasons in mind. Besides being acceptable to everyone including atheists and agnostics, 'Truth as God' implies that each one is called upon to fall back on his own resources and to be an ardent seeker of Truth. It also avoids any equivocation that is characteristic of the concept of God. When one is in search of God, one naturally turns to all the sources of knowledge of God like the religious scriptures, the saints, the seers and so on, which are beset with controversies.[46]

N.K. Bose interpreted the change as relieving a *satyagrahi* from the necessity of any theological or at least any specific theological belief.

> With this changed creed, he could easily accommodate as fellow-seekers those who looked on Humanity or any other object as their god, and for which they were prepared to sacrifice their all. By enthroning Truth on the highest pedestal, Gandhi thus truly became a catholic, and lost all trace of separateness from every other honest man who worshipped gods other than his own.[47]

Further, one can safely say that Gandhi experienced a double communion in his daily life – a direct and intimate communion with God on the one hand and on the other a personal communion with the teeming millions of human beings all through the day. It is this communion that led Gandhi to assert Truth rather than God. So Gandhi wrote in the *Harijan*: "I claim to know my millions. All the 24 hours of the day I am with them. They are my first care and last, because I recognize no God except the God that is to be found in the hearts of the dumb millions. They do not recognize His presence; I do. And I worship the God that is Truth or Truth which is God through the service of these millions."[48]

Attributes of God

Speaking about the attributes of God which is Truth, Gandhi said that God and His attributes are not like subject and predicate but each attribute of God is substantive. Therefore Gandhi wrote: "He and His Laws are one. The Law is God. Anything attributed to Him is not a mere attribute. He is the attribute. He is Truth, Love and Law and a million other things that human ingenuity can name."[49] This is precisely what infiniteness means.

Yet, Gandhi gave a number of attributes to God which is Truth. He wrote:

> To me God is Truth and Love; God is ethics and morality; God is fearlessness. God is the source of Light and Life and yet He is above and beyond all these. God is conscience. He is even the atheism of the atheists . . . He is the searcher of hearts. He transcends speech and reason. He knows us and our hearts better than we do ourselves. He does not take us at our word for He knows that we often do not mean it, some knowingly and other unknowingly. He is a personal God to those who need His personal presence. He

> is embodied to those who need His touch. He is the purest essence. He simply is to those who have faith. He is all things to all men. He is in us and yet above and beyond us.[50]

However, he was of the opinion that Truth is the embodiment of all attributes.

Gandhi also said that where there is Truth, there is also knowledge, which is true. Hence *Chit* or knowledge is associated with the name of God. *Chit* is also understood as pure consciousness. That is the reason why Shankara defined *Chit* as consciousness without a subject (*ashraya*) and without an object (*vishya*). "It is neither individualized – my consciousness – nor concretised – consciousness of blue. What is more, it is the only reality, Sat is *chit*."[51] Further, "where there is true knowledge there is always bliss (*Ananda*). There sorrow has no place."[52] Just as Truth is eternal, bliss, which emanates from it, is also eternal. Hence God is *Sat-chit-ananda*. In other words, Truth becomes the basis of the Trio of God.

Gandhi accepted the fact that of the three transcendental attributes, Truth is basic. He even claimed that every religious founder too gave similar emphasis to Truth. For he wrote:

> Truth is the first thing to be sought for, and Beauty and Goodness will then be added unto you. That is what Christ really taught in the Sermon on the Mount. Jesus was, to my mind, a supreme artist because he saw and expressed Truth; and so was Muhammad, the Koran being the most perfect composition in all Arabic literature – at any rate, that is what scholars say. It is because both of them strove first for Truth that the grace of expression naturally came in and yet neither Jesus nor Muhammad wrote on art. That is the Truth and Beauty I crave for, live for, and would die for.[53]

It, therefore, implies that Beauty is necessarily contained in Truth. Gandhi explained this thus: "I see and find beauty in Truth or through Truth. All Truths, not merely true ideas, but truthful faces, truthful pictures, or songs are highly beautiful. People generally fail to see Beauty in Truth, the ordinary man runs away from and becomes blind to the beauty in it. Whenever men begin to see Beauty in Truth, then true art will arise."[54] Further Gandhi claimed that Truth may show itself in forms which may not be outwardly beautiful at all. Of Socrates Gandhi said that he was the most truthful man of his time and yet his features were said to have been the ugliest in Greece. "To my mind," wrote Gandhi, "he was beautiful because all his life was a striving after Truth, and you may remember that his outward form did not prevent Phidias from appreciating the beauty of Truth in him, though as an artist he was accustomed to see Beauty in outward forms also!"[55]

Another attribute of Truth, which is God, is life. "You feel vitality in you when you have got Truth in you."[56] Truth also gives joy. Gandhi says, "Truth gives perennial joy . . . Bliss is a permanent thing of which you cannot be robbed. You may be sent to the gallows, or put to torture; but if you have Truth in you, you will experience an inner joy."[57] Citing the example of Bradlaugh, who had to suffer a lot for thus speaking the truth, Gandhi says that he delighted in it and said that truth is its own reward. Not that he was quite insensible to the joy resulting from the observance of truth. This joy however is not worldly, but springs out of communion with the divine.[58] In other words, Gandhi believed that divine joy is in-built in the very suffering that one has to undergo for pursuing the path of Truth. A corollary to this quality of joy is that belief in Truth makes one an optimist. Gandhi said: "I believe in Truth and therefore I have no doubt in the future of this country or the future of humanity . . . I trust in God Who knows how to confound the wisdom of men."[59]

Further, for Gandhi God translated as Truth is also the source of peace. A seeker after Truth experiences peace of mind. In his talk to Dr. Dodd, Gandhi said: "in the midst of humiliation and so-called defeat and a tempestuous life, I am able to retain my peace, because of an undying faith in God, translated as Truth."[60]

From the above analysis, one can conclude that for Gandhi the only reality that is existent is God. To him God alone is *sat*. And he called it as Truth. In that respect world is mere appearance or *asat* in the sense that it is not permanent. Here Gandhi comes closer to the advaitic concept of *Maya*. Writing to Balkrishna Bhave, he said:

> I do not know with certainty what Sankaracharya meant by *Maya*. This is what I believe. The world, which we see and believe in, is mere appearance; it is a product of our imagination. But in its true essence it does not exist. We do not know what that essence is. We say it is *Brahman*, but we characterize all descriptions of the latter as inadequate – *neti, neti* (not that, not that). The world also is *Brhaman* and not different from it. The difference which we see is mere appearance.[61]

Gandhi transferred this God-intoxication to Truth-intoxication, which made him see the world as appearance to the concept of Truth. And this is Truth in its absolute sense.

Gandhi was quick to admit the difficulties that are involved in this pursuit of Truth. Gandhi listed them in *Harijan*:

> A Himalayan expedition has its prescribed conditions of success. Difficulty of fulfilling the conditions does not make the expedition impossible. It only adds interest and zest to the search. Well, this expedition in search of God or Truth is infinitely more than numberless Himalayan expeditions and, therefore, much more interesting. If we have no zest for it, it is because of the weakness of our faith.[62]

The first step in this expedition in experiencing Truth was to make the world's faith in God one's own. And Gandhi called that faith as amounting to experience. However, this description of faith as experience is to tamper with truth. Hence, Gandhi said: "it may perhaps be more correct to say that I have no word characterising my belief in God"[63] Further, Gandhi was of the opinion that in order to see Truth in its universal ramifications, one must love the meanest of creation as oneself and be involved in all fields of life. "That is why my devotion of Truth has drawn me into the field of politics; and I can say without the slightest hesitation, and yet in all humility, that those who say that religion has nothing to do with politics do not know what religion means."[64] Thus for Gandhi, worship of God implies service of the poor. "I cannot imagine better worship of God than that in His name I should labour for the poor even as they do."[65]

However, Gandhi acknowledges that the Absolute Truth which is God is not analysable. "A God who can be analysed by my poor intellect won't satisfy me. Therefore, I do not try to analyse Him."[66] It is here that Gandhi comes up with his doctrine of relative truth. For he said: "I go behind the relative to the absolute and get my peace of mind."[67]

Relative Truth

Everyone endeavours to approach Absolute Truth. But it is inaccessible and elusive. So one would have to be content with what Gandhi calls relative truth. However, this relative truth at each stage is as good as the Absolute Truth. To explain the concept of relative truth, Gandhi distinguished it from Absolute Truth. "Relative truth is the truth as we perceive it in relation to a particular set of circumstances. It is not the whole truth. What may be true under one set of circumstances may not be true in relation to a different set of circumstances . . . In contradistinction with relative truth is the absolute truth – the ultimate reality – which alone is, was and forever shall be."[68]

Gandhi was of the opinion that Truth as experienced by humankind by its very nature is bound to be relative. "You cannot possibly say that what is best for you is the best for all. Quinine may be the only means of saving life in your case, but a dangerous poison in the case of another."[69] Further, while Gandhi was second to none in his inward quest for the totality of transcendental truth which philosophers call by the name of reality, he perceived that that quest would be only partial if he did not address himself to the truth of daily life which was immanent and which was like a reflection of or a window on Reality itself. He saw that human life as all other life and its progress was the immediate and urgent concern of each conscient individual, who aimed at seeking truth.[70] This type of truth he called relative truth. Besides, the finite human being cannot grasp the whole truth, not even relative truth. "What may, therefore, appear as truth to one person may appear as error to another. And yet both of them may be right from their relative points of view like the seven blind men of Hindustan."[71]

One of the reasons why Gandhi upheld relative truth is that no human being can claim that "he is absolutely in the right or that a particular thing is wrong because he thinks so, but it is wrong for him so long as that is his deliberate judgement. It is therefore meant that he should not do that which he knows to be wrong, and suffer the consequence whatever it may be."[72] Further, Gandhi believed that human being could never realize perfect truth so long as he/she is imprisoned in this mortal frame. He/she can only visualize it in his/her imagination. Hence human being has to be content with relative truth.

From a social point of view, the immanent truth of the day-to-day life experiences was important for Gandhi. In fact, Diwakar says that Gandhi had a supreme passion to perceive it, realise it and establish it. But this does not mean that his quest of the transcendent aspect of truth, which is the ground of all existence, was not less intense. In fact, the path of his quest for the transcendent truth itself lay in his search for the truth of daily life. "That is why he used to say that God is in the hearts of all men and beings and that all life is one and that the search for truth or God has to be through love, the law of identity and through unselfish as well as unstinted service."[73]

Gandhian understanding of relative truth is unique in as much as it is neither a conservative nor an absolutist position. In this context, Joan Bondurant's comment is worth quoting:

> Truth, with Gandhi, is the one persisting goal. But conservatives are often seekers for peace rather than truth. This was so for Plato and it tended to be so for Burke. That 'truth' was, for Gandhi, relative truth is of striking significance. For absolutes are more congenial to the conservative mind. The development of a technique for discovering relative truths, and for resolving conflicts among them, is Gandhi's special contribution.[74]

Further, Gandhi holds that his understanding of relative truth does not lead to relativism. He himself gives the reason for it when he wrote: "Seeing that the human mind works through innumerable media and that the evolution of human mind is not the same for all, it follows that what may be truth for one may be untruth for another."[75] Bondurant also agrees with this view because relative truth is related to Absolute Truth. "The Gandhian concept of truth, in its non-absolutistic sense, escapes some of the practical difficulties of ethical relativism through its interrelationships with non-violence as an operative in *satyagraha*."[76] A person is required to be non-violent towards another precisely because the truth that the imperfect human beings perceive is bound to be manifold in accordance with all the manifold aspects and according to the varied subjective conditions.

Since relative truth is different for different people, tolerance becomes a necessity. In fact, for Gandhi, the golden rule of conduct is mutual tolerance. This is because "we will never all think alike and we shall see Truth in fragment and from different angles of vision. Conscience is not the same thing for all. Whilst, therefore, it is a good guide for individual conduct, imposition of that conduct upon all will be an insufferable interference with everybody's freedom of conscience."[77] This tolerance has to cover every aspect of the ways of life and thought of others even though they may be different, except where the difference is fundamental.

Relative truth involves self-suffering on the part of the seeker. It may happen that what appears to be truth to one person will appear as untruth to another person. But this need not deter the seeker from his/her quest because suffering is yet one way of worship.

> Where there is honest effort, it will be realized that what appears to be different truths are like the countless and apparently different leaves of the same tree. Does not God Himself appear to different individuals in different aspects? Yet we know that He is one. But Truth is the right designation of God. Hence there is nothing wrong in every one following Truth according to his lights. Indeed it is his duty to do so. Then if there is a mistake on the part of any one so following Truth, it will be automatically set right. For the quest of Truth involves *tapas* – self-suffering, sometimes even unto death. There can be no place in it for even a trace of self-interest. In such selfless search for Truth nobody can lose his bearings for long. Directly he takes to the wrong path, he stumbles and he is thus redirected to the right path. Therefore the pursuit of Truth is true *bhakti*. It is the path that leads to God.[78]

Relative truth also implies humility on the part of the seeker. Since relative truth is meant to lead one Absolute Truth, which is hidden, the practice of humility by the votary of truth will enable him/her to remove the veil that hides Truth. Gandhi said:

> A votary of truth has to be humble as the dust. His humility increases with his observance of truth. I see this every moment of my life. I have a much vivider sense of Truth and of my own littleness that I had a year ago. The wonderful implication of the great '*Brahma Satyam Jaganmitya*' (Brahman is real, all else unreal) grows on me from day and day. It teaches us patience. This will purge us of harshness and add to our tolerance. It will make us magnify the molehills of our errors into mountains and minimize the mountains of others' errors into molehills. The body persists because of egoism. The utter extinction of the body of egoism is *moksha*. He who has achieved this will be the very image of Truth, or one may call it Brahman.[79]

Inner Voice

The relative truth that is within the grasp of human being is to be sought in one's conscience. In other words, relative truth implies that one must act according to the dictates of one's conscience. The etymological meaning of conscience is 'truth knowledge.' "The dictionary meaning is 'faculty distinguishing between right and wrong and influencing conduct accordingly.'"[80] Gandhi called it as the voice of God, the inner voice or the still small voice. It is "like the Voice from afar and yet quite near. It was as unmistakable as some human voice definitely speaking to me, and irresistible."[81] Further, he said: "It is the voice of "God which is Truth", the voice of purified reason, instinct, conscience. Its whispering is heard in every heart but not everybody possesses the faculty of listening to it."[82]

Gandhi insisted that God does speak to the devotee clearly and distinctly at the appropriate moment. Giving an instance where things take place that cannot possibly happen apart from God, Gandhi wrote:

> It relates to my 21 days' fast for the removal of untouchability.[83] I had gone to sleep the night before without the slightest idea of having to declare a fast the next morning. At about 12 o'clock in the night something wakes me up suddenly, and some voice, - within or without, I cannot say – whispers 'Thou must go on a fast.' 'How many days?' I ask. The voice again said, 'Twenty-one days.' 'When does it begin?' I ask. It says, 'You begin tomorrow.' I went quietly off to sleep after making the decision.[84]

Thus Gandhi affirmed that his inexplicable actions are really due to inner promptings.

It is possible that the Inner voice may mean a message from God or the Devil, for both are wrestling in the human breast. Here Gandhi appealed to the fruits or the acts to determine the nature of the voice. Another criterion to decide whether the Inner voice is really from God is that "there should be no sliding back (on what one had heard), just as there is no forgetting it by one who has learnt to swim."[85]

Thus, Gandhi claimed that the inner voice is its own proof. So, it is all the more important to follow it and there is no question of going back. Hearing the "inner voice" is a class of experience by itself. The "inner voice defies description."[86] In the final test it is its own seal and sanction. "Sometimes we . . . feel that we receive an inspiration from within."[87] "There come to us moments in life when we need no proof from without. A little voice within us tells us: 'You are on the right track, move neither to your left nor to your right, but keep to the strait and narrow way'"[88] There are moments when "you must act, even though you cannot carry your best friends with you."[89]

One must beware of self-deception while talking of inner voice. It could be just a picture of one's elongated self that is before oneself. One can also misuse the concept of inner voice. But because of dangers, genuine claims of inner voice cannot be suppressed. Therefore, one must train oneself seriously in order to listen to one's inner voice. Hence Gandhi said:

> Before one is able to listen to that voice, one has to go through a long and fairly severe course of training, and when it is the inner voice that speaks, it is unmistakable. The world cannot be successfully fooled for all time. There is, therefore, no danger of anarchy setting in because a humble man like me will not be suppressed and will dare to claim the authority of the inner voice, when he believes that he has heard it.[90]

Such a laborious, disciplined and strict training of conscience enables one to be hesitant to assert oneself, to be always humble, never boisterous, always compromising, always ready to listen and ever willing and even anxious to admit mistakes.[91] In other words, self-purification becomes a pre-requisite to hear the inner voice. For, "the divine music is incessantly going on within ourselves, but the loud senses drown the delicate music."[92] In fact, the cost of listening to the inner voice is great. Gandhi said:

> I must not suppress the voice within, call it 'conscience,' call it the 'prompting of my inner basic nature'. There is something within me impelling me to cry out my agony . . . . That something in me which never deceives me tells me now, 'You have to stand against the whole world although you may have to stand alone . . . . Do not fear. Trust that little thing which resides in the heart. It says, 'Forsake friends, wife, all; but testify to that for which you have lived, and for which you have to die.[93]

Stressing of the need for humility in listening to the inner voice, Gandhi said that there is a need for zeroing oneself.

> . . . The renunciation precedes the certainty. It was only after and because he had surrendered himself completely to the spirit of Truth which is God and ceased to have a separate will of his own, or to put it differently, when he had reduced himself to 'zero' that he arrived at the certainty that the voice that he heard was not an echo of his "elongated self" but the voice of God.[94]

Silence plays a great role in listening to the inner voice. To quote Gandhi:

> A seeker after truth has to be silent. I know the wonderful efficacy of silence. I visited a Trappist monastery in South Africa. A beautiful place it was. Most of the inmates of that place were under a vow of silence. I enquired of the Father the motive of it, and he said that the move was apparent. 'We are frail human beings. We do not know very often what we say. If we want to listen to the still small voice that is always speaking within us, it will not be heard if we continually speak'.[95]

Finally, obedience to the inner voice results in joy. Citing his own example, Gandhi wrote: "I felt refreshed"[96] as a result of his decision to go on a fast in accordance with the promptings of the inner voice.

While admitting the significance of the Gandhian concept of inner voice as a means to arrive at relative truth, one wonders whether it is possible to grant that all can train their conscience so as to see the truth in them correctly and hear the voice of conscience properly. Even if that is granted, there is no guarantee that all will act only according to the dictates of the inner voice and not selfishly. These questions do not negate the fact that Gandhi was able to live an authentic truthful life following the dictates of his conscience not only in his personal life but also in social and political domains. In fact, every aspect of his life exhibited his devotion to truth. His love for truth led him to embrace non-violence as a creed and policy of life and this he translated into the political sphere by introducing the concept of *satyagraha* as a weapon to fight against injustice and oppression. Besides, his obsession with truth gave a new direction to different spheres of human life – social, economic and even in journalism.

EFFECTS OF TRUTH ON GANDHI

Gandhi's life of truth encompassed many dimensions. He exerted a divine influence on his followers, dispensing the magic of truth all around. It made him detect untruth easily. There was no place for applying cunning diplomacy in politics. His adherence to truth enabled him to show equanimity on all occasions and to attend to even minute details in day-to-day life. This section deals with these changes that Gandhi experienced as a result of his devotion to truth.

Gandhi's meticulous pursuit of truth could be observed from the way he carried out his daily activities. Truth was always natural to him. In fact, his mental make-up was conducive to be truthful. Truth was his life's only desire. He wrote: "My desire is to close this life searching for truth, acting truth and thinking truth and that alone, and I request the blessings of the nation that that desire of mine may be fulfilled."[97] The people who lived with him credited Gandhi with supernatural powers. Reacting to their observation, he says that the only powers he has are derived from his "scrupulous regard for truth, an unquenchable industry, fair play to opponents, readiness always to admit mistakes, and an incessant appeal to reason."[98] It is in this context, that one examines the different qualities that Gandhi demonstrated as a result of truth-living.

The magnetic personality of Gandhi transmitted a divine power on people who came in contact with him. Writing about her first meeting with Gandhi in the Ashram on 7 November 1925, Madelein Slade, whom Gandhiji later renamed as Mirabehn, said: "As I entered, a slight brown figure rose up and came toward me. I was conscious of nothing but a sense of light. I fell on my knees. Hands gently raised me up, and a voice said: 'You shall be my daughter.' . . . Yes, this was Mahatma Gandhi, and I had arrived."[99]

The meticulous pursuit of truth gave Gandhi the power to gauge any untruth that was around him. Pyarelal wrote:

> Gandhi's unremitting striving for truth endowed him with clarity of thinking, a mastery of details and finally that "unerring hunch" which aroused the envy and admiration of seasoned diplomats and statesmen of the orthodox school. It further gave him that uncanny instinct, almost like the sixth sense – the result of uttermost refinement and heightened sensitivity of the psyche – which enabled him to detect untruth and corruption not visible to the common eye.[100]

His devotion to truth enabled him to eschew cunningness in his political enterprises. He said: "I believe cunning is not only morally wrong but also politically inexpedient, and have therefore always discountenanced its use even from the practical standpoint."[101]

This scrupulous pursuit of truth enabled Gandhi to equate an oversight with sin. Thus during his negotiations with the Nawab of

Bhopal, Gandhi found himself guilty of an oversight. It shook him to his depths. He arraigned himself before the tribunal of his conscience and accused himself of gross negligence, "which is criminal in a public man."[102] Not satisfied with it, he made a confession of his error before the evening prayer gathering. "Friends may say that it was no sin but a mere oversight – a trivial mistake. I draw no distinction between error and sin. If a man commits a bona fide mistake and confesses it with a contrite heart before his Maker, the merciful Maker sterilises it of all harm."[103]

Gandhi showed equanimity of the highest order in the face of dangers and even in times of bereavement of dear ones. On the 28 June 1946, Gandhiji left Delhi for Poona. In the small hours of the night while proceeding at full speed between Neral and Karjat, the special train bearing him bumped against some boulders which seemed to have been deliberately placed on the track to derail it. The dynamo of the rear bogie was wrecked and the ironwork under the engine damaged. But for the presence of mind of the engine driver, Mr. Pereira, who pulled up the train in time, there might have been a terrible accident. "Whilst for over two hours during the night gangs of mechanics were at work, loosening and removing the wrecked steel structures, Gandhiji continued to sleep the sleep of the just and the innocent amidst the din and clangour of hammer blows. Asked next morning if he knew what had happened during the night, he exclaimed, 'Oh! I was not aware of it!'"[104] Or again, on hearing the death of Rasik, son of Harilal who died in Delhi on 8 February, 1929, Gandhi wrote from Sind to Devadas on 9 February: "The telegram arrived when food was being brought in for me. I took my meal as usual and kept on working as I ate . . . Rasik's death certainly pains me, but that is only because of selfishness . . "[105]

Confession of one's guilt forms part of the life of a truth-seeker. Gandhi said:

> A man of truth must ever be confident if he has also equal need to be diffident . . . His consciousness of the fallibility of human nature must make him humble and therefore ever ready to retrace his steps immediately he discovers his error. It makes no difference to his confidence that he has previously made Himalayan blunders. His confession and penance make him, if anything, stronger for future action. Discovery of errors makes the votary of truth more cautious of believing things and forming conclusions, but once he has made up his mind, his confidence must remain unshaken.[106]

He insisted that this confession should be done immediately – the moment the error is discovered. He wrote: "I have ever followed the maxim that one should not let the sun go down upon one's error without confessing it."[107] In fact, his *Autobiography* is a frank and humble confession of his own shortcomings.

A lover of truth is concerned with minute details. In one of his visits to Sevagram, Gandhi examined the dormitory of the boys regarding minute things such as how to patch up torn bed sheets, etc. He told the teachers:

> All these may appear to you to be trifles but all big things are made up of trifles. My entire life has been built on trifles. To the extent to which we have neglected to inculcate the importance of little things on our boys, we have failed or rather . . . I have failed. For it was I who launched the experiment of Nai Talim but could not find time to conduct it myself and had to leave it to others. A sense of cleanliness, tidiness and sanitation, in my opinion, constitutes the very core of Nai Talim.[108]

Concern for minutest of details also implies that the votary must exercise the greatest caution in his dealings with others. To allow a human being to believe a thing which one has not fully verified is to compromise truth. It also implies that not only telling lies is untruth, but guilty silence or hiding one's state of mind from one's guardians is also against truth. Truth has to be uttered even in matters of gentility. To say untruth out of politeness is hypocrisy. A meticulous care regarding the intake of food items is a matter of importance for truth-seekers. Truth does not entertain partiality even for one's own dear ones. A profession like that of a lawyer is not a liar's profession. In fact, as a lawyer, Gandhi never took up a false case. He never coached the witnesses. He believed that it was possible to practise law without compromising truth.

In business too, Gandhi promoted truthfulness. Truthfulness in matters of money made Gandhi to write in *Navajivan* an article under the title "My Shame and Sorrow" wherein he highlighted the details of the various irregularities committed by Chaganlal Gandhi and Kasturba in handling money. The offence of Kasturba was that she kept a sum of four rupees that a visitor to the Ashram had offered to her. Although she handed it over to Chhaganlal Joshi, the Secretary of the Ashram, when the latter asked for it, nevertheless, it was a transgression.[109]

Scrupulous accounting of public money is another quality of a truth seeker.

A person of truth will perform his/her duties out of a sense of selflessness seeing them as willed by God. The strain thus accrued does not cause any serious tension. Gandhi once remarked: "In the course of self-examination, I often ask myself whether the terrific strain to which I subject my system in pursuit of my mission is a sign of self-will or a mark of His grace. The test is this: If I break down under the strain, it was the result of self-will, attachment, impatience for results; but if my labour was solely in pursuance of His will, His grace should be with me and I should be able to bear up under the strain."[110]

Another characteristic feature of a votary of truth is that he does not indulge in generalizations. Writing in *Harijan*, Gandhi said: "Some priests may be bad. Some temples, churches and mosques exhibit corruption. But this does not mean that all priests are bad or that all the churches, temples and mosques are hotbeds of corruption and superstition. A votary of truth cannot derive sweeping conclusions from some instances."[111]

Punctuality is another quality of a truthful person. Gandhi told a companion: "He alone can claim to have faith who in life ceaselessly endeavours to observe the law of God. For, as I have often said, He and His law are one. The mark of a man of faith is that he is always awake and alert in every little thing. I claim to have faith in God, but then I keep my routine with clock-like regularity in respect of eating, drinking, rest and work."[112] Further in a letter Gandhi wrote: "He who is punctual in everything, will not fall ill and in any event will experience imperturbable calm. This is made possible by ceaseless remembrance of God's name. Let His name, therefore, abide with you always."[113] Hence to the votary of truth, punctuality is an important quality that gives peace.

Devotion to truth enabled Gandhi to acknowledge the goodness in others without any bias. Commenting on the selfless and free services rendered by Simmonds, an expert stenographer during his London deputation in 1906, Gandhi said: "I have often experienced that benevolence is by no means peculiar to the brown skin."[114] Further, Gandhi genuinely appreciated even his own enemies and was all out to meet his critics face to face and tried to win them over. Thus during his London deputation in 1906, Gandhi spent three Sunday evenings with Shyamji Krishnavarma who was critical of Gandhi volunteering his help to the Government of South Africa during the Zulu Rebellion.[115] Gandhi also humbly accepted the remarks of critics for reforms. While commenting on Katherine Mayo's book under the title *Mother India*, which denounced Hindus and Hinduism, Gandhi wrote: "We may repudiate the cha.ge as it has been framed by her, but we may not repudiate the substance underlying the many allegations she has made. It is a good thing to see ourselves as others see us. We need not even examine the motives with which the book is written. A cautious reformer may make some use of it."[116]

Thus to Gandhi, truth meant not only verbal truth but truthful living – complete accord between profession and practice, thought, word and deed. There was a physical, mental and spiritual consistency of life as a result of his attachment to truth. Further, truth must be sought in one's every activity. Gandhi wrote: "How beautiful it would be, if all of us, men and women, devoted ourselves wholly to Truth in all that we might do in our waking hours, whether working, eating, drinking, or playing, till dissolution of the body makes us one with Truth? God as Truth has been for me a treasure beyond price; may He be so to every one of us."[117] But this was not an easy task for him. It requires attentive and ceaseless striving. Gandhi himself acknowledged this when he wrote: "the path of truth is as narrow as it is straight. It is like balancing oneself on the edge of a sword. By concentration an acrobat can walk on a rope. But the concentration required to tread the path of Truth is far great. The slightest inattention brings one tumbling to the ground. One can realize Truth only by the ceaseless striving."[118]

NON-VIOLENCE AS MEANS TO REALIZE TRUTH

Gandhi considered truth as his life's only ambition and the means to achieve this goal was non-violence. In enunciating his principle of non-violence, Gandhi was influenced by the teachings of different religious seers. His understanding of non-violence is based on a unique philosophy of means and ends wherein he gave importance to both. Gandhi also stipulated a number of conditions in order to practise non-violence, which in turn enabled him to attain truth. All these issues are discussed in this section.

To Gandhi, both truth and non-violence became very precious, even more precious than *moksha*. He said: "I cannot consider anything dearer to me than *moksha*. Yet even that *moksha* I would renounce if it were to conflict with truth and non-violence."[119] Gandhi abhorred the idea of comparing truth and non-violence. This is because as Gandhi himself said: "Ahimsa and Truth are my two lungs. I cannot live without them."[120] However, if such comparison must be instituted, he said: "I would say that truth is superior even to non-violence. For untruth is tantamount to violence. The lover of truth is bound to make a discovery of non-violence sooner or later."[121] Further, if cohesive force is necessary for material (atomic) world which is nothing but blind matter, it is all the more necessary for animate beings especially, the humans. This force is love or non-violence.

The insight into non-violent technique was already noticed in young Moniya.[122]

> "When brothers and sisters quarrel with each other," the mother would argue, "they square it out among themselves. If your brother hits you, you can return the blow." In answer, Moniya would say: "Well, then let him hit me. I won't," and add as an afterthought: "Should you not, mother, prevent my brother from beating me, instead of asking me to imitate him?" Dumbfounded, the mother would hug her darling and exclaim: "Moniya, wherefrom has all this come to you? Who has taught you all this? and she would wonder what destiny awaited her little one.[123]

Gandhi received an object lesson in non-violence when he made a clean confession to his father.[124] Further, in understanding the principle of non-violence, Gandhi was influenced by the teachings of the Buddha. Sacredness of animal life was emphasised in Buddhist teachings. This, according to Gandhi, implied upholding the sanctity of all life. This is possible only through the principle of non-violence.[125] Another influence that overwhelmed Gandhi's understanding of non-violence was the life and teachings of Jesus especially 'the Sermon on the Mount'. Romain Rolland too made a deep impact on Gandhi. Speaking about him Gandhi said: "He lived Truth and Non-violence as he saw and believed them from time to time. He responded to all suffering. He revolted against wanton human butchery..."[126]

The Indian seers also influenced Gandhi in his pursuit of truth through non-violence. In fact, the impossibility of full realization of Truth in this mortal body led these seekers after Truth to the appreciation of *ahimsa*.

> The question, which confronted him was: "Shall I bear with those who create difficulties for me, or shall I destroy them?" The seeker realized that he who went on destroying others did not make headway but simply stayed where he was, while the man who suffered those who created difficulties marched ahead, and at times even took the others with him. The first act of destruction taught him that the Truth, which was the object of his quest, was not outside himself but within. Hence the more he took to violence; the more he receded from Truth. For in fighting the imagined enemy without, he neglected the enemy within.[127]

Gandhi defined non-violence as the active force of the highest order. "It is soul-force or the power of Godhead within us."[128] Although negatively non-violence implies non-injury in thought, word and action to any other being, in its positive sense, non-violence is purest love. Gandhi said:

> To express purest love is like walking on the edge of a sword. ... We never know when we are not selfish even when we fancy we are all love. The more I think of it, the more I feel the Truth of what I have often said. Love and truth are two faces of the same coin and both most difficult to practise and the only things worth living for. A person cannot be true, if he does not love all God's creatures; truth and love are therefore the complete sacrifice.[129]

Thus non-violence is the way of love for the meanest of creation as oneself; it is the path of self-suffering through which one detects and transforms untruth into truth.

Conditions for Non-violence

Pure non-violence, according to Gandhi, is hurt by every evil thought, by anger, by wishing ill to anybody, by hatred, by fear, by selfishness, by lying, by undue haste and by attachment. Therefore, conditions for non-violence are that one must avoid these evils conscientiously. Non-violence in thought implies that there is no room for harbouring ill-will in one's heart even though it is not expressed in acts. Gandhi said: "By non-violence or peace I mean the peace, which comes through inner strength. If I have that peace, that non-violence, I won't have any hate in me.... Non-violence works organically, not mechanically."[130]

Gandhi claimed that it takes a fairly strenuous course of training to attain a mental state of non-violence. In daily life it has to be a course of discipline to control one's anger.

> Unless there is a hearty cooperation of the mind the mere outward observance will be simply a mask, harmful both to the man himself and to others. The perfect state if reached only when mind and body and speech are in proper coordination. But it is always a case of intense mental struggle. It is not that I am incapable of anger, for instance, but I succeed on almost all occasions to keep my feelings under control.[131]

Injuring the feelings of others day in and day out is a subtle form of violence. In fact, for Gandhi, it is very much worse than even murders. Non-violence in words means that one must avoid the use of harsh language. Gandhi lamented the false belief of some people, who think that in order to be truthful one must use callous language. But the fact is that truth really suffers when it is harshly put. "Truth being itself fully strong is insulted when an attempt is made to support it with harshness."[132]

Non-violence avoids any hatred in one's heart against another even if he/she is an enemy. Hatred should give way to self-suffering. Gandhi says that hatred has its origin in fear. The two are the reverse and obverse of the same coin. The desire to kill is, therefore, "in inverse proportion to the readiness to die."[133] It is the fear of the opponent that gives rise to hatred in us. But in the dictionary of non-violence "there is no such word as an external enemy."[134] When that recognition comes, fear goes and with that hatred must by itself cease. "Thus his (the opponent's) conversion implies our conversion, too."[135] The inner logic of non-violence is this: hatred is born out of fear and one is ready to kill another only when one is afraid of one's death. Gandhi's percept is that one must convert oneself and be ready to die, and then befriend the other and create conversion in him/her.

Therefore, non-violence implies fearlessness. In fact, Gandhi said that the true test of love or *ahimsa* is fearlessness.

> "Perfect love casts out all fear." Conversely, fear is an indication of the absence of love or Ahimsa towards the object of our fear. But it is no use making a show of bravery when there is fear in the heart. It won't work. Instances have been known of children fearlessly playing with snakes without coming to harm. "But if a grown-up person who was afraid of snakes tried to play with one, it would detect fear in the very touch and probably bite him."[136]

It is the same with human beings. Hence fearlessness does not mean that one does not perceive danger; instead, it implies that even when one perceives danger, one is ready to trust in God. "To see the danger clearly and yet to remain unperturbed in the face of it, trusting in God's goodness, is true wisdom."[137]

Further, fearlessness distinguishes non-violence from violence. Cultivation of bravery is common to both violence and non-violence. There is, however, one difference. The courage of violence "does not mean emancipation from fear, but discovering the means of combating the cause of fear."[138] The votary of non-violence has to cultivate "the capacity for sacrifice of the highest type in order to be free from fear."[139]

Another condition for non-violence is avoidance of selfishness. *Ahimsa* is not simply non-injury but non-injury without selfishness. Therefore, "ahimsa does not simply mean non-killing. *Himsa* means causing pain to or killing, any life out of anger or for a selfish purpose, or with the intention of causing injury. Refraining from so doing is ahimsa."[140]

Non-violence is hurt by lying. One must never say 'yes' when one means 'no,' whatever be the consequences. Truth and non-violence admit of no exceptions. But then one is not bound always to answer questions that may be asked. One can refuse to answer instead of telling a lie. Gandhi expressed these views in answer to a problem raised by Bertrand Russell. "I once in the course of a country walk saw a tired fox at the last stages of exhaustion still forcing himself to run. A few minutes afterwards I saw the hunt. They asked me if I had seen the fox, and I said I had. They asked me which way he had gone, and I lied to them."[141] The person made the initial mistake of admitting that he/she had seen the fox. However, "when it is relevant, truth has to be uttered, however unpleasant it may be. Irrelevance is always untruth and should never be uttered."[142]

Undue haste too impairs non-violence. Hence concentration is required to tread the path of non-violence. This concentration is far greater than the concentration that an acrobat uses to walk on a rope. "The slightest inattention brings one tumbling to the ground. One can realize Truth and Ahimsa only by ceaseless striving."[143] Gandhi's remark on this subject is worth quoting:

> God has given us power to see only the step in front of us, and it should be enough if Heavenly light reveals that step to us. We

can then sing with Newman, 'One step enough for me'. And we may be sure from our past experience that the next step will always be in view. In other words, the impenetrable darkness is nothing so impenetrable as we imagine. But it seems impenetrable when, in our impatience, we want to look beyond that one step.[144]

Still, another condition for non-violence is detachment. According to Gandhi, "it is impossible for a man with 'possessions' to observe Ahimsa even in the gross meaning of that term. A man of property must adopt measures for its security involving the punishment of whoever tries to steal it. Only he can observe Ahimsa who holds nothing as his own and works away in a spirit of total detachment."[145] Detachment also involves one's wife, son and friends besides one's possession. Only when all these are subordinated to truth and non-violence, can a person become a true *Satyagrahi.*[146]

Gandhi also spoke of the *ahimsa* of the brave. "The minimum that is required of a person wishing to cultivate the Ahimsa of the brave is first to clear one's thought of cowardice and in the light of the clearance regulate his conduct in every activity, great or small."[147] Thus, for example, a fellow passenger threatens one's son with assault and when the father reasons with him/her he/she then turns upon him. If then the father takes the blow with grace and dignity, without harbouring any ill will against him, he exhibits the *ahimsa* of the brave. The only criterion of ahimsa of the brave is death. Gandhi wrote: "If someone killed me and I died with prayer for the assassin on my lips, and God's remembrance and consciousness of His living presence in the sanctuary of my heart, then alone would I be said to have the non-violence of the brave."[148]

Thus, non-violence became Gandhi's only means of arriving at truth. It turned out, for Gandhi, not merely a personal virtue to be pursued but a quality that needs to be practised at every level of group, community and nation. While addressing the Gandhi Seva Sangh, he said: "For me non-violence is something to be shunned if it is a private virtue. My concept of non-violence is universal. It belongs to the millions.... Anything that cannot reach the millions is not for me.... We were born to prove that truth and non-violence is not just a rule for personal conduct. It can become the policy of a group, a community, a nation."[149]

In his interactions with other people including his opponents, non-violence enabled Gandhi to make concessions, compromises and adjustments but without compromising his principles. He told people to their face the most unpalatable truths but in a manner that did not hurt them. The object was never to overreach the opponent. Instead he made the opponent a fellow-seeker in the quest of truth.

> He aimed not at destroying his power; he transformed and annexed it. In argument he did not seek to overbear or coerce the opponent by intellectual bludgeoning but to win him by showing, or rather helping him to see for himself, the flaw in his position. In doing so, he sometimes discovered a gap in his own. It made the opponent's mind receptive instead of resistant. In the end there was no "victor" or "vanquished" feeling left. Both sides shared in an equal measure the thrill and joy of the discovery of truth and its vindication.[150]

Means and Ends

For Gandhi, both non-violence and truth are inseparable. They are "so intertwined that it is practically impossible to disentangle and separate them. They are like the two sides of a coin, or rather of a smooth unstamped metallic disc. Who can say, which is the obverse, and which is the reverse? Nevertheless, *Ahimsa* is the means; Truth is the end."[151] To explain this intimate interrelationship between truth and non-violence, Gandhi expounded his unique philosophy of means and ends.

Gandhi wrote: "There is such a close connection between the means and the ends that it is difficult to say which of the two is more important. Or we may say that the means is the body and the end is the soul. The end is invisible; the means is visible."[152] This relationship is very intimate. In order to reach the goal of peace, for example, the means had to be peaceful and consistent with the goal. Thus violence could not end violence. Therefore, Gandhi insisted on the use of the right means to reach the right end. "The means may be likened to a seed and the end to a tree. There is the (same) inviolable connection between the means and the end as there is between the seed and the tree."[153]

Further, Gandhi held that means take preponderance over the end. He said:

> They say, 'means are after all means.' I would say, 'means are after all everything.' As the means so the end. There is no wall of separation between the means and the end. Indeed, the Creator has

> given us control (and that too very limited) over means, none over the end. Realization of the goal is in exact proportion to that of the means. This is a proposition that admits of no exception.[154]

Thus Gandhi held that the means, which are in the control of human beings, if properly used, will lead one to the end. When means are taken care of, it will automatically take care of the end.

Therefore, Gandhi insisted on the importance of the purity of means. Addressing a gathering of the workers from Maharashtra, in his first public address after his release from the Aga Khan Detention Camp, Gandhi said: "The phenomenal awakening of the masses during the last 25 years has been entirely due to the purity of our means. And to the extent that untruth and violence has crept in, they have hindered our progress."[155] Further on the eve of the historic Dandi march, 11 March1930, Gandhi delivering the remarkable speech on the Sabarmati sands at Ahmedabad, said: "I have faith in the righteousness of our cause and the purity of our weapons. And where the means are clean, there God is undoubtedly present with His blessings. And where these three combine, there defeat is an impossibility."[156]

The same means sometimes can be used either for exploitation or for emancipation. Thus under the East India Company's regime the spinning wheel had become the symbol of the exploitation and slavery of the artisans, and the arrogance of the rulers. But in the hands of Gandhi, the same wheel became the symbol of non-violence and deliverance of the masses through it. "The same knife that took away life in the hands of a butcher could become the means of saving life in the hands of a surgeon."[157] Therefore, the means are judged according to the results they produce.

In this way, Gandhi gave emphasis to the means, namely, non-violence. Writing in *Young India*, Gandhi said: "For me the only certain means of knowing God is non-violence."[158] Ahimsa is not the goal. Truth is the goal. "But we have no means of realising truth in human relationship except through the practice of Ahimsa . . . Ahimsa being the means we are naturally more concerned with it in our everyday life. It is Ahimsa, therefore, that our masses have to be educated in. Education in truth follows from it as a natural end."[159]

Further, in the political field, Gandhi applied the same doctrine of non-violence in order to fight against unjust laws and systems that crippled the dignity and the worth of human being. However, he was quick to assure that he hated only the evil system and not the evildoer. He made a sharp distinction between human being and the system. His non-cooperation was "with an attitude that was responsible for the system which has seized us in its serpentine coils and which, was reducing us to dust."[160] Gandhi called this non-violent and truthful fight against unjust political and social systems as *satyagraha.*

SATYAGRAHA

Gandhi was not merely interested in the pursuit of Truth as a personal virtue and in his personal capacity. Rather, he was keen on making it into a social movement for fighting untruth and violence. He wanted truth and non-violence to be "organised in a powerful movement, not based merely on the goodness of the individual but on the goodness organised to withstand organised evil."[161] It is this powerful movement, organised by Gandhi as a social weapon to fight evil and injustice as well as a means to inspire the masses with self-confidence in resisting with their own strength against all tyranny that is known as *satyagraha.* In this section, besides discussing the meaning and the characteristic features of *satyagraha,* we shall deal at length with the various pre-requisites needed for one to undertake it. The eleven vows that Gandhi proposed to his *ashramites* will serve as basic conditions for the success of *satyagraha.*

The *satyagraha* movement took its origin during the historic meeting that was held at Johannesburg on 11 September 1906 by Indians in the Transvaal in South Africa. Initially the movement was called passive resistance. But Gandhi found this term to be too narrowly constructed and it is supposed to be the weapon of the weak and is characterised by hatred and violence. This was, of course, contrary to his ideals of truth and non-violence. Therefore, he offered a nominal prize through *Indian Opinion* to the reader who made the best suggestion on the subject. As a result, Maganlal Gandhi coined the word *sadagraha* and won the prize. But later it was changed into *satyagraha* (*sat* = truth; *agraha* = firmness)[162]. It is the truth-force or a clinging to truth.

Gandhi explained the meaning of *satyagraha* thus:

> . . . Tolstoy called it also Soul-Force or Love-Force, and so it is. Carried out to its utmost limit this force is independent of pecuniary or other material assistance; certainly, even in its elementary form

> it is free of physical force or violence. Indeed, violence is the negation of this great spiritual force, which can only be cultivated or wielded by those who will entirely eschew violence. It is the force that may be used as well in political as in domestic affairs. It may be used by individuals as well as by communities. Its universal applicability is a demonstration of its permanence and invincibility.[163]

In other words, the essence of *satyagraha* is that it is a battle of Right against Might.

"The laws that govern the power of Satyagraha, Gandhiji maintained, are as objective and concrete as physical laws. There is, however, one important difference between the laws of Satyagraha and the laws of physical science. The laws of physical science are inert laws; those governing Satyagraha are living laws subject to the principle of growth, evolution, adaptation and change."[164] While scientific laws deal with natural functioning, the laws of *satyagraha* deal with human functioning. But just because they are dealing with human beings, they do not become subjective and variant; instead, they are objective and universal in the sense that if the *satyagrahi* has no fear and exhibit love for the opponent, it is sure to change the heart of the oppressor. Likewise, if one is free from anger and pride, one is sure to listen to the inner voice with clarity.

In adopting passive resistance or *satyagraha* as Gandhi called it, he was influenced by various factors. Gandhi knew of its use by Indians living in certain princely states. He admitted that it was the New Testament, which really awakened him to the rightness and value of Passive Resistance; he was particularly influenced by the Sermon on the Mount. The *Bhagavad-Gita* deepened the consciousness created by the New Testament, and Tolstoy's *The Kingdom of God is Within You* gave this ideal a permanent form. He was also influenced by Ruskin and Thoreau, particularly the former's *Crown of Wild Olive*.[165]

Another important influence on Gandhi's notion of *satyagraha* was Kasturba, Gandhi's own wife. From the days of their early married life he found out that Kasturba was a girl with a mind of her own and she was not willing to accept the husband's authority and obey him, unless what he said appealed to her head and heart. He could make her miserable but he could not make her do what he wanted unless he carried conviction to her. It made him realize that the basic principle for carrying the opponent with you is the underlying desire to be able to make him/

her see your point of view and to have respect and affection for him/her.[166]

The above influences reinforced Gandhi's concept of *satyagraha*. Pyarelal observes:

> ... we do not need to destroy the opponent or weaken his power in order to win the battle of right against wrong. We can transform and annex it by the alchemy of vicarious suffering – Ahimsa or non-violence. He gave it the name Satyagraha – "soul- force" or "truth-force"; the power that accrues from a conscious realization of one's identity with the whole creation and ... the Supernal Reality, which is Truth or God, and which expresses itself in human relationships as love. It makes no difference by what name we call Him, or even whether we recognize His existence or not. Since He is Himself both the Law-giver and the Law, to deny His existence no more affects the operation of His law than ignoring the law of gravitation can prevent an apple from falling.[167]

In this way, it can be said that s*atyagraha* as advanced by Gandhi was unique. "My truthfulness, I feel, is peculiarly my own. My Ahimsa is an intense feeling and the Satyagraha born of a blending of the two is indeed indescribable."[168]

Satyagraha thus excludes every form of violence. It avoids the destruction of government property like railways, buildings, bridges and telegraph because evil does not reside there but rather a self-immolation of the purest type would convert the evildoer. In fact, the name 'Phoenix' which he gave to his new experiment began in Durban after reading John Ruskin's *Unto This Last* is noteworthy. A Greek legend attributed to the bird Phoenix qualities of purity, sacrifice and immortality. The bird is supposed to be alone without a mate. It immolates itself and is re-born from its own ashes.[169] Another reason for eschewing violence in *satyagraha* is that "man is not capable of knowing the absolute truth and therefore not competent to punish."[170]

A feature of Gandhian concept of *satyagraha* is compromise. Life is made of compromises. Compromise means that both the parties make large concessions on all points except where a principle is involved. "Ahimsa, simply because it is purest, unselfish love often demands such compromises. The conditions are imperative. There should be no self in one's action, no fear, no untruth, and it must be in furtherance of the cause of Ahimsa. The compromise must be natural to oneself, not imposed from without."[171]

The *satyagrahi* must be ready for compromise even at the last minute. Thus during his struggle against Asiatic Registration Act in South Africa, as the Asiatic Registration Act was still the subject matter of correspondence between the Imperial Government and the Transvaal authorities, Gandhi appealed to the Europeans through the columns of the *Star* saying that the anti-Asiatic party having now obtained what it wanted, it should not be impossible to arrive at a reasonable compromise even at that stage and save British Indians from being considered untrustworthy and feloniously inclined. He put before them his offer of voluntary registration, so that those who were bona fide holders of permits and were honest would be automatically separated from those who were not.[172]

Still another feature of *satyagraha* is that it avoids all forms of secrecy, even those born of good intentions. This is because Gandhi believed that secrecy is against the very concept of truth on which *satyagraha* rests. Gandhi deplored the secret activities of some congress workers who went underground during the Quit India movement. He said: "No secret organization, however big, could do any good. Secrecy aims at building a wall of protection round you. Ahimsa disdains all such protection ... We have to organize for action a vast [mass of] people that have been crushed under the heel of unspeakable tyranny for centuries. They cannot be organized by any other than open, truthful means."[173] Secrecy is also sinful and a symptom of violence especially when the *satyagrahi* is involved in the cause of the dumb millions. It hurts the *satyagraha* movement. Hence Gandhi said that only by adhering to truth and Non-violence can we bring back lustre to the lustreless eyes of crores of Indians fighting for freedom.[174]

Pre-requisites for *Satyagraha*

The aim of *satyagraha* is voluntary self-suffering without any ill will towards the opponent in order to awaken the inherent goodness in his/her heart and through which the *satyagrahi* strives for more and more self-purification. To achieve this end, their faith must become stronger and stronger. It also requires an austere living. All this calls for training and to this purpose Gandhi opened training grounds both in South Africa and India which he named as *ashrams*. The training consists in the practice of the eleven vows, which he stipulated to all his *satyagrahis* for observance. The vows include truth, non-violence, celibacy, non-stealing, non-possession, control of the palate, fearlessness, removal of untouchability, bread-labour, unity of religions and *swadeshi*. Here truth is one of the vows and yet for Gandhi it is the basic vow and it is for its sake that other vows are observed. These vows are highlighted in his *From Yeravda Mandir: Ashram observances.*[175] To sustain the observance of these vows, the *satyagrahi* needs divine assistance, which he/she invokes through prayer, Ramanama, fasting and silence. In this section, a brief attempt is made to understand the concept of vow, the different vows that Gandhi stipulated and the means to sustain the practice of these vows.

Gandhi defined vow as an unflinching determination that helps one against temptation. For him, "taking vows is not a sign of weakness, but of strength. To do at any cost something that one ought to do constitutes a vow. It becomes a bulwark of strength. A man who says that he will do something 'as far as possible' betrays either his pride or his weakness."[176] Vows can be taken only on points of universally recognised principles. Other qualities of vow-taking include moderation and sobriety. "The taking of vows that are not feasible or that are beyond one's capacity would betray thoughtlessness and want of balance. Similarly a vow can be made conditional without losing any of its efficacy or virtue.... Self-restraint is the very keystone of the ethics of vow taking. For instance, one cannot take a vow of self-indulgence, to eat, drink and be merry."[177] God being the very image of vow is the model. "God would cease to be God if He swerved from His own laws even by a hair's breadth."[178] This implies that vows should be fulfilled in the spirit and in the letter in which they are taken. Vows are meant for the purpose of self-purification and self-realization. "They are to a man what anchor is to a ship. A ship without anchor is tossed to and fro and finally broken on the rocks; without vows, human beings meet a similar fate."[179]

The vow of **truth** includes all other vows. This is because truth is the anchor of *satyagraha*. In fact *satyagraha ashram* owes its very existence to the pursuit and the attempted practice of Truth. Further, the sole justification for human existence on earth itself, according to Gandhi, is devotion to Truth. "All our activities and even the very breath of our life should be centred on Truth. Without Truth it is impossible to observe any principles or rules in life."[180] The vow of truth does not merely imply speaking the truth. "There should be Truth in thought, Truth in speech and Truth in action."[181] Thus, the *satyagrahi* through an unflinching adherence to truth fights the unjust and oppressive systems.

The second vow that Gandhi gave his a*shramites* is **non-violence**. In his search after truth, the first and most important means is non-violence. It implies, as seen above, both non-injury in thought, word and deed and positive love towards all created beings. Non-violence is not a mechanical thing. "You do not become non-violent by merely saying, 'I shall not use force'. It must be felt in the heart ... When there is that feeling it will express itself through some action. It may be a sign, a glance, even silence. But, such as it is, it will melt the heart of the wrong-doer and check the wrong."[182] Thus the vow of non-violence is the result of assiduous training which is already described earlier.

Brahmacharaya or celibacy, the third vow, means non-self-gratification. "A man, whose activities are wholly consecrated to the realization of Truth, which requires utter selflessness, can have no time of the selfish purpose of begetting children and running a household. Realization of Truth through self-gratification should, after what has been said before, appear a contradiction in terms."[183] In fact, observing *brahmacharya* is one of the means to the end, which is seeing Brahman or union with Brahman. "Without brahmacharya no one may expect to see Him, and without seeing Him one cannot observe brahmacharya to perfection."[184] Even for married persons, Gandhi suggested that they must behave as if they were not married in order to realize Truth. If the married couple can think of each other as brother and sister, they are freed for universal service. The married men must treat all the women in the world as sisters, mothers or daughters. Then their love becomes free from all impurities of lust. In this way, Gandhi says, married persons can strive for Truth.[185]

Non-stealing is another Gandhian vow. People who claim to know Truth cannot steal things. Stealing makes a person untruthful in his/her action. But most people are consciously or unconsciously more or less guilty of theft. One may not steal what belongs to others. But one steals at times what belongs to oneself, as is done, for instance, by a father who eats something secretly, keeping his children in the dark about it. Common property cannot be removed secretly without proper permission. Things found on the roadside cannot be taken away as they belong to the ruler. Stealing also implies that we should not receive anything that we do not need. Hence unnecessary multiplication of wants is actually stealing. Further it is theft mentally to desire acquisition of anything belonging to others, or to cast a greedy eye on it. Likewise, many people are guilty of stealing ideas of others. Plagiarism is a form of stealing.[186]

The next vow is **non-possession**. It implies that a seeker after Truth cannot hold anything against tomorrow. "God never stores for the morrow: He never creates more than what is strictly needed for the moment. If there, we repose faith in His providence, we should rest assured, that He will give us every day our daily bread, meaning everything that we require."[187] Gandhi applied this principle to thoughts as well. "A man who fills his brain with useless knowledge violates that inestimable principle. Thoughts, which turn us away from God, or do not turn us towards Him, constitute impediments in our way."[188] Further, Gandhi held that from the standpoint of pure Truth, the body too is a possession. "It has been truly said, that desire for enjoyment creates bodies for the soul. When this desire vanishes, there remains no further need for the body, and man is free from the vicious cycle of births and deaths."[189]

The vow of non-possession also includes the concept of voluntary poverty, which, according to Gandhi, implies reduction of desires and wants. In fact, "Civilization, in the real sense of the term, consists not in the multiplication, but in the deliberate and voluntary reduction of wants. This alone promotes real happiness and contentment, and increases the capacity for service."[190] Great men like Jesus, Muhammad, the Buddha, Nanak, Kabir, Chaitanya, Shankara, Dayananada and Ramakrishna exercised an immense influence over and moulded the character of thousands of men and women. They were all men who deliberately embraced poverty as their lot.[191] Such "renunciation made for the sake of dedicated and selfless service is an ineffable joy of which none can deprive one, because that nectar springs from within and sustains life."[192] Besides, ease and comfort are a mental state. Voluntary poverty also enables one to identify oneself with those one serves. "In order to serve the poor one must make oneself poor."[193]

Gandhi was accused of having possessions while preaching poverty. He confessed that his travel had become costly, as he had to travel by second class due to his poor health. His food was also not a poor person's food. His friends met all the expenses incurred. But he did not own any property. Hence he said: "For me dispossession has been a positive gain. I would like people to compete with me in my contentment. It is the richest treasure I own. Hence it is perhaps right to say that though I preach poverty, I am a rich man."[194]

The vow of **control of the palate** is closely connected with the observance of the vow of *brahmacharya*. Food has to be taken like medicine. "It is . . . breach of this observance to take anything just for its pleasant taste. It is equally a breach to take too much of what one finds to one's taste."[195] The body is injured by over-eating which can be partially impaired only by fasting. Gandhi thought that common kitchen relieved people of having to think out the menu for each day.

The vow of **fearlessness** connotes freedom from all external and internal fears. Externally, one must get rid of fear of disease, bodily injury and death, of dispossession, of losing one's nearest and dearest, of losing reputation or giving offence, and so on. "All external fear is the baseless fabric of our own vision. They revolve around the body as the centre and will therefore disappear, as soon as we get rid of attachment for the body."[196] Further, one must also fear the internal foes. Thus one must be rightly afraid of animal passion, anger and the like. Fearlessness is a *sine qua non* for the growth of noble qualities like Truth and love. Gandhi quotes the words of Pirtam who says, "The Path of Hari (the Lord) is the path of the brave, not of cowards." Hari here means Truth, and the brave are those armed with fearlessness, not with the sword, the rifle or other carnal weapons, which are affected only by cowards."[197] Hence Gandhi exhorts his *satyagrahis* to do the right thing fearlessly even if others desert them. Otherwise, the right thing will go on decreasing in the midst of growing hypocrisy and untruth.[198]

The **removal of untouchability** is another vow. By insisting on it, Gandhi wanted to assert that untouchability is not only not part and parcel of Hinduism, but also a plague. It is the bounden duty of every Hindu to fight against it. To remove this curse, he suggested that people must consider it a sin. They should atone for it by fraternizing with untouchables, associating with them in a spirit of love and service, deeming themselves purified by such acts, redressing their grievances, helping them patiently to overcome ignorance and other evils due to the slavery of age, and inspiring other Hindus to do likewise.

Untouchability is against the practice of Truth and non-violence. A seeker after Truth treats everyone as equal by loving him or her as he/she loves his/her own self. He/she should visualise the removal of untouchability from a spiritual standpoint and should worry about its material or political consequences.[199]

Bread labour, another vow, according to Gandhi, is a veritable blessing to one who would worship Truth. This was first stressed by a Russian writer named T.M. Bondaref. Tolstoy gave it wide publicity. By bread labour, Gandhi meant that to live human beings must work. The *Gita* enjoins in the third chapter that one who eats without offering sacrifice eats stolen food. Sacrifice here, according to Gandhi, can only mean Bread labour. If all had worked for their bread, then all distinctions of rank would be obliterated. The worldwide conflict between the capital and the labour, between the rich and the poor would cease to exist. The rich will be there but they would consider themselves to be only trustees of their property and would use it mainly in the public interest.[200] This vow also implies that every type of work is important. "No work that is done in His name and dedicated to Him is small. All work when so done assumes equal merit. A scavenger who works in His service shares equal distinction with a king who uses his gifts in His name and as a mere trustee."[201]

The vow of **unity of religions** means respect and reverence for all religions. Gandhi did not like the term tolerance. It is because tolerance can imply a gratuitous assumption of the inferiority of other faiths to one's own. Instead, Gandhi spoke of entertaining the same respect for the religious faiths of others as what we accord to our own. In this way, one can admit the imperfections of one's own religion. This is what a seeker after Truth should do.

> If we had attained the full vision of truth, we would no longer be mere seekers, but would have become one with God, for Truth is God. But being only seekers, we prosecute our quest, and are conscious of our imperfection. And if we are imperfect ourselves, religion as conceived by us must also be imperfect. We have not realized religion in its perfection, even as we have not realized God. Religion of our conception, being thus imperfect, is always subject to a process of evolution and re-interpretation.[202]

Thus if all faiths outlined by human beings are imperfect, the question of comparative merit does not arise. All faiths constitute a revelation of Truth, but all are imperfect and liable to error. "Tolerance obviously does not disturb the distinction between right and wrong, or good and evil. The reference here throughout is naturally to the principal faiths of the world. They are all based on common fundamentals. They have all produced great saints."[203]

Reverence for other faiths does not mean that one must be blind to the faults of other religions. One must be keenly alive to the defects of one's own religion. One must try to overcome those defects instead of leaving one's own religion and embrace other religions. When one considers all religions with an equal eye, it is possible to blend into one's own faith every acceptable feature of other faiths.[204]

To the question, why there should be so many different faiths, Gandhi said: "the Soul is one, but the bodies which She animates are many. We cannot reduce the number of bodies; yet we recognize the unity of the Soul. Even as a tree has a single trunk, but many branches and leaves, so is there one true and perfect Religion. But as it passes through the human medium, it becomes many."[205] Imperfect people interpret the one Religion differently. All are right from their own standpoint, but it is impossible that everybody is wrong. Hence we need tolerance, which is not indifference towards other faiths but a more intelligent and purer love for them. Tolerance removes all traces of fanaticism. "True knowledge of religion breaks down the barriers between faith and faith. Cultivation of tolerance for other faiths will impart to us a truer understanding of one's own."[206]

The acceptance of the doctrine of Equality of Religions does not abolish the distinction between religion and irreligion. We do not propose to cultivate toleration for irreligion. But a person who seeks Truth and love will not bear hatred towards an irreligious person; instead help that person to see the error of his/her ways, or he/she will point out our error, or each will tolerate the other's differences of opinion.[207]

The vow of ***Swadeshi*** means the spirit, which restricts persons to the use of services available in the immediate surroundings to the exclusion of the more remote. However, he said: "A votary of *Swadeshi* will never harbour ill-will towards the foreigner; he will not be actuated by antagonism towards anybody on earth. *Swadeshism* is not a cult of hatred. It is a doctrine of selfless service that has its roots in the purest *Ahimsa*, that is, love."[208] Gandhi extended this principle of *swadeshi* to religion as well and said: "I must restrict myself to my ancestral religion. That is, the use of my immediate religious surrounding. If I find it defective, I should serve it by purging it of its defects."[209]

Discipline for *Satyagraha*

Besides the eleven vows, Gandhi also proposed many measures of discipline for making *satyagraha* a powerful method. Humility, sacrifice, prayer that includes repetition of *Ramanama*, fasting and silence are the different means through which Gandhi wanted people to practice *satyagraha*.

Stressing the need for **humility**, Gandhi himself wrote:

> Truth without humility would be an arrogant caricature. He who wants to practise truth knows how hard it is. The world may applaud his so-called triumphs. Little does the world know his falls. A truthful man is a chastened being. He has need to be humble. A man who wants to love the whole world including one who calls himself his enemy knows how impossible it is to do so in his own strength. He must be as mere dust before he can understand the elements of Ahimsa.[210]

Humility implies acknowledging one's imperfections and making amends for them. In a letter to Mirabehn, Gandhi wrote: "If I succeed in emptying myself utterly, God will possess me. Then ... everything will come true; but it is a serious question when I shall have reduced myself to zero."[211]

Therefore, Gandhi was of the opinion that one who cultivates truth, non-violence, celibacy and other vows must be humble. In humility, one is able to perceive truth even in the midst of dangers and precarious existence. It helps to avoid any indifference to the source of all life. Only arrogance can make one to be apathetic to the existence of God.

The life of a *satyagrahi* must be one of unbroken cycle of **sacrifice**. For this, the person must live not for the satisfaction of the senses but only for the service of God. His life then becomes a sacrament or a symbol of self-sacrifice. Writing on 4 July 1908 in Gujarati in *Indian Opinion* under the heading "Self-Sacrifice," Gandhi said: "Satyagraha and self-interest do not go together. Satyagraha always calls for sacrifice of self. ... We rejoice in this opportunity (for sacrifice) as though it were a nuptial occasion, and want every Indian to do the same. Satyagraha will reveal its real meaning now."[212] In order to be effective, the sacrifice must be "... willing and ... made in faith and hope, without a trace of ill will or hatred in the heart ... there is nothing that such sacrifice cannot achieve."[213]

If *satyagraha* seems to fail, Gandhi called for self-introspection, which should lead to self-purification. This purification, according to Gandhi, consisted of several things. From the societal point of view, purification was freedom from contamination by participation in an evil order – staying away unspotted from the world. In a more personal sense, purification meant deliverance from anger, greed, pride and fear. In a positive sense, purification meant the fulfilment of one's dharma – religious duties – which in the human sphere were a reflection of natural laws in the order of the universe. Finally, in a personal and positive sense, such purity was to be evidenced by the *satyagrahi* in daily practice of virtue, in a detached sense, such as the *Gita* commands.[214] The problem remains as to how such self-purification is to be achieved so that Truth may be realized and its power evidenced. To this end, Gandhi proposed the practice of the eleven vows that are discussed above.

A *satyagrahi* must be a person of **prayer**. Prayer means "an earnest desire to be filled with the spirit of Truth. This desire should be present all the twenty-four hours. But our souls are too dull to have this awareness day and night. Therefore, we offer prayer for a short time in the hope that a time will come when all our conduct will be one continuously sustained prayer."[215] It is "a heart search ... a call to humility ... a call to self-purification."[216] It is "a yearning of the heart to be one with the Maker, an invocation for His blessing."[217] It is "a confession of one's unworthiness and weakness and is not to be performed with the lips, but with the heart."[218] "For those who are filled with the presence of God in them, to labour is to pray. Their life is one continuous prayer or act of worship."[219] For those who act only to sin, to indulge themselves, and live for self, no time is too much for prayer. But for the ordinary mortals there is a middle path. They are not so exalted to say that all their acts are a dedication nor are they so far gone as to be living purely for self. Hence, all religions set apart times for general devotion.[220]

Meditation is a form of personal prayer, which every religion subscribes to. For Gandhi, meditation consisted in "closing the eyes and ears of the mind to all else, except the object of one's devotion."[221] Therefore, Gandhi said that a person while praying may be said to worship "his own glorified self,"[222] the divine essence, the truth that is within oneself, within the soul of every being. "At prayer time, our speech is addressed to ourselves and is intended to shake off our torpor. Some of us are intellectually aware of God. ... None has seen Him face to face. We desire to . . . realise Him, to become one with Him ... through prayer."[223]

The Repetition of *Ramanama* is another form of personal prayer that Gandhi recommended as a tool for the practice of *satyagraha*. The philosophy behind *Ramanama* is this: "Constant repetition of a word-symbol connoting the Ultimate Reality, or whatever aspect of it appeals to one, with concentration till it results in such a silence of intellect, will and feeling, that the divine Word can be uttered within the soul."[224] It forms part of the spiritual exercises prescribed in almost all religions. "If the word is simply repeated 'all whole, and not broken up or undone' by discursive analysis, the Fact for which the word stands will end by presenting itself to the soul in the form of an integral intuition."[225] Gandhi used the name of Ram for the repetition.

The effects of *Ramanama* are many. It gives a living faith in oneself and in others. A person who repeated *Ramanama* and thereby cleansed his inner being could not tolerate the filth outside. Since soul is the governing principle of human being, one can treat one's body through *Ramanama*. However it will be meaningless farce when at the same time one is drugging one's system with medicines.[226] *Ramanama* banishes fear. Gandhi as a child was frightened of ghosts and spirits. Rambha, his nurse, suggested the repetition of *Ramanama* as a remedy for his fear.[227] Gandhi, in his turn, offered the same talisman to the refugees at Laksham Refugee Camp.

> God resides in the hearts of the pure always. If you walk in fear of Him, you need fear no one on earth. Why should you be afraid of the cry of Allah-o-Akbar? The Allah of Islam is the same as the Rama of Hindus – the protector of the innocent. If you believe in Ramanama you will not think of leaving East Bengal. To run away from danger instead of facing it is to deny one's faith in man and God and even oneself. It were better far to drown oneself than live to declare such bankruptcy of faith.[228]

Gandhi also insisted on congregational prayer. "Man is both an individual and a social being. As an individual he may have his prayer during all the waking hours, but as a member of society he has to join in the congregational prayer."[229] It is a means for establishing the essential human unity through common worship. "Mass singing of Ramadhun and the beating of Tal are its outward expression. If they are not a mechanical performance but are an echo of the inner unison, as they should be, they generate a power and an atmosphere of sweetness and fragrance which has only to be seen to be realized."[230] Its success depends upon the purity of the leader and the faith of the audience. Gandhi said: "I know instances in which the audience had faith and the leader was an impostor. Such cases will continue to happen. But truth like the sun shines in the midst of the darkness of untruth. Their result as in my case will be known probably after my death."[231]

The fruit of prayer should be looked for not in any "extraneous evidence but in the transformed conduct and character of those who have left the real presence of God within."[232] One of the benefits of prayer is peace. He said: "In spite of despair staring me in the face on the political horizon, I have never lost my peace. In fact I have found people who envy my peace. That peace, I tell you, comes from prayer."[233] He claimed that one could discover truth and the method of applying it, that is, *satyagraha* or soul force by patient endeavour and silent prayer.[234] Gandhi also felt that God always heard his prayer. "I have found Him nearest at hand when the horizon seemed darkest – in my ordeals in jails when it was not all smooth sailing for me. I cannot recall a moment in my life when I had a sense of desertion by God."[235]

Fasting is still another means for sustaining the morale of the *satyagrahi*. Fasts can be undertaken only in obedience to the inner voice. It is not something mechanical nor is it according to one's whims and fancies. Gandhi wrote:

> I am not responsible for these fasts. I do not undertake them for my amusement. I would not torture the flesh for the love of fame. Though I bear joyfully the pangs of hunger and many other physical discomforts of fasting, let no one imagine that I do not suffer. These fasts are bearable only because they are imposed upon me by a higher power and the capacity to bear the pain also comes from that Power.[236]

Thus the grace of God becomes a necessary condition for fasting. This is because "when a man starves his senses through fasting, the objects of those senses disappear from him, but not the yearning for them; the yearning too departs when he beholds the Supreme."[237] Further, Gandhi said that it requires complete self-purification, much more than what is required in facing death with retaliation. There can be no room for selfishness, anger, lack of faith, or impatience in a pure fast. However, mortification of the flesh is allowed when the flesh rebels against one and of course, not for its own sake. It can be resorted to against a lover, not to extort rights but to reform him/her. In this way, fasting should be inspired by perfect truth and perfect non-violence.[238]

Gandhi was of the opinion that fast must be the last weapon that a votary of *ahimsa* resorts to. Only when all human ingenuity has failed, the votary can undertake fast. Gandhi also enumerated the fruits of fasting. He wrote: "This fasting quickens the spirit of prayer, that is to say, the fasting is a spiritual act and, therefore, addressed to God. The effect of such action on the life of the people is that when they at all know the person fasting their sleeping conscience is awakened."[239] In fact, Gandhi held that only one act of perfect sacrifice would suffice for the world. "Such is held to be the example of Jesus ... A man who was completely innocent offered himself as a sacrifice for the good of others, including his enemies, and became the ransom of the world. It was a perfect act. ... It enshrines an eternal law – the law of vicarious and innocent suffering taken in its true sense."[240]

Gandhi believed that fasting is a remedy for getting rid of untruth in an institution like *ashram*. Obviously, such fasts are undertaken by the head of the institution. He stipulates a number of qualities that the penitent must possess in such cases. The wrongdoer should have love for the penitent. He/she may have love for the wrongdoer and the wrongdoer should recognize it. The penitent himself/herself must be one of the parties wronged. Mere friendship is no reason for one to fast. A penitent for another's wrongdoing must himself/herself be guiltless of similar misconduct. The pot may not call the kettle black. He must otherwise also be a person of purity and appear as such to the wrongdoer and must not have any personal interest to serve. The penitent must not have any anger in him/her. The wrong act must be patent, accepted as such by all and spiritually harmful, and the doer must be aware of its nature.[241] Further, such fasts have a threefold influence, firstly, over the penitent, secondly, over the wrongdoer and thirdly, over the congregation. "The penitent becomes more alert, examines the innermost recesses of his own heart and takes steps to deal with any personal weakness that he may discover. If the wrongdoer has any pity, he becomes conscious of his own fault, is ashamed of it and resolves never to sin any more in the future. The congregation takes a course of self-introspection."[242]

Fasting can have a coercive element. Gandhi said that fasting in its real sense should not be construed as coercion. "Love compels; it does not coerce. In the same way, truth too compels, and so does right if once we acknowledge that right is might as it indisputably is. But surely one cannot describe the overwhelming effect of love, of truth or of right by the term coercion, as it is commonly understood."[243] Further to avoid any element of coercion, Gandhi suggested that one's intention for fasting must be clarified and expressed as such well in advance. Even after being aware of the danger of moral coercion involved in fasting, if one is sure of the rightness of such an act, then one must undertake the fast following the dictates of the inner voice.

Silence becomes another means to sustain the *satyagrahi* in his/her resolve. Gandhi found several advantages of silence. He wrote: "Silence has now become both a physical and spiritual necessity for me. Originally it was taken to relieve the sense of pressure. Then I wanted time for writing. After, however, I had practiced it for some time, I saw the spiritual value of it. It suddenly flashed across my mind that that was the time when I could best hold communion with God,"[244] and to listen to the "Voice of the Great Silence."[245] "The Divine Radio is always singing if we could only make ourselves ready to listen to it, but it is impossible to listen without silence."[246] Silence also helps the *satyagrahi* to clarify his/her perception of Truth. "Our life is a long and arduous quest after Truth, and the soul requires inward restfulness to attain its full height."[247] Besides, proneness to exaggerate, to suppress or modify the truth, wittingly or unwittingly, is a natural weakness of a human being. Silence, according to Gandhi, can surmount such difficulties.

Thus, *satyagraha* became the great movement in the pursuit of truth in the midst of oppression and structural violence. It helped in the removal of segregation laws in South Africa and won independence for India in a unique way unknown to the world. It differed from the then known concept of passive resistance with which the Western thinkers were familiar with. For, *satyagraha* is a movement based on truth, on soul force and aimed at changing the opponent's heart through self-suffering. It was based on love and was completely free from any desire to defeat or degrade the opponent. There was no room for untruth in it.[248] In contrast, passive resistance is based on expediency and has the scope for the use of arms when a suitable occasion arrives in order to inflict suffering on the opponent.

TRUTH APPLIED TO FIELDS OF ACTION

Truth as an all-comprehensive concept had its ramifications in all branches of human activity. Gandhi, as it were, saw every event that occurred in his life, in the society and in the world at large with the eyes of truth just as a person with red goggles sees everything red. Nothing was spared from the scrupulous scrutiny based on truth and non-violence. Everything was judged from the perspective of an honest and sincere seeker after truth. Thus political concerns, economic activities, societal moorings and even the journalistic outlook came under its purview. After all, truth governed the universe and all that it contains. In this section, an attempt is made to analyse how Gandhi applied his understanding of truth to his political, social, economic, educational and journalistic activities.

Truth in Politics

Gandhi firmly believed that truth and non-violence are not meant for personal salvation but to sanctify the secular world of politics. In the hands of Gandhi, politics took on a new meaning. Everything that was concerned with politics acquired a new direction. Mr. Casey, the Governor of Bengal, after meeting Gandhi, said: "amongst saints he is a statesman, and amongst statesmen a saint."[249] Gandhi did not compartmentalize different human activities; instead saw a fundamental unity in human life. For him religion was the source of all activities. "My politics and all other activities of mine are derived from my religion. I go further and say that every activity of a man of religion must be derived from his religion, because religion means being bound to God, that is to say, God rules your every breath. If you recognize that truth, naturally God regulates every activity of yours."[250]

Gandhi's revolt against the British was not merely a political necessity but a truth pursuit. Being *advaitic* in outlook, he was outraged at the silencc of the millions of his fellowmen and women whose life was just a lie, a cowardly existence and therefore, a denial of God under the British rule. He realised that he could not pursue his spiritual path unless he fought for them. It was this moral imperative that made him rise against the oppressive power of the British. Gandhi wrote: "my motive has been purely religious ... I could not be leading a religious life unless I identified myself with the whole of mankind: and this I could not do unless I took part in politics."[251]

Thus, for Gandhi, the Quit India movement resolution of 8 August 1942 was not a mere political slogan but a cry of the soul of India for self-realisation. This cry was not raised out of one's helplessness, but out of a firm expression of one's right as well as demands of the exploiters' right path. It was wholly a spiritual pursuit, not merely personal, but setting right even the path of the exploiter. He announced that the movement was due to his faith in non-violence and in God. "Action is my motto. I am not anxious about the result. I must work with the instruments that God has placed at my disposal. I cannot create a new universe for myself. I have lived for the dumb millions. I have faith they won't forsake me. I am, therefore, able to work without losing hope. I know all will be well in the end but we have to pass through the purgatory."[252] Thus Quit India movement became a spiritual pursuit.

Humility and acceptance of the just decisions of the leaders pervaded Gandhian principles in politics. During the negotiations with Cabinet Mission, the Congress Working Committee could not agree with Gandhi on issues such as the use of the British army for the maintenance of internal order, on his insistence on being left alone to settle directly with the Muslim League after the British had quit and his readiness to face chaos and anarchy in preference to peace imposed by British arms. Hence, during the final phase of negotiations, Gandhi withdrew himself from the discussions and yet as a gentleman, he accepted and defended the decisions of the Working Committee.[253] It was his humility that enabled him to accept and defend the decisions of the Working Committee although he was not a party to it. Gandhi at times acknowledged his own position as dark when an apparent rift between him and the Working Committee members took place and accepted the Committee's decision.[254]

In politics, Gandhi held that duty is the only right. This is because "rights accrue automatically to him who duly performs his duties. In fact the right to perform one's duties is the only right that is worth living for and dying for. It covers all legitimate rights. All the rest is grabbing under one guise or another and contains in it seeds of Himsa."[255] This also implied that politics was not a means to seize power. There was a section among Congressmen, who held that the best use that the Congress could make of the Constituent Assembly was to capture it, declare it to be a sovereign body and turn it to a revolutionary body after the pattern of the States General in France. Gandhi strongly deprecated that line of thinking. "Not while I am alive," he remarked. "To become sovereign you have to behave in a sovereign way."[256]

It is in this context that Gandhi defined his concept of *swaraj* or complete independence. "Swaraj for me means freedom for the meanest of our countrymen. ... I am not interested in freeing India merely from the English yoke. I am bent upon freeing India from any yoke whatsoever. I have no desire to exchange 'king log' for 'king stork'."[257] This independence must be achieved through truth and non-violence and as such there is no room for fraud or falsehood. It is never exclusive and therefore, wholly compatible with interdependence within or without.

Therefore, when the individual freedom of the masses is safeguarded, then there is true democracy. This freedom must be exercised with responsibility. However, it is possible for some people to exercise their freedom without responsibility. Then there is the problem of controlling them. Hence, Gandhi said that the "individual freedom can have the fullest play only under a regime of unadulterated Ahimsa."[258] Further, for Gandhi, "democracy must in essence mean the art and science of mobilizing the entire physical, economic and spiritual resources of all the various sections of the people in the service of the common good of all."[259] In other words, common good is the sole goal of mobilization of all resources. Such a democracy can succeed only through a science of non-violence.

The democracy that Gandhi proposed was not the rule of the majority. "For the rule of majority when it becomes coercive is as intolerable as that of a bureaucratic minority. We must patiently try to bring round the minority to our view by gentle persuasion and argument."[260] This is because "intolerance betrays want of faith in one's cause."[261] Further, "in matters of conscience the law of the majority has no place."[262] Gandhi's endeavour in emphasising the weaknesses of democracy was that as a great human institution, it can be abused. He proposed to reduce the possibility of such abuse to a minimum. Hence, he projected truthful and non-violent means to arrive at democracy.

Thus, Gandhi's conception of non-violent democracy tended towards pure or enlightened anarchy. He said:

Political power means capacity to regulate national life through national representatives. If national life become so perfect as to become self-regulated, no representation becomes necessary. There is then a state of enlightened anarchy. In such a state everyone is his own ruler. He rules himself in such a manner that he is never a hindrance to his neighbour. In the ideal state therefore, there is no political power because there is no State. But the ideal is never fully realized in life. Hence the classical statement of Thoreau that that Government is best which governs the least.[263]

Gandhi knew that power politics existed everywhere. However, non-violence and truth also existed in a measure much larger than that. After all, Truth which is God pervades everywhere. However, for the time being, His existence is hidden from human being. But God cannot disappear forever. Such a faith, Gandhi claims, can sustain the political life in the world.[264]

Finally, in today's politics, one wins a point only by accusing the other. In contrast, Gandhi never accused the other, even his own opponent. He always saw a good point in the opponent. When there was a bad point in the opponent, even then he criticised only the evil point and not the evil-doer. On the contrary, he loved him/her. In this way, without hurting the other, he was able to point out the evil in him/her. In this context, Casey, the then Governor of Bengal wrote: "He [Gandhi] can make his point publicly with an opponent and yet leave his opponent without any feeling of bitterness – when he likes ... Gandhi seldom, if ever, speaks ill of any man. I discussed several men with him who had used him harshly but he managed to find some good to say of them and no ill ... He trusts those who trust him."[265]

Truth in Social Realm

Gandhi's social philosophy, in its ultimate sense, makes an individual resolute in identifying oneself with the entire creation and to be unbound from the bondage of the physical body. But he ruled out all means save truth and non-violence for the realisation of the goal of individual freedom, equality and brotherhood; in other words, "the Kingdom of Heaven upon Earth."[266] However, Gandhi emphasised the wellbeing of all the individuals and not merely of a few lucky ones. In enunciating such social principles, Gandhi subscribed to the views of John Ruskin whose book *Unto This Last* made a lasting impression on him. He coined a new term, *Sarvodaya*, to express these social ideals.

Commenting about the principle of *Sarvodaya* during a prayer meeting, Gandhi said:

> Man should earnestly desire the well being of all God's creation and pray that he might have the strength to do so. In desiring the well-being of all lies his own welfare; he who desires only his own or his community's welfare is selfish and it can never be well with him ... It is essential for man to discriminate between what he may consider to be good and what is really good for him.[267]

Gandhi also distinguished *sarvodaya* from the utilitarian theory of Jeremy Bentham and J.S. Mill. He wrote:

> A votary of Ahimsa cannot subscribe to the utilitarian formula (of the greatest good of the greatest number). He will strive for the greatest good of all and die in the attempt to realize the idea. ... The greatest good of all inevitably includes the good of the greatest number .... The utilitarian to be logical will never sacrifice himself. The absolutist will even sacrifice himself.[268]

One of the social concerns that took much of the time of Gandhi was the upliftment of the low castes whom he called *Harijans* – children of God - by purging away the curse of untouchability. However, he revolted against this unjust social structure non-violently. In 22 October 1925 during a public meeting at Bhuj, the capital of Kutch, Gandhi noticed that the untouchables had been seated at the back of the compound in a corner fenced round with ropes. Gandhi requested the audience to let the untouchables mix with the rest, but they were not in a mood to listen to him. So Gandhi said: "The majority being on your side has not hurt me, and has certainly not made me angry. Now let everyone remain where he is; I alone will go over to that side and take my seat there, for I have a special duty in this place and on this occasion."[269] He then went and sat amidst the untouchables, from where he addressed the gathering.

In fact, the *Harijan* service became his life's endeavour. He says that he can live for some days at least without the daily bread, but he cannot live without *Harijan* service for one single minute.

> It is a constant prayer to the Almighty that this blot of untouchability may be removed in its entirety from Hinduism and that the millions of caste-Hindus may see the Sun of Truth which shines upon us, if we would only remove the scales from our eyes, as I have

> repeatedly said in these columns. My life is a dedication to this cause and I shall consider no penance too great for the vindication of this Truth.[270]

Gandhi promoted peace in society through the institution of peace brigades. Speaking about the qualities of peace brigades, Gandhi wrote: [they]

> ... must have a living faith in non-violence. This is impossible without a living faith in God. A non-violent man can do nothing save by the power and grace of God. Without it he won't have the courage to die without anger, without fear and without retaliation. Such courage comes from the belief that God sits in the hearts of all and that there should be no fear in the presence of God.[271]

The messenger of peace must also have equal regard for all the principal religions of the world. This respect implies that the peace brigade must possess a knowledge of the general principles of the different faiths professed in the country.

Further, Gandhi was apprehensive of the evil effects of modern civilization. He was influenced by Edward Carpenter's *Civilization: Its Cause and Cure*, which he read on 7 September 1909. It made a deep impression on his mind. Carpenter was a vegetarian and a believer in simplicity and democracy. He considered civilization a kind of disease which the various races of humans have to pass through. But he regretted that there was no known case of a nation recovering from it and returning to health. The malady of civilization led to progressive loss of unity, community and purpose, and increase in private property. For a cure, it was necessary to move towards a return to nature and community of human life, including a simplification of domestic life and clothing. Open air, clean and pure food especially fruits and grains (vegetarian diet) and the company of animals would help.[272]

Being influenced by the writings of Edward Carpenter, G.K. Chesterton and Tolstoy, Gandhi wrote *Hind Swaraj*. In this book, Gandhi explained his views about the exploitation of the poor by the middle or rich class. He held that machinery, industrialization and the rise of professional classes such doctors, lawyers and administrators maintained the British rule in India whether they realized it or not. They joined hands with the British rulers in exploiting the poor masses. They copied British ways of living, which pampered the body and famished the soul.

Real freedom should facilitate Indians to decide their own destiny and formulate their economic, political and social structure in accordance with their own moral principles, instincts and traditions.[273]

Thus while rejecting the Western civilization for its competition and non-moral industrial growth, Gandhi emphasised that civilization is a mode of life, which made humans lead a moral life and be a master of himself/herself. It was that mode of conduct, which points out to human being the path of duty. This is in agreement with the Eastern principle which says 'truth alone conquers,' that truth knows no mishap, that the strong and the weak have alike a right to secure justice. This excludes the Western principle of 'Might is Right.'[274]

Truth in Economics

Gandhi, as a true seeker after truth, brought the economic activities of people under the purview of truth and non-violence. Therefore, he wrote:

> True economics never militates against the highest ethical standard, just as all true ethics to be worth its name must at the same time be also good economics. An economics that inculcates Mammon worship, and enables the strong to amass wealth at the expense of the weak, is a false and dismal science. It spells death. True economics, on the other hand, stands for social justice, it promotes the good of all equally including the weakest, and is indispensable for decent life.[275]

Every economic activity must be guided by these principles. Gandhi unequivocally rejected large-scale industries of mass production because it violated truth and non-violence. However, he was not for taking India back to the medieval period. His emphasis was on the use of appropriate technology, prevention of pollution of the atmosphere, and halting of the reckless squandering of natural resources by mass production. Preservation of the self-respect of humans through dignity and joy of creative work, which could satisfy one's creative urge, was also an important aspect of the problem.[276]

Regarding class struggle in the capitalist economic structure, Gandhi said:

> Class struggle has always been there. It can be ended if the capitalists voluntarily renounce their role and become all labourers. The other

> way is to realize that labour is real capital, in fact, the maker of capital. What the two hands of the labourer would achieve, the capitalist would never get with all his gold and silver. Can anyone live on gold? But labour has to be made conscious of its strength. It has to have in one hand Truth, and in the other non-violence and it would be invincible.[277]

The reason for this is that capitalists are trustees for the welfare of the labouring class. So, ideally both labour and capital must supplement and help each other. They should be a great family living in unity and harmony.

Further, Gandhi accepted donations from the capitalists and also gave his blessings and at times they were conditional. When a friend objected to such a show of affection towards the capitalists, Gandhi said that one cannot curse a rich person because he/she is rich. One can be blessed provided one contributes to the welfare of the poor. In this way, blessings for the rich depend upon their conduct towards the poor. Gandhi wrote: "My blessings will haunt like a ghost anyone who contravenes the condition attaching to it. If anyone after this barters the interests of the poor, my blessings will recoil upon him like a curse."[278]

Gandhi actively engaged himself in an economic activity, namely, the task of propagating *charkha* and *khadi*. For him, *charkha* was the "symbol of unity of Indian humanity, of its economic freedom and equality and, therefore, ultimately, in the poetic expression of Jawaharlal Nehru, 'the livery of India's freedom.'[279] The message of the spinning wheel, according to Gandhi, was one of "simplicity, service of mankind, living so as not to hurt others, creating an indissoluble bond between the rich and the poor, capital and labour, the prince and the peasant."[280] The process of emancipation of India through the application of *charkha* implies that the villagers take it up as a means for their survival while the city people spin by way of sacrifice showing an example to the villagers. Spinning wheel has also a spiritual benefit. "It helped in the pursuit of *Brahmacharya*; it was known to still the passions of those who have turned it in the fullness of faith. It was a powerful means of cultivating steadiness."[281]

Truth in Education

For Gandhi, "education is an all-round drawing out of the best in child and man – body, mind and spirit. Literacy is not the end of education nor even the beginning."[282] It consists in acquiring knowledge of what is worth knowing about. "The only thing worth knowing about is the atman. True knowledge is thus knowledge of the self. But in order to attain this knowledge, one has to know literature, history, geography, mathematics, etc. All these are by way of means."[283]

Therefore, the teachers while imparting all the knowledge in the world to their students should inculcate truth and purity in them. Otherwise, Gandhi said, they betray them and set them down the road to perdition. "Knowledge without character is a power for evil only, as seen in the instances of so many talented thieves and 'gentlemen rascals' in the world."[284] The students, in their turn, must translate their knowledge into their daily life. Otherwise, moral impurity will spread like a hidden epidemic causing havoc among them. Hence Gandhi told a group of students in Sri Lanka: "Character cannot be built with mortar and stone. It cannot be built by hands other than your own. The Principal and the Professor cannot give you character from the pages of books. Character building comes from their very lives and really speaking, it must come from within yourselves."[285]

In his experiments in education, Gandhi introduced the concept of basic education or *Nai Talim*. It is the education through handicrafts. This is part of his search after truth. He wrote:

> The root of this new education goes much deeper. It lies in the application of truth and love in every variety of human activity, whether in individual life or a corporate one. The notion of education through handicrafts rises from the contemplation of truth and love permeating life's activities. Love requires that true education should be easily accessible to all, and should be of use to every villager in his daily life.[286]

Truth in Journalism

Gandhi did not take up journalism for its sake but merely as an aid to his mission of service in the pursuit after truth. Gandhi wrote: "my mission is to teach by example and precept under severe restraint the use of the matchless weapon of *Satyagraha*, which is a direct corollary of non-violence and truth."[287] Therefore, he did not write in anger or in malice or merely to excite passion. But he wrote to uphold truth. He meticulously avoided superficiality, one-sidedness, inaccuracy and dishonesty that have crept into modern journalism.

Speaking about the *Indian Opinion*, Gandhi wrote: "*Indian Opinion* was a mirror, a part of my life . . . Changes in the journal were indicative of changes of my life."[288] It became the mouthpiece of the Indian community, an organ of its toils and a compendium of the orders of the day for the *satyagrahis*. The readers looked forward to it for a reliable account of the *satyagraha* campaign as also of the real conditions of Indians in South Africa. In it was reflected, as in a mirror, the entire landscape of the life of the Indian community in South Africa – its hopes and objectives, its successes and failures, as also the ups and downs of its struggle. As Gandhi put it, *Indian Opinion* was an "open book to whoever wanted to gauge the strength and weakness of the community, be he a friend, an enemy or a neutral"[289]

Speaking about the aims of newspapers, Gandhi wrote: "one of the objects of a newspaper is to understand popular feeling and to give expression to it; another is to arouse among the people certain desirable sentiments; and the third is fearlessly to expose popular defects."[290] A still further aim of newspapers is to educate the people and apprise them of current trends in the history of the world. Therefore, the newspaper editors and staff must check the veracity of the news they print despite the difficult circumstances in which they work. Gandhi was also against making newspaper a means of earning a living or as an instrument of making profits. This will lead to a number of evils.

Gandhi deplored the tendency of equivocation and the failure to cultivate the courage to speak the truth. He wrote: "In order to get over certain restrictions like the 'Seditious Writing Act' and the 'Defence of India Act', newspapers evolved a style of writing which makes it possible to interpret what they say on a particular matter, which may seem to fall within the purview of these Acts, in two different ways."[291] Such tendencies only harm the country.

Regarding advertisements, Gandhi insisted on truth. "It is a habit with people ... to treat the printed word in a book or a newspaper as gospel truth. There is need, therefore, for extreme caution in drawing up advertisements. Untruths are most dangerous."[292] Immoral advertisements must be scrupulously avoided. "I do believe that if advertisements should be taken at all there should be a rigid censorship instituted by newspaper proprietors and editors themselves and that only healthy advertisements should be taken.... The evil of immoral advertisements is overtaking even what are known as the most respectable newspapers and magazines."[293] Further, the established practice of newspapers to derive their main income from advertisements has resulted in inconsistencies, which according to Gandhi, were deplorable. The very newspaper, which in its editorial columns strongly deplores the drink-evil, publishes advertisements in praise of drink. One can notice similar anomalies with regard to evils like smoking, use of tobacco, etc.[294]

CONCLUSION

In conclusion, it can be said that truth as developed and lived by Gandhi shows that his attachment to truth is phenomenal. Truth encompassed his every activity. It must be borne in mind that his understanding of truth was not static; instead it was a very dynamic and ever growing concept. Not only his understanding of the concept of truth grew day by day, but also his living out of that truth found newer expressions in his daily life. Therefore, he was ready to be inconsistent in his teachings even at the cost of criticism. For, he firmly believed that consistency means stagnation. Professor Gilbert Murray, while defending his inconsistency, said that it is impossible for someone to be completely consistent, and moreover, "complete consistency is absurd."[295] Therefore, improvement and growth require inconsistency.

Further, one can notice that many of the concepts that Gandhi emphasised were inspired by sources belonging to other religions and cultures, which he clearly acknowledged. Thus for example, Gandhi derived the concept of *satyagraha* partly from Jesus, the concept of *sarvodaya* from Ruskin, the concept of bread labour from T.M. Bondaref and Tolstoy. However, Gandhi rediscovered them in his own Hindu tradition. At times, he even re-interpreted the traditional concepts when he did not directly find equivalences. In this way, Gandhi contributed to the mutual fecundity of different cultures and religions.

Gandhi's equating of God with Truth and the subsequent reversal to 'Truth is God' made his conception of truth unique, and his distinction between Absolute Truth and Relative Truth made his analysis of truth very enriching. Finally, his derivation of every other concept from truth made his whole approach to life truly 'satyo-centric.' It is in this 'satyo-centrism' that enabled Gandhi to resolve the different baffling issues in the theology of religions. This will be discussed in the next chapter.

NOTES

1. Gandhi, Autobiography, p. 3.
2. *Young India*, 21-8-1924, 279; as cited by M.K. Gandhi, *In Search of the Supreme*, ed. V.K. Kher, vol. 1 (Ahmedabad: Navajivan Publishing House, 1961), p. 128. Henceforth, Gandhi, *In Search of the Supreme*, vol. 1.
3. Gandhi, Autobiography, p. 4.
4. Cf. Gandhi, Autobiography, reprint 1976, p.2.
5. Harishchandra was a great king, renowned for his unflinching adherence to truth. Visvamitra, a well-known sage, wanted to test the king. He caused the king to dream that he had gifted away his kingdom to Visvamitra. Next day while the king was narrating his dream to his people, lo, there was Visvamitra, come to claim the kingdom. The king was so truthful that he gave away the kingdom and made ready to walk out with his wife and child with nothing except the clothes they wore. But that was only the beginning. The sage demanded daksina, in addition, without which no gift is complete. The king had now nothing except himself, his wife, and his son. He asked his wife to take employment as a maidservant in Kashi, which was outside his former kingdom, and himself became a bondsman. That was how the daksina was paid. Then began trials and tribulations, which have hardly a parallel even in legend. The story proceeds to relate many pathetic incidents, which bring out the cheerful sufferings of the royal family and king's utter adherence to his pledged word. The climax was reached when the royal bondsman was charged by his master to execute the queen now turned maid-servant for some fault she had committed. Visvamitra in his zeal to test the king had managed to bring about even such a situation. The king did not fail. Harischandra began to do his duty as a bondsman, raised a sword over the head of his queen to strike her down. Visvamitra then melted. Staying the hand of the king, he said: "O king, there is none so great as you in all three worlds. You are the most truthful of all human beings." Cf. Diwakar, Saga of Satyagraha, pp. 6-7.
6. Gandhi, Autobiography, p. 6.
7. In fact, immediately after reaching England, Dr. Mehta asked Gandhi to stay with a family in Richmond to gain experience of English life and customs. Seeing how Gandhi starved at lunch and dinner due to his vow not to touch meat, one of his friends almost coxed him to eat meat. But he was able to withstand such pressures. Gandhi explains the incident in his Autobiography. Cf. Gandhi, Autobiography, reprint, 1976, pp. 34-35. At another time, a woman other than his wife moved Gandhi to lust while attending a Vegetarian Conference at Portsmouth.

The timely warning of a good companion saved him. Cf. Gandhi, Autobiography, reprint, 1976, p. 53

8. Gandhi, Autobiography, pp. 74-75.
9. Gandhi, Autobiography, p. 29.
10. Pyarelal, *Mahatma Gandhi - Early Phase*, vol. 1, reprint (Ahmedabad: Navajivan Publishing House, 1986), p. 628. Henceforth, Pyarelal, Early Phase.
11. Pyarelal, Early Phase, p. 675.
12. Count Leo Tolstoy, *The Kingdom of God is Within You*, trans. A Delano (London: Walter Scott Ltd., 1894), p. 376; Henceforth, Tolstoy, The Kingdom of God is Within You.
13. Tolstoy, The Kingdom of God is Within You, p. 362; Emphasis in the original.
14. Tolstoy, The Kingdom of God is Within You, pp. 361-362.
15. Heinrich Zimmer, *Philosophies of India* (New York: Pantheon Books, 1951), p.160. Henceforth, Zimmer, Philosophies of India.
16. Zimmer, Philosophies of India, p.171.
17. *Collected Works of Mahatma Gandhi*, 28, pp. 427-428; as cited by Sushila Nayar, *Mahatma Gandhi, Salt Satyagraha – The Watershed*, vol. 6 (Ahmedabad: Navajivan Publishing House, 1995), p. 10. Henceforth, Nayar, Salt Satyagraha.
18. Pyarelal, Early Phase, pp. 276-277.
19. *Young India*, 21-1-1926; as cited by M.K. Gandhi, *Truth is God (Gleanings from the writings of Mahatma Gandhi bearing on God, God-realization and the Godly way)*, ed. R.K. Prabhu, 11th reprint (Ahmedabad: Navajivan Publishing House, 1998), pp. 10-11. Henceforth, Gandhi, Truth is God.
20. Diwakar, Saga of Satyagraha, p. 21.
21. *Harijan*, 27-11-1949, p. 340; as cited by M.K. Gandhi, *In Search of the Supreme*, ed. V.B. Kher, vol. 2 (Ahmedabad: Navajivan Publishing House, 1961), p. 15. Henceforth, Gandhi, *In Search of the Supreme*, vol. 2. This is part of a letter addressed to Jamnalal from Sabarmati Central Prison on 17-3-1922.
22. M.K. Gandhi, *From Yeravda Mandir: Ashram Observances*, trans. Valji Govindji (Ahmedabad: Navajivan Publishing House, 1932), p. 3. Henceforth, Gandhi, From Yeravda Mandir.
23. Conversations of Gandhiji, 1949, pp. 35-36; as cited by M.K. Gandhi, *The Selected Works of Mahatma Gandhi – The Voice of Truth*, ed. Shriman Narayan, vol. 6, 4th reprint (Ahmedabad: Navajivan publishing House, 1997), p. 97. Henceforth, Gandhi, The Voice of Truth.

24. *Conversations of Gandhiji*, 1949, pp. 35-36; as cited by Gandhi, The Voice of Truth, p. 97.

25. *An Atheist with Gandhi*, 1958, p. 30; as cited by Gandhi, The Voice of Truth, p. 100.

26. Cf. Diwakar, Saga of Satyagraha, p. 1.

27. The *Chandogya Upanishad*, Swami Swahananda, trans. (Madras: Sri Ramakrishna Math, 1984), p. 416. Henceforth, Swahananda, The Chandogya Upanishad.

28. Swahananda, *The Chandogya Upanishad*, pp. 416-417.

29. The *Brhadaranyaka Upanishad*, trans. not mentioned (Madras: Sr. Ramakrishna Math, 1979), p. 128.

30. Cf. George Pattery, Gandhi – The Believer: An Indian Christian Perspective (Delhi: ISPCK, 1996), p. 89. Henceforth, Pattery, Gandhi – The Believer.

31. K.L. Seshagiri Rao, "On Truth: A Hindu Perspective," Philosophy East and West, XX, No. 4, October 1970, p. 381. For further readings on Hindu perspective of Sat, cf., Pattery, Gandhi – The Believer, pp. 89-92.

32. Italicized for emphasis only and not in the original.

33. James K. Mathews, *The Matchless Weapon Satyagraha* (Bombay: Bharatiya Vidya Bhavan, 1989), p. 70. Henceforth, Mathews, The Matchless Weapon.

34. *Young India*, 31-12-1931, pp. 427-428; as cited by Gandhi, The Voice of Truth, p. 98.

35. *Ashram Observances in Action*, 1959, p. 37; as cited by Gandhi, *The Voice of Truth*, pp. 96-97.

36. *Selected Letters* – I, p. 56; as cited by Shriman Narayan, ed., *The Selected Works of Mahatma Gandhi: Selected Letters*, vol.5 (Ahmedabad: Navajivan Publishing House, 1968), pp. 356-357. Henceforth, Narayan, Selected Letters.

37. *Selected Letters* – I, p. 38; as cited by Narayan, Selected Letters, p. 356.

38. *Selected Letters* – I, p. 55; as cited by Narayan, Selected Letters, p. 356.

39. *Harijan*, 27-3-1949, p. 26; as cited by Joan V. Bondurant, *Conquest of Violence: The Gandhian Philosophy of Conflict* (Bombay: Oxford University Press, 1959), p. 19; Emphasis in the original. Henceforth, Bondurant, Conquest of Violence. This letter was written on 9 July 1932.

40. *The Diary of Mahadev Desai*, vol.1, p. 160; as cited by Narayan, Selected Letters, pp. 351-352.

41. Cf. D.G. *Tendulkar, Mahatma*, vol. 2 (Bombay: Jhaveri and Tendulkar, 1952), p. 249. Henceforth, Tendulkar, Mahatma.

42. Tendulkar, Mahatma, p. 312.

43. Tendulkar, Mahatma, p. 176.

44. *Young India*, 31-12-1931, p. 424; as cited by Gandhi, *In Search of the Supreme*, vol. 1, p. 11.

45. *Collected Works of Mahatma Gandhi*, vol. 49, p, 223; as cited by Sushila Nayar, *Mahatma Gandhi, Preparing for Swaraj*, vol. 7 (Ahmedabad: Navajivan Publishing House, 1996), p. 19. Henceforth, Nayar, Preparing for Swaraj.

46. Cf. R.R. Diwakar, "Gandhi: From 'God is Truth' to 'Truth is God,'" *Gandhi Marg* (February 1983), pp. 617-626.

47. N.K. Bose, *Studies in Gandhism*, 2nd ed. (Calcutta: Indian Associated Publishing Co., 1947), p. 269.

48. *Harijan*, 11-3-1939, p. 44; as cited by Gandhi, *In Search of the Supreme*, vol.1, p. 29.

49. *Harijan*, 16-2-1934; as cited by Gandhi, Truth is God, p.21.

50. *Young India*, 5-3-1925, p. 80; as cited by Gandhi, *In Search of the Supreme*, vol. 1, p. 15.

51. Nayar, *Preparing for Swaraj*, p. 19; Emphasis in the original.

52. Gandhi, *From Yeravda Mandir*, p. 3.

53. *Young India*, 20-11-1924; as cited by Gandhi, Truth is God, pp. 110-101.

54. *Young India*, 13-11-1924; as cited by Gandhi, Truth is God, p. 99.

55. *Young India*, 13-11-1924, p. 377; as cited by Gandhi, The Voice of Truth, pp. 288-289.

56. *Conversations of Gandhiji*, 1949, pp. 35-36; as cited by Gandhi, The Voice of Truth, p. 97.

57. *Conversations of Gandhiji*, 1949, pp. 35-36; as cited by Gandhi, The Voice of Truth, p. 97.

58. Cf. *Young India*, 23-1-1930; as cited by Gandhi, Truth is God, p. 39.

59. *Young India*, 13-8-1925, p. 277 at 279; as cited by Gandhi, *In Search of the Supreme*, vol. 2, p. 269.

60. *Harijan*, 14-9-1934, p. 245; as cited by Gandhi, *In Search of the Supreme*, vol. 2, p. 270.

61. *Collected Works of Mahatma Gandhi*, vol., 50, p. 392; as cited by

Nayar, *Preparing for Swaraj*, p.19; Emphasis in the original. This letter was written on 20 August 1932.

62. *Harijan*, 21-9-1934, p. 252; as cited by Gandhi, *In Search of the Supreme*, vol.1, pp. 25-26.
63. Gandhi, Truth is God, p. 4.
64. Gandhi, Truth is God, pp. 4-5.
65. *Young India*, 20-10-1921; as cited by M.K. Gandhi, *India of My Dreams*, 6th reprint (Ahmedabad: Navajivan Publishing House, 1997), p. 114. Henceforth, Gandhi, India of My Dreams.
66. Pyarelal, *Mahatma Gandhi, The Last Phase*, vol. 9, book I, part I, 2nd reprint (Ahmedabad: Navajivan Publishing House, 1997), p. 58. Henceforth, Pyarelal, The Last Phase, book 1.
67. Pyarelal, The Last Phase, book 1, p. 58.
68. Pyarelal, The Last Phase, book 1, 325.
69. *Harijan*, 13-1-1940; as cited by M.K. Gandhi, *All Religions are True*, ed. Anand T. Hingorani (Bombay: Bharatiya Vidya Bhavan, 1962), p. 123. Henceforth, Gandhi, All Religions are True.
70. Cf. Diwakar, Saga of Satyagraha, p. 24.
71. Pyarelal, The Last Phase, book 1, p. 325.
72. *Collected Works of Mahatma Gandhi*, vol., 10, p. 49; as cited by Sushila Nayar, *Mahatma Gandhi – Satyagraha at Work*, vol. 4 (Ahmedabad: Navajivan Publishing House, 1989), 503. Henceforth, Nayar, Satyagraha at Work.
73. Diwakar, Saga of Satyagraha, p.22.
74. Bondurant, Conquest of Violence, p. 164.
75. *Young India*, 31-12 -1931, pp. 427-28.
76. Bondurant, Conquest of Violence, pp. 20-21.
77. *Young India*, 23-9-1926; as cited by Gandhi, Truth is God, p. 62.
78. From Yeravda Mandir, (1957 Edn.), Chapter XIII; as cited by Gandhi, *In Search of the Supreme*, vol. 2, p. 11; Emphasis in the original.
79. To a Gandhian Capitalist, pp. 49-50; as cited by Narayan, Selected Letters, pp. 144-145. This is taken from a letter that Gandhi wrote to Jamnalal Bajaj on 16 March 1922.
80. *Young India*, 23-9-1926, p.333; as cited by M.K. Gandhi, *In Search of the Supreme*, ed. V.B. Kher, vol. 3 (Ahmedabad: Navajivan Publishing House, 1962), p. 40. Henceforth, Gandhi, *In Search of the Supreme*, vol. 3.
81. *Harijan*, 8-7-1933; as cited by Gandhi, *In Search of the Supreme*, vol. 1, pp. 311-312.

82. *Young India*, 31-12-1931, p. 428; as cited by Pyarelal, *Mahatma Gandhi, The Last Phase*, vol. 10, part 2, reprint (Ahmedabad: Navajivan Publishing House, 1997), pp. 743-744. Henceforth, Pyarelal, The Last Phase, part 2.

83. This fast took place on 8th May 1933. On that day, he was released from prison and was taken to Parnakuti, Lady Thackerry's house in Poona, where Gandhi successfully completed the twenty-one day ordeal.

84. *Harijan*, 10-12-1939, p. 369 at p. 373; as cited by Gandhi, *In Search of the Supreme*, vol. 1, p. 252.

85. *Harijan*, 7-10-1939; as cited by Gandhi, *In Search of the Supreme*, vol. 1, p. 255.

86. *The Diary of Mahadev Desai*, vol. I, Ahmedabad, 1953, p. 275;as cited by Pyarelal, The Last Phase, part 2, p. 744.

87. *The Diary of Mahadev Desai*, vol. I, Ahmedabad, 1953, p. 275;as cited by Pyarelal, The Last Phase, part 2, p. 744.

88. Hingorani, ed., *God is Truth*, Bombay, 1957, p. 33;as cited by Pyarelal, The Last Phase, part 2, p. 744.

89. *Young India*, 4-8-1920, p. 3; as cited by Pyarelal, The Last Phase, part 2, p. 744.

90. *Harijan*, 18-3-1933, p. 7; as cited by Gandhi, *In Search of the Supreme*, vol. 1, p. 260.

91. Cf. *Young India*, 21-8-1924, p. 278; as cited by Gandhi, *In Search of the Supreme*, vol. 1, pp. 262-263.

92. *Harijan*, 13-6-1936, p. 141; as cited by Pyarelal, The Last Phase, book I, p. 323.

93. Gandhi, *In Search of the Supreme*, vol. 1, p. 261. It is part of the speech that Gandhi delivered in English on Quit India Resolution at the historic All India Congress Committee Session at Bombay on 8 August 1942.

94. Pyarelal, The Last Phase, part 2, 746.

95. *Young India*, 6-8-1925, p. 273; as cited by Gandhi, *In Search of the Supreme*, vol. 3, p. 328. It is part of the address of Gandhi to the missionaries at Calcutta Y.W.C.A. on 28 July 1925.

96. *Harijan*, 8-7-1933, p. 4; as cited by Gandhi, *In Search of the Supreme*, vol. 1, p. 312.

97. *Collected Works of Mahatma Gandhi*, vol. 16, p. 175; as cited by Narayan, Selected Letters, p. 382.

98. *Young India*, 13-4-1921, p. 113 at p.114; as cited by Gandhi, *In Search of the Supreme*, vol. 2, p. 236.

99. Mira Behn, The Spirit's Pilgrimage (London: Longmans, 1960), p. 66.
100. Pyarelal, The Last Phase, book I, p. 188.
101. Nayar, Satyagraha at Work, p. 394.
102. *Harijan*, 20-10-1946, p. 367; as cited by Pyarelal, The Last Phase, book I, p. 330.
103. Pyarelal, The Last Phase, book I, p. 330.
104. Pyarelal, The Last Phase, book I, p. 232.
105. *Collected Works of Mahatma Gandhi*, vol. 39, p. 432; as cited by Nayar, Salt Satyagraha, pp. 190-191.
106. *Young India*, 10-9-1925, p. 309; as cited by Gandhi, *In Search of the Supreme*, vol. 1, p. 65.
107. *Harijan*, 20-10-1946, p. 365; as cited by Gandhi, *In Search of the Supreme*, vol. 1, p. 168. One can notice a parallel in "Be angry but do not sin; do not let the sun go down on your anger." (Eph 4:26; RSV).
108. Pyarelal, The Last Phase, book I, p. 135.
109. Cf. *Collected Works of Mahatma Gandhi*, vol. 40, pp. 209-212; as cited by Nayar, Salt Satyagraha, p. 196.
110. Nayar, Salt Satyagraha, 100.
111. *Harijan*, 11-3-1933, p. 4; as cited by Gandhi, *In Search of the Supreme*, vol. 1, p. 233.
112. Pyarelal, The Last Phase, part 2, pp. 242-243..
113. Pyarelal, The Last Phase, part 2, p. 243.
114. Nayar, Satyagraha at Work, p. 29.
115. Cf. Nayar, Satyagraha at Work, p. 11.
116. *Collected Works of Mahatma Gandhi*, vol. 34, pp. 530-547; as cited by Nayar, Salt Satyagraha, p. 98.
117. *From Yeravda Mandir*, Chapter I; as cited by Gandhi, Truth is God, p.21. Here one can notice a parallel in the writings of St. Paul. He wrote: "So, whether you eat or drink, or whatever you do, do all to the glory of God." (1 Cor 10:31; RSV).
118. Gandhi, From Yeravda Mandir, p.5.
119. *Collected Works of Mahatma Gandhi*, vol. 25, p. 127; as cited by Narayan, Selected Letters, p. 388.
120. *Young India*, 21-10-1926, p. 364; as cited by Mathews, The Matchless Weapon, p. 68.
121. *The Diary of Mahadev Desai*, vol. I, p. 177; as cited by Narayan, Selected Letters, pp. 480-481.

122. Cf. The parents of young Gandhi called him affectionately Moniya.
123. Pyarelal, Early Phase, p. 195.
124. During the meat-eating period, Gandhi also indulged in smoking. To buy cigarettes, he had to steal money from the servants. He even tried to commit suicide in sheer disgust at the fact that he could not do anything without elder's permission. Finally, he decided write out the confession and submit it to his father. Gandhi's father was then suffering from a fistula and was confined to bed. He read it through, and pearl-drops trickled down his cheeks, wetting the paper. For a moment he closed his eyes in thought and then tore up the note. Gandhi could see his father's agony. Those pearl-drops of love cleansed his heart, and washed his sin away. This was for Gandhi, an object lesson in Ahimsa. Cf. Gandhi, Autobiography, pp. 22-24.
125. Cf. *Young India*, 24-11-1927, p. 392; as cited by Gandhi, *In Search of the Supreme*, vol. 3, p. 296.
126. Gandhi's Press Statement, 10-1-1945; as cited by Pyarelal, The Last Phase, book I, p. 101.
127. Gandhi, From Yeravda Mandir, p.5.
128. *Harijan*, 12-11-1938, p. 327; as cited by M.K. Gandhi, *My God* (Ahmedabad: Navajivan Publishing House, 1999), pp. 17-18. Henceforth, Gandhi, My God.
129. My Dear child, pp. 53-54; as cited by Narayan, Selected Letters, pp. 474-475.
130. *Young India*, 20-3-1930, p. 98; as cited by Gandhi, *In Search of the Supreme*, vol. 2, pp. 59-60.
131. *Young India*, 1-10-1931, p. 285 at p. 287; as cited by Gandhi, *In Search of the Supreme*, vol. 2, p. 58.
132. *Young India*, 17-9-1925, p. 317; as cited by Gandhi, *In Search of the Supreme*, vol. 2, p. 19.
133. *Young India*, 23-1-1930, p. 27; as cited by Pyarelal, The Last Phase, book I, p. 320.
134. *Harijan*, 13-10-1940, p. 318; as cited by Pyarelal, The Last Phase, book I, p. 320.
135. *Harijan*, 7-4-1946, p. 70; as cited by Pyarelal, The Last Phase, book I, p. 320.
136. *Harijan*, 5-5-1946, p. 114; as cited by Pyarelal, The Last Phase, book I, pp. 320-321.
137. *Harijan*, 7-4-1946, p. 73; as cited by Pyarelal, The Last Phase, book I, p. 320.

138. *Harijan*, 1-9-1940, p. 268; as cited by Pyarelal, The Last Phase, part 2, pp. 617-618.

139. *Harijan*, 1-9-1940, p. 268; as cited by Pyarelal, The Last Phase, part 2, pp. 617-618.

140. *Collected Works of Mahatma Gandhi*, vol. 31, p. 545; as cited by Nayar, Salt Satyagraha, p. 36. The context of this teaching of Gandhi is this: with the approval of Gandhiji, the Municipality killed some 60 stray dogs – some of them rabid. Gandhi received many angry letters accusing him of being violent. So Gandhiji in a series of articles in *Navajivan* and later in *Young India* explained the parameters of ahimsa in practice.

141. *Harijan*, 9-6-1946, p. 170 at 171; as cited by Gandhi, *In Search of the Supreme*, vol. 2, p.22.

142. *Harijan*, 21-12-1947, p. 473; as cited by Gandhi, *In Search of the Supreme*, vol. 2, p. 18.

143. From Yeravda Mandir, trans. V.G. Desai (1957 Edn.), Chap. II; as cited by Gandhi, *In Search of the Supreme*, vol. 2, p. 25.

144. *Harijan*, 2-4-1934; as cited by Gandhi, Truth is God, p.33.

145. Ashram Observances in Action, trans. V.G. Desai (1957 Edn.), Chap. III; as cited by Gandhi, *In Search of the Supreme*, vol. 2, p. 32.

146. Cf. *Harijan*, 27-11-1949, p. 340; as cited by Gandhi, *In Search of the Supreme*, vol. 2, p. 16.

147. *Harijan*, 17-11-1946, p. 404; as cited by Gandhi, *In Search of the Supreme*, vol. 2, p. 40.

148. Prayer Speech, 16-6-1947; Pyarelal, The Last Phase, part 2, p. 327.

149. *Collected Works of Mahatma Gandhi*, vol. 71, p. 264; as cited by Sushila Nayar, Mahatma Gandhi, Final Fight for Freedom, vol. 8 (Ahmedabad: Navajivan Publishing House, 1997), p. 12. Henceforth, Nayar, Final Fight. The meeting took place at Malikanda near Dakha on 20 February 1940.

150. Pyarelal, The Last Phase, book I, pp. 186-187.

151. Gandhi, From Yeravda Mandir, p.7.

152. *Collected Works of Mahatma Gandhi*, vol. 23, p. 69; as cited by Narayan, Selected Letters, p. 399.

153. *Collected Works of Mahatma Gandhi*, vol. 10, pp. 45-6; as cited by Nayar, Satyagraha at Work, p. 502.

154. *Young India*, 17-7-1924; as cited by Gandhi, India of My Dreams, p. 65.

155. Gandhiji's speech before the Congressmen from Maharashtra, 29-6-1944; as cited by Pyarelal, The Last Phase, book I, p.22.

156. Gandhi, The Voice of Truth, p.28.

157. Pyarelal, The Last Phase, book I, p. 52.

158. *Young India* 3 -4-1924; as cited by Jag Parvesh Chander, ed., *Teachings of Mahatma Gandhi* (Lahore: The Indian Printing Works, 1945), p. 266.

159. Pyarelal, The Last Phase, book I, p. 214.

160. *Collected Works of Mahatma Gandhi*, vol. 31, pp. 44-45; as cited by Nayar, *Salt Satyagraha*, pp. 26-27.

161. J.B. Kripalani, *Gandhi: His Life and Thought, Builders of Modern Indian Series*, ed. R.R. Diwakar, rev. ed. (New Delhi: Publications Division, Ministry of Information and Broadcasting, Government of India, 1991), p. 408.

162. The word sadagraha means firmness in a good cause. Although Gandhi liked the word, it did not fully represent the whole idea that he wanted to connote or signify. As a result, he corrected the word from sadagraha to satyagraha which means firmness in truth. Cf. Gandhi, Autobiography, p. 266.

163. C.F. Andrews, *The Position of British Indians in the Transvaal*, pp. 13-14; as cited by Nayar, Satyagraha at Work, pp. 85-86.

164. Pyarelal, The Last Phase, book I, p. 324.

165. Cf. Huttenback, R.A., Gandhi in South Africa, p. 169; as cited by Nayar, Satyagraha at Work, p. 82.

166. Cf. Nayar, Satyagraha at Work, p. 122.

167. Pyarelal, Early Phase, p. 19.

168. *Collected Works of Mahatma Gandhi*, Vol. 16, p. 147; as cited by Narayan, Selected Letters, pp. 396-397.

169. Prabhudas Gandhi, *My Childhood with Gandhiji*, pp. 35-37; as cited by Nayar, Satyagraha at Work, p. 283.

170. M.K. Gandhi, Speeches and Writings of Mahatma Gandhi, 4th ed. (Madras: Natesan, [n.d.]), p. 506; as cited by Bondurant, Conquest of Violence, p. 16.

171. *Harijan*, 17-10-1936, p. 284; as cited by Gandhi, *In Search of the Supreme*, vol. 1, p.144.

172. Cf. *Collected Woks of Mahatma Gandhi*, vol. 6, p. 502; as cited by Nayar, Satyagraha at Work, p. 76.

173. Nayar, Final Fight, p. 387.

174. Cf. *Gandhiji's Press Statement*, 28-7-1944; as cited by Pyarelal, The Last Phase, book I, p. 35.

175. Cf. M. K. *Gandhi, From Yeravda Mandir*: Ashram Observances, trans. Valji Govindji (Ahmedabad: Navajivan Publishing House, 1932).

176. M.K. Gandhi, From Yeravda Mandir, trans. V.G. Desai (1957 Edn.), Chapter XIII; as cited by Gandhi, *In Search of the Supreme*, vol. 2, pp. 4-5.

177. *Young India*, 22-8-1929, p. 278; as cited by Gandhi, *In Search of the Supreme*, vol. 2, p. 8.

178. *From Yeravda Mandir*, V.G. Desai (1957 Edn.), Chapter XIII; as cited by Gandhi, *In Search of the Supreme*, vol. 2, p. 5.

179. *Collected Works of Mahatma Gandhi*, vol. 14, p. 97; as cited by Narayan, Selected Letters, p. 449.

180. Gandhi, *From Yeravda Mandir*, p. 3.

181. Gandhi, *From Yeravda Mandir*, pp. 3-4.

182. *Harijan*, 9-3-1940, p. 31; as cited by Pyarelal, The Last Phase, part 2, pp. 506-507.

183. *From Yeravda Mandir*, trans. V.G. Desai (1957 Edn.), Chap. III; as cited by Gandhi, *In Search of the Supreme*, vol. 2, p. 66.

184. *From Yeravda Mandir*, trans. V.G. Desai (1957 Edn.), Chap. III; as cited by Gandhi, *In Search of the Supreme*, vol. 2, p. 73.

185. Cf. Gandhi, From Yeravda Mandir, p. 9.

186. Cf. Gandhi, From Yeravda Mandir, pp. 13-15.

187. Gandhi, From Yeravda Mandir, p. 15.

188. From Yeravda Mandir, trans. V.G. Desai (1957 Edn.), Chap. III; as cited by Gandhi, *In Search of the Supreme*, vol. 2, p. 107.

189. Gandhi, From Yeravda Mandir, p. 16.

190. *From Yeravda Mandir*, trans. V.G. Desai (1957 Edn.), Chap. III; as cited by Gandhi, *In Search of the Supreme*, vol. 2, p. 106.

191. Cf. G.A. Natesan, Speeches and Writings of Mahatma Gandhi, Madras: 1933, p. 353; as cited by Gandhi, India of My Dreams, p. 55.

192. *Harijan*, 1-2-1942, p. 42; as cited by Gandhi, *In Search of the Supreme*, vol. 1, pp. 267-268.

193. *Collected Works of Mahatma Gandhi*, vol. 48, pp. 50-58; as cited by Nayar, Salt Satyagraha, p. 371.

194. *Young India*, 30-4-1925, p.149; as cited by Gandhi, *In Search of the Supreme*, vol. 2, p. 246.

195. Gandhi, From Yeravda Mandir, p. 11.

196. Gandhi, From Yeravda Mandir, p. 19.

197. M.K. Gandhi, *The Message of the Gita* (Ahmedabad: Navajivan Publishing House, 1996), p. 34.

198. Cf. *Harijan*, 2-6-1946; as cited by M.K. Gandhi, Ramanama (Ahmedabad: Navajivan Publishing House, 1949), p. 16. Henceforth, Gandhi, Ramanama.

199. Cf. Gandhi, From Yeravda Mandir, p. 20.

200. Cf. Gandhi, From Yeravda Mandir, p. 22.

201. *Young India*, 25-11-1926; as cited by Gandhi, India of My Dreams, p.63.

202. Gandhi, From Yeravda Mandir, p. 23. Gandhian understanding of religious plurality is further discussed at length in the next chapter.

203. Gandhi, From Yeravda Mandir, p. 24.

204. Cf. Gandhi, From Yeravda Mandir, p. 23.

205. Gandhi, From Yeravda Mandir, p. 24.

206. Gandhi, From Yeravda Mandir, p. 24.

207. Gandhi, From Yeravda Mandir, p. 26.

208. *From Yeravda Mandir*, (1957), p. 66; as cited by Gandhi, The Voice of Truth, p.339; Emphasis in the original.

209. G.A. Natesan, *Speeches and Writings of Mahatma Gandhi* (Madras: 1933), pp. 336-344; as cited by Gandhi, India of My Dreams, p. 120.

210. *Young India*, 25-6-1925; as cited by Gandhi, Truth is God, p. 36.

211. *Gandhiji to Mirabehn*, 4-1-1947; as cited by Pyarelal, *Mahatma Gandhi, The Last Phase*, vol. 9, book 2, part I, 2nd reprint (Ahmedabad: Navajivan Publishing House, 1997), p.118. Henceforth, Pyarelal, The Last Phase, book 2.

212. *Collected Works of Mahatma Gandhi*, vol. 8, pp. 319-322; as cited by Nayar, Satyagraha at Work, p. 295.

213. *Harijan*, 8-9-1945, p. 305; as cited by Pyarelal, The Last Phase, book I, p. 245.

214. Cf. Mathews, The Matchless Weapon, pp. 122-123.

215. M. K. Gandh, *Ashram Observances in Action* (Ahmedabad: 1955), p. 37; as cited by Pyarelal, The Last Phase, book 2, p.66.

216. *Harijan*, 8-6-1935, p. 132; as cited by Pyarelal, The Last Phase, book 2, p.66.

217. Gandhi, *In Search of the Supreme*, vol. 1, p. 169.

218. *Young India*, 24-9-1925, p. 331; as cited by Gandhi, *In Search of the Supreme*, vol. 1, p.171.

219. M.K. Gandhi, *In Search of the Supreme*, vol. 1, p. 170.

220. Cf. *Young India*, 10-6-1926, p. 211; as cited by Gandhi, *In Search of the Supreme*, vol. 1, p. 170.

221. *Harijan*, 18-8-1946, p. 265; as cited by Pyarelal, The Last Phase, book 2, p. 66.

222. *Harijan*, 18-8-1946, p. 267; as cited by Pyarelal, The Last Phase, book 2, p.66.

223. M.K. Gandhi, *Ashram Observances in Action* (Ahmedabad: 1955), p. 36; as cited by Pyarelal, The Last Phase, book 2, p.66.

224. Aldous Huxley, *The Perennial Philosophy* (London: 1946), p. 320; as cited by Pyarelal, The Last Phase, book 2, p. 164.

225. Aldous Huxley, *The Perennial Philosophy* (London: 1946), p. 320; as cited by Pyarelal, The Last Phase, book 2, p. 164.

226. Gandhi, *Ramanama*, pp. 28-29.

227. Gandhi, *Autobiography*, p.27.

228. Pyarelal, The Last Phase, book 2, p. 19.

229. *Young India*, 8-9-1927, p. 294 at 295; as cited by Gandhi, *In Search of the Supreme*, vol. 1, p. 201.

230. *Harijan*, 3-3-1946, p. 25; as cited by Gandhi, *In Search of the Supreme*, vol. 1, pp. 204-205.

231. *Harijan*, 21-7-1946, p.229; as cited by Gandhi, *In Search of the Supreme*, vol. 1, p. 205.

232. *Young India*, 11-10-1928, pp. 34-341; as cited by Pyarelal, The Last Phase, book 2, p. 66.

233. *Young India*, 24-9-1931, p. 272 at p. 274; as cited by Gandhi, *In Search of the Supreme*, vol. 1, p. 186.

234. Cf. *Young India*, 1-6-1921, p. 174; as cited by Pyarelal, The Last Phase, book 2, p. 65.

235. *Harijan*, 24-12-1938, p. 392 at p. 395; as cited by Gandhi, *In Search of the Supreme*, vol.1, p. 188.

236. *Harijan*, 24-8-1934, p. 223; as cited by Gandhi, *In Search of the Supreme*, vol. 1, p. 258. A similar passage is found in the writings of St. Paul. "My grace is sufficient for you, for my power if made perfect in weakness." (2 Cor 12:9; RSV).

237. Gandhi, *In Search of the Supreme*, vol. 2, p. 72.

238. Cf. *Selected Letters*-II, pp. 46-47; as cited by Narayan, Selected Letters, pp. 402-403.

239. *Harijan*, 24-12-1947, p. 476; as cited by Gandhi, *In Search of the Supreme*, vol. 1, p. 278.

240. *Harijan*, 27-10-1946, pp. 372-373; as cited by Pyarelal, The Last Phase, book I, p. 303.
241. *Ashram Observances in Action*, Chapter 1 (1959 Edn.), pp. 12-22; as cited by Gandhi, *In Search of the Supreme*, vol.1, pp. 285-286.
242. *Ashram Observances in Action*, Chapter 1 (1959 Edn.), pp. 12-22; as cited by Gandhi, *In Search of the Supreme*, vol. 1, p. 284.
243. *The Epic Fast*, p. 14; as cited by Nayar, Preparing for Swaraj, p. 65.
244. *Harijan*, 1-12-1938; as cited by Gandhi, Truth is God, p. 57.
245. *Harijan*, 1-12-1938; as cited by Gandhi, Truth is God, p. 56.
246. *Harijan*, 1-12-1938; as cited by Gandhi, Truth is God, p. 56.
247. *Harijan*, 10-12-1938; as cited by Gandhi, Truth is God, p. 57.
248. Cf. M.K. Gandhi, *Satyagraha in South Africa*; as cited by Shriman Narayan, ed., *The Selected Words of Mahatma Gandhi* (Ahmedabad: Navajivan Publishing House, 1968), pp. 156-157. Henceforth, Narayan, The Selected Words.
249. Casey, *An Australian in India* (London: 1947), p. 61; as cited by Pyarelal, The Last Phase, book I, p. 146.
250. *Harijan*, 2-3-1934, p. 19 at p. 23; as cited by Gandhi, *In Search of the Supreme*, vol. 3, p. 179.
251. Dr. Radhakrishnan, ed., *Mahatma Gandhi: Essays and Reflections on His Life and Work* (London: Allen & Unwin Ltd., 1939), p. 143.
252. Pyarelal, The Last Phase, book I, pp. 44-45.
253. Cf. Pyarelal, The Last Phase, book I, p. 228.
254. Cf. Prayer Speech, 25-6-1946; as cited by Pyarelal, The Last Phase, book I, p. 230.
255. *Harijan*, 27-5-1939; as cited by Gandhi, India of My Dreams, p. 19.
256. *Harijan*, 4-8-1946, p. 245; as cited by Pyarelal, The Last Phase, book I, p. 237.
257. *Young India*, 12-6-1924, p. 195; as cited by Gandhi, The Voice of Truth, p. 442.
258. *Harijan*, 25-5-1939, p. 143; as cited by Gandhi, The Voice of Truth, p. 446.
259. *Harijan*, 27-5-1939, p. 143; as cited by Gandhi, The Voice of Truth, p. 446.
260. *Young India*, 26-1-1922; as cited by Gandhi, India of My Dreams, pp. 20-21.
261. *Young India*, 2-2-1921; as cited by Gandhi, India of My Dreams, p. 20.

262. *Young India*, 4-8-1920, p. 3; as cited by Gandhi, The Voice of Truth, p. 462.

263. *Young India*, 2-7-1931, p. 162; as cited by Gandhi, The Voice of Truth, p. 436.

264. Cf. *Harijan*, 29-9-1946, p. 332; as cited by Gandhi, *In Search of the Supreme*, vol. 2, pp. 315-316.

265. Casey, *An Australian in India* (London: 1947), p. 61; as cited by Pyarelal, The Last Phase, book I, p. 146.

266. Pyarelal, The Last Phase, book 2, p. 189.

267. *Harijan*, 20-10-1946, p. 367; as cited by Pyarelal, The Last Phase, book I, p. 330.

268. *Young India*, 9-12-1926, p. 432; as cited by Gandhi, The Voice of Truth, p. 230.

269. Mahadevbhaini Diary (Gujarati), vol. 8, pp. 315-319; *Collected Works of Mahatma Gandhi*, vol. 18, pp. 377-80; as cited by Nayar, Salt Satyagraha, p.8.

270. *Harijan*, 26-8-1933, p. 1; as cited by Gandhi, *In Search of the Supreme*, vol. 2, p. 267.

271. *Harijan*, 18-6-1938; as cited by Gandhi, India of My Dreams, p. 284.

272. James D. Hunt, *Gandhi in London* (1978), p. 150; as cited by Nayar, Satyagraha at Work, p. 490.

273. Cf. Nayar, Satyagraha at Work, pp. 494-499.

274. Cf. *Young India*, 11-2-1920; as cited by Gandhi, India of My Dreams, p. 39.

275. *Harijan*, 8-10-1937, p. 292; as cited by Gandhi, The Voice of Truth, pp. 321-322

276. Cf. Nayar, Satyagraha at Work, p. 510

277. *Hindustan Times*, 5-1-1946; as cited by Gandhi, The Voice of Truth, p.433.

278. Pyarelal, The Last Phase, book I, p. 107.

279. Constructive Programme, (1961), pp. 12-13; as cited by Gandhi, The Voice of Truth, p. 385.

280. *Young India*, 17-9-1925, p. 321; as cited by Gandhi, The Voice of Truth, p. 321.

281. Nayar, Salt Satyagraha, p. 26.

282. *Harijan*, 31-7-1937, p. 197; as cited by Gandhi, The Voice of Truth, p. 507.

283. *Collected Works of Mahatma Gandhi*, vol. 26, p. 362; as cited by Narayan, Selected Letters, p. 441.

284. *Young India*, 21-2-1929, p. 58; as cited by Gandhi, The Voice of Truth, p. 529.

285. With Gandhiji in Ceylon, (1928), pp. 89-90; as cited by Gandhi, The Voice of Truth, p. 529.

286. *Harijan*, 21-12-1947, p. 480; as cited by Gandhi, The Voice of Truth, p. 505.

287. *Young India*, 2-7-1925, p. 232; as cited by Gandhi, The Voice of Truth, pp. 313-314.

288. Gandhi, Autobiography, p. 286.

289. M.K. Gandhi, *Satyagraha in South Africa*; as cited by Narayan, The Selected Words, p. 145.

290. *Hind Swaraj or Indian Rule*, (1962), p. 19; as cited by Gandhi, The Voice of Truth, p. 313.

291. *True Education*, (1962), pp. 171-1973; as cited by Gandhi, The Voice of Truth, p. 312.

292. *Harijan*, 24-8-1935, p. 283; as cited by Gandhi, India of My Dreams, p. 283.

293. *Young India*, 25-3-1926; as cited by Gandhi, India of My Dreams, p. 282.

294. *True Education*, (1962), pp. 171-173; as cited by Gandhi, The Voice of Truth, p. 311.

295. Gılbert Murray, "The Soul As It Is and How To Deal With It," *Hibbert Journal*, 16 (1917-1918) 2, 198; as cited by Mathews, The Matchless Weapon, p. 151.

3

'SATYO-CENTRISM': A FRAMEWORK FOR THE THEOLOGY OF RELIGIONS

The concept of truth as derived and inferred from the life and thought of Gandhi is all-comprehensive. The nature of truth is so holistic that it has a profound significance in understanding the philosophical issues involved in religious plurality and in interreligious concerns. If we can unravel this dimension of truth among different religions, it is hoped, it will present a solution to the problem at hand, namely, providing a viable and rational basis for interreligious relations.

Therefore, this chapter will begin with an analysis of how Gandhi understood and lived religious plurality from the perspective of truth. It will then proceed to examine the concept of uniqueness of Christ, as an illustration, which caused hurdles among Christians in arriving at a meaningful relationship among other religions and how Gandhi, by applying the benchmark of truth, was able to understand it from his perspective. Using the same criterion it is hoped to solve the problem of uniqueness of religions as well as similar problems that can cause concern in interreligious relationships. A truth-oriented understanding of religious concepts that enabled Gandhi to live interreligiously, thus, paves the way for a 'satyo-centric' theology of religions.

The contention here is that if 'satyo-centrism' can resolve the controversies that surround the question of the uniqueness of Christ with which Gandhi was not so much involved, it can explain and interpret religious pluralism of which he was an active promoter. To arrive at this, the chapter will also discuss how Gandhi was able to rise above the existing religions to arrive at the Religion of Truth wherein one can experience the oneness of all religions and from where every religion can draw vital energy not only for its sustenance but also for understanding other religious traditions in such a way that all religions can live side by side in fellowship and mutual cooperation.

RELIGIOUS PLURALITY: A GANDHIAN PERSPECTIVE

Gandhi's religious endeavour consisted in understanding and in imbibing those teachings bequeathed to humankind by the prophets of the world, which helped him to understand religions in terms of truth, with his limited intelligence that God had given him. His devotion to truth helped him in this task. To achieve his aim, Gandhi allowed himself to be rooted in his own religion and cultivated a sincere appreciation for other religions. His religious experiences that included even conflicts within himself and with others helped him to conclude that all religions are not only imperfect but also equal. After all, every religion attempts to approximate the Absolute Truth. Hence Gandhi endeavoured to strive after interreligious cooperation and fellowship through different ways.

As a young boy, Gandhi visited the temple frequently with his mother, listened to the reading of the *Gita* during the illness of his father and religious discourses that his father had with different sages who visited his home. As pointed out earlier, the rigorous fasts that his mother undertook touched the tender heart of the young boy with religious fervour. Gandhi learnt the habit of repeating the name of Rama from his nurse Ramba. All these childhood experiences instilled in Gandhi a sincere devotion to his native religion.

Later, Gandhi himself defined the Hindu creed he lived as a

> search after Truth through non-violent means. A Man may not believe even in God and still call himself a Hindu. Hinduism is a relentless pursuit after truth and, if today it has become moribund, inactive, irresponsive to growth, it is because we are fatigued, and as soon as the fatigue is over, Hinduism will burst forth upon the world with a brilliance perhaps unknown before. Of course, therefore, Hinduism is the most tolerant of all religions.[1]

Further, Gandhi also disputed the description that Hindus believed in many gods and are idolaters. Although they do say there are many gods, they also declare unmistakably that there is One God, God of gods. Hindus believe that there is a world inhabited by superior beings called gods whom we do not see but who nevertheless exist just as there is a world inhabited by men and another by beasts. The problem arose because of the rendering of the word *deva* or *devata* for which we have to find a better term than god. For, God is *Ishvara*, *Devadhideva*, God of gods.[2]

Gandhi also had a specific love for the *Gita*. For him, "the Gita is pure religious discourse given without any embellishment. It simply describes the progress of the pilgrim soul towards the supreme goal."[3] Speaking about the effect he had on reading the *Gita*, Gandhi wrote: "The Gita became an infallible guide of conduct. It became my dictionary of daily reference. Just as I turned to the English dictionary for the meanings of English words that I did not understand, I turned to this dictionary of conduct for a ready solution of all my troubles and trials."[4]

Despite his predilection for Hinduism, Gandhi was not a fanatic; instead, being a sincere seeker of truth, he was quick to point out the accretions that had accumulated in it. It "is a living organism liable to growth and decay, and subject to the laws of nature . . . . The changes in the seasons affect it . . . . Hinduism is like the Ganges pure and unsullied at its source, but taking in its course the impurities on the way."[5] Further, Gandhi held that the uniqueness of one's religion must be protected by non-violence, self-sacrifice and penance and not by coercion.

Gandhi's devotion to truth also enabled him to appreciate other religions. To understand other religions, Gandhi acquainted himself with the religious scriptures of different religions as well as the writings of great thinkers. While in prison, Gandhi read the *Gita* in the morning and the Koran in English translation at noon. He used the Bible to teach English to his Chinese Christian fellow prisoners. He also read Ruskin, Socrates, Tolstoy, Huxley, Carlyle and Bacon.[6]

It must be noted that Gandhi's openness and impartiality with regard to religion was already noticed when he was a child. When disputes arose among the players, young Gandhi invariably acted as the peacemaker. He never made any distinction between Hindu, Muslim, Parsi and others.[7] This openness continued when Gandhi went to England in 1888 for studying law. During his stay in England, Gandhi came across two theosophist brothers. They introduced him to various religious scriptures like the *Gita* and *The Light of Asia.* He also came in contact with Madame Blavatsky and Mrs. Besant who advised him to join the society[8].

Some of his Christian friends introduced Gandhi to the reading of the Bible. The books of the Old Testament did not inspire him. But the New Testament produced a different impression; especially the Sermon on the Mount had a deep impression on him. He compared it to the *Gita.* He learnt that renunciation is the highest form of religion. He was also acquainted with atheism especially of Bradlaugh. But Gandhi was prejudiced against it as it did not appeal to him.[9]

Just as Gandhi's Christian friends were trying to win him over to Christianity, his Muslim friends were trying to induce him to study Islam. "As a seeker after truth he welcomed their efforts to show to him the light, obtained a copy of the Sale's translation of the *Koran* and other books on Islam and read them with due care and reverence."[10] While in South Africa, his receptive mind, ever ready to accept fresh values from other religious traditions, took the motto of the Trappist monastery at Pine Town, *Ora et labora.* This was later embodied in essence in his own creed – service to God through selfless service to humanity.[11]

All these acquaintances with different religions resulted in an intra-personal conflict within Gandhi. He wondered whether he should convert himself to any other religion leaving behind his ancestral faith. This conflict had two-fold dimensions. "Objectively, it was a question regarding the status of religions: which religion was really a true religion? Subjectively, it was concerned with the response he had to give to the issue: should he be converted to any other religion at all? Both the questions are intimately connected with each other. It is only by solving the first that he could answer the second."[12] However, as a sincere seeker after truth, Gandhi drew himself into a prolonged process in resolving the conflict. He took guidance from Raychandbhai,[13] a businessman who was absorbed in godly pursuits, who advised him to be patient and to study Hinduism more deeply. He held that before getting oneself converted to another religion, one must know one's own religion thoroughly. This spurred Gandhi to study not only Hinduism deeply but also other religions as well by reading books on various religions given by his friends. Gandhi interspersed his study of religions with prayer asking God for guidance. He was fully open to His will.

Gandhi writes: "For a time I struggled with the question: which was the true religion out of which I knew. To feel my way I waited upon God, seeking His guidance."[14] Gandhi also put into practice various principles that he learned from the different religions as a result of his study. All these helped him to resolve the conflict by remaining a good Hindu at the same time having sincere love and respect for other religions.[15]

The result of this conflict that arose within him on account of his living contact with numerous followers of other religions and the subsequent resolution of the same was that Gandhi became the most accommodative person of any religious tradition other than his own. Further, it also helped Gandhi to observe that not only Hinduism but every religion is imperfect. Speaking at a prayer meeting, Gandhi said that no religion as it existed in the present-day world was entirely free from blemish. Islam gave to the world some of the noblest characters in history but unwanted accumulations had gathered in the practices of Muslims, which ran counter to the fundamental teachings of Islam. Similarly, Christian nations professed to follow Jesus, who taught humankind to love even their enemies. But they were responsible for two major world wars in a single generation. Likewise, Hinduism, which was based on the doctrine of the oneness of all creation, had allowed a diabolical wrong to be perpetrated on the so-called untouchables in the name of religion.[16]

This imperfection in religions stems from the fact that human beings, who profess and live the different faiths, are themselves imperfect. Although all religions constitute a revelation of Truth as absolute, this truth is revealed only relatively. Hence every religion like the rain-drops of pure water that become diluted or polluted as soon as they come in contact with Mother Earth, is alloyed with impurities.[17] For Gandhi, "different religions are beautiful flowers from the same garden, or they are branches of the same majestic tree. Therefore they are equally true, though being received and interpreted through human instruments equally imperfect."[18]

Thus, Gandhi held that all religions are equal, in spite of, or because of, the imperfections in them. One cannot secretly harbour the thought that one's neighbour's faith is inferior to one's own. This equality is not physical but primarily a mental state and refers to the interiority. When one says that human beings are absolutely equal, it implies that this equality is of souls and not of bodies. So too is religion. "We need to think of and to assert equality because we see great inequalities in the physical world. We have to realize equality in the midst of this apparent external inequality."[19] He compared this equality of religions to the leaves on a tree. "No two leaves are alike, yet there is no antagonism between them or between the branches on which they grow. Even so, there is an underlying unity in the variety which we see in God's creation."[20]

Every religion is growing in its attempt to reach the Absolute Truth. Hence the question of inferiority or superiority of religions does not arise. He explains this as follows:

> . . . [the] finer the line you draw, the nearer it approaches Euclid's true straight line, but it never is the true straight line. The tree of Religion is the same; there is not that physical equality between the branches. They are all growing, and the person who belongs to the growing branch must not gloat over it and say, 'Mine is the superior one.' None is superior, none is inferior, to the other.[21]

The acceptance of the equality of religions does not in any way negate the distinction between religion and irreligion. There is no room for cultivation of toleration for irreligion. However, Gandhi held that "a person who seeks Truth and love, will not bear hatred towards an irreligious brother instead help him to see the error of his ways, or he will point out our error, or each will tolerate the other's difference of opinion."[22]

The equality of religions is also implied from the fact that God reveals to everyone equally. Anyone who is open will hear Him in day to day life. It is similar to the presence of music that is broadcast through the radio waves. Only a transistor that is attuned properly to the waves can receive it. Gandhi said: "My firm belief is that He reveals Himself daily to every human being but we shut our ears to the still small voice. We shut our eyes to the Pillar of Fire in front of us."[23] However, this revelation of God is distinct for each human being. Hence Gandhi claimed: "The God of my imagination rules my life, and not the God of your imagination."[24]

In accepting both the possibility of imperfection in, and the subsequent equality of religions, Gandhi confirmed the fact of the plurality of religions. He wrote: "Personally, I think the world as a whole will never have, and need not have, a single religion."[25] One of the reasons for this plurality is that God, though One, appears differently to different people. "Everyone has his own conception of God. For instance, I believe myself to be a Hindu but I know I do not worship God in the same manner as many of the Hindus do."[26] "Different temperaments and climatic conditions"[27] too favoured the fact of plurality of religions. Another reason is that Truth which is God for Gandhi has no form. "Therefore every one will form such an idea or image of truth as appeals to him, and there will be as many images of truth as there are men."[28] Further Gandhi wrote: "Rama, Rahaman, Ahurmazda, God or Krishna are all attempts on the part of man to name that invincible force which is the greatest of all forces. It is inherent in man, imperfect he though be, ceaselessly to strive after perfection."[29] Gandhi was of the opinion that humans try to describe God in their own poor language and their attempt is bound to be plural.

Besides, for Gandhi reality was multiform and ever changing. Hence it follows that "no statement can hold good at all times and in all ways and in all places, and it is, therefore, impossible to pledge ourselves to an inflexible creed. Nor may anyone claim exclusive truth for his own."[30] His acquiescence of the Jaina theory of *Syadvada* also contributed to the acceptance of the plurality of religions. The doctrine that truth is relative to our standpoint also became the basis of his understanding of religions. The natural law of 'unity in diversity' confirmed Gandhi's faith in religious plurality. "In nature there is a fundamental unity running through all the diversity we see about us. Religions are no exception to the natural law."[31] The fact that conscience even in well trained persons is different shows that religious plurality is inevitable. "Even amongst the most conscientious persons, there will be room enough for honest differences of opinion."[32]

Already in South Africa, Gandhi realized this truth about religions, namely, religious plurality is a fact of life. Hence Gandhi called for interreligious cooperation by tolerating other religions without disparaging them. Thus, while advertising the books published by the Esoteric Christian Union in Natal Mercury, Gandhi wrote: "the system of thought expounded by the books advertised . . . is . . . a system of religion which teaches universality . . . In that system, there is no reviling of Mohamed or Buddha . . . It reconciles the other religions with Christianity which, in the opinion of the authors, is nothing but one mode (among many) of the presentation of the same eternal truth."[33]

Such interreligious cooperation is necessary because the core of religious teaching is love and kindness. "All religions teach that we should all live together in love and mutual kindness."[34] The fact that every religion has produced great saints shows that every religion has certain good features. Tolerance implies that one should accept these right features and not the evils. Further, since imperfect humans interpret the one Religion differently, everybody is right from his own perspective. Therefore tolerance becomes a necessity. Tolerance does not mean indifference but a more intelligent and purer love for different religions. In this way, Gandhi said that in the context of religious differences, "the golden rule of conduct ... is mutual toleration seeing that we will never all think alike and that we shall always see Truth in fragment and from different angles of vision."[35]

In order to promote mutual tolerance and cooperation among religions, Gandhi proposed a reverent study of the sayings of different teachers of humankind. One should cultivate equimindedness towards all other faiths and should never have the slightest desire to criticize any of the religions merely because they are not one's own. Tolerance also would mean that exclusive understanding of a religion is not only a disservice to itself but also to the very fabric of religious harmony. When people professing different religions live the religious principles they believe in, in an authentic manner, mutual cooperation is possible. For, "Truth has to be lived if it is to fructify."[36] It is by living their religion, that the various followers of different religions will be able to add to the sum total of human search. "We should by living the life according to our lights share the best with one another, thus adding to the sum total of human effort to reach God."[37]

Interreligious collaboration can be instilled by promoting the observance of religious injunctions and by celebrating the festivals of different religions and through interreligious prayer. Thus while living in Tolstoy Farm[38], Gandhi encouraged the Muslim youngsters to observe the *Ramzan* fast. He himself decided to observe *pradosha* and asked the Hindu, Parsi and Christian youngsters to join him. In fact, many of the inmates of the Farm welcomed his proposal and began to fast. The result of these experiments was that all were convinced of the value of fasting, and a splendid *esprit de corps* grew up among them. To avoid offending the religious susceptibilities, all the inmates of the Farm took to vegetarianism, irrespective of their religious affiliations. They relished the vegetarian diet.[39]

The celebration of festivals of different religions would facilitate one to recognize the essential oneness. On Christmas day, in a short message to members of the Ashram, Gandhi said:

> We, who have equal regard for all religions, should make it a point to celebrate all such occasions.... Let us turn the searchlight inward ... purge ourselves of all dross (and) realise the oneness of God and the essential sameness of His word. We should ... bear witness to our faith by being ready to lay down our life for what we hold to be true or right.... Let us on this occasion remember and mediate on the fact that Christ mounted the Cross for what he held to be the Truth.[40]

For Gandhi, interreligious prayer became an instrument of interreligious living and an antidote to bigotry. Thus during the communal disturbances in Noakhali, Gandhi introduced congregational public prayer of a cosmopolitan character, in which all could join. He used it to inculcate bravery, which comes from a living faith in God, upon the victims of violence and to teach the lessons of tolerance, just dealing and brotherhood among the perpetrators of the outrages as well as among the victims.[41] "Congregational prayer," said Gandhi, "is a means for establishing the essential human unity through common worship."[42] It became an integral part of his technique of non-violent mass action. Since congregation consists of individuals, it goes without saying that congregational worship can have no meaning for one who has never prayed himself but at the same time, individual prayer must be a lame affair if it does not result in a yearning of realizing unity with the masses through congregational worship. Success would ultimately depend on the purity of the leader and the faith of the audience.[43]

It must be kept in mind, that interreligious prayer must give equal reverence to all religions. To this end, Gandhi incorporated prayers and verses from various religions in his Ashram worship. "Such additions enriched the prayer and helped in reaching the hearts of a larger audience than before."[44] During congregational prayers, it is not necessary to sort out the intricate stories and meanings attached to different divinities. Instead, what is more important is to realise the presence of God. For, going deep into such matters is not part of one's quest for truth.[45]

The use of various names of God in interreligious worship caused some problems to Gandhi. Thus some Muslims accused him for coupling the names of Rama and Krishna with Rahim and Karim. It was blasphemous and offended Muslim ears. This was a painful surprise for Gandhi. It betrayed intolerance and narrowness of mind. It was untrue that he was trying to corrupt Islam by coupling the Hindu incarnations of Rama and Krishna with the One God of Islam. He claimed to be a humble man of God. He had never invited, on principle, anybody to change his religion. His object was ever to make Muslims better Muslims, Hindus better Hindus, and Christians better Christians. His religion was not exclusive but expansive and all-inclusive. Rama, Allah and God were to him convertible terms.[46]

Further, when one of the ashramites modestly but firmly argued that the worship of Sarasvati, Ganesh and the like was violence to truth on the ground that no such divinities really existed and hence stopped reciting verses containing names of such divinities, Gandhi said that if one begins to condemn verses on the strength of this argument, it would be tantamount to an attack on the very basis of Hinduism. Even if one is not sure of the existence of certain deities, still they could be used in interreligious worship because every name is ultimately the description of one God, although devoted poets have given a local habitation and a name of His countless aspects. As a true devotee, one must transcend such particularities and embrace the one universal God.[47]

Thus Gandhi firmly believed in the fact of religious plurality. It became a necessity for him as a worshipper of truth. Therefore, he strove to safeguard and to inculcate plurality, by taking a serious view on the controversies that endangered religious harmony. As a man of truth, naturally, he tried to resolve them by appealing to an all-embracing concept of truth. For, he held that Truth, which is not only absolute but also relative, is acceptable to all religions. Each religion contains relative truth and endeavours to reach near the Absolute Truth. Gandhi also respected the individuality of each religion and allowed it grow at its own pace. He did not attempt to simplify and unify religions by merely combining different beliefs taken from them. He also avoided blending the deities of different religions. All these helped Gandhi to avoid the dangers of relativism[48] and syncretism in his understanding of religious plurality. His interreligious experiences together with his devotion to truth facilitated him to deal with certain problems that arise in a multi-religious context in a manner acceptable to different religious traditions, if they are sincere and open. This can pave the way for a 'satyo-centric' theology of religions.

TOWARDS A 'SATYO-CENTRED' THEOLOGY OF RELIGIONS

The theology of religions attempts to understand and relate with other religious traditions. However, there are difficulties in the understanding of unique features of religions that pose an impediment in forging genuine relationships among religions. One must accept the fact that there are such features peculiar to each religion and that they must be respected. After all, it is these features that give identity to the religions. But the followers of one religion cannot understand the categories that are peculiar to other religions. Hence there is a genuine need to use common categories that are acceptable to all the religions in order to understand the unique features present in different religions. The category of truth as evolved by Gandhi can help in understanding the problem areas in every religion. The reason for invoking such a category is not only that Gandhi himself made use of it successfully in resolving his own intra-personal conflicts that arose in the context of religious plurality and interreligious conflicts as shown in the previous section of this chapter but also that it is philosophically sound as shown in the second chapter.

Each religion, as a result of its unique features, has its problem areas when it relates to other religions. It must be borne in mind that these are not problem areas for the religion concerned. They turn out to be problems only in a multi-religious context. We take here the problem of uniqueness of Christ as an example for our consideration. For Christianity, Christological concerns regarding uniqueness of Jesus become a problem area while it relates with other religious traditions. Gandhi, with his yardstick of truth and from the experiences gained in resolving intra-personal and interreligious conflicts in the context of religious plurality was able to detect the causes for the problem of Christian uniqueness and attempted to resolve them. Hence, in the next section we will first discuss the Christological concerns regarding uniqueness of Jesus in general and then from the viewpoint of eight different positions held by different scholars. The latter part of this section will examine Gandhi's benchmark of truth, as applied to the same concern.

Christological Concerns

In the context of Christian theology, Christological concerns do not centre on the theme of uniqueness of Christ. If at all there is any problem, it will be a family problem: how to understand the varied interpretations of uniqueness within the large galaxy of theological viewpoints within the Christian context. However, when Christianity encountered other religious traditions and began to dialogue with them, the Christian theologians came to a painful awareness of other traditions' claims to uniqueness. Here the problem that Christian theology faced was with regard to the very claim to the uniqueness of Jesus. This necessarily led one to the question of the validity of other religions, or else, one had to question the validity of one's own religious tradition. This actually gave rise to the new discipline of the theology of religions. Thus the Christological questions formed the real core of the theology of religions for the Christians. In other words, one cannot just brush aside Christology from any serious discussion on the theology of religions.

In fact, overlooking the question of Jesus is to be less than honest in one's encounter with those of other faiths. Harvey Cox wrote:

> For the vast majority of Christians, including those most energetically engaged in dialogue, Jesus is not merely a background figure. He is central to Christian faith. Not only do the Christian dialoguers recognize this, but so do their Muslim, Buddhist, Shinto, Hindu, and Jewish conversation partners. Wherever one starts ... any honest dialogue between Christians and others will sooner or later ... have to deal with the figure of Jesus.[49]

Whereas some Christians are reluctant to bring up Jesus for discussion, frequently it is precisely the question of Jesus that non-Christian participants seem most eager to involve themselves in a discussion about Jesus. Harvey Cox admits that in the past he too, in an effort to stay clear of controversy and any appearance of insensitivity to others, avoided talking about Jesus too quickly. But, he continues, "I soon discovered my interlocutors wanted me to, and their bearing sometimes suggested that they did not believe they were really engaged in a brass-tacks conversation with a Christian until that happened."[50] This tremendous interest in the person of Jesus by followers of other faiths should not be surprising. For, as historian Jaroslav Pelikan remarks: "Regardless of what anyone may personally believe about him, Jesus of Nazareth has been the dominant figure in the history of Western culture for almost twenty centuries."[51]

The issue of the uniqueness of Jesus in relation to other religious epiphanies is central to the debate on the theology of religions among the Christians, together with its backing in the doctrine of incarnation. For the Christian Church, the uniqueness of Jesus is inescapable. Wolfhart Pannenberg said: "Of course, if Jesus is to be understood as the incarnate son of God, then the claim to Christian uniqueness is inevitable."[52] Alan Race is of the opinion that Christology was always destined to become the focus for the tension between the spirit of dialogue, with its disclosure of something 'more' and the theoretics of dialogue that concentrated on granting permission for dialogue in the first place. Stanley J. Samartha already identified this Christological tension in his preparations for the WCC's *Guidelines on Dialogue*: "How to state in a theologically credible way the relation between the *universality* of God's love and justice as Creator and the *particularity* of God's revelation in Jesus Christ."[53]

With regard to the relationship that exists between the commitment to dialogue and the theology of religions in the Catholic Church, Alan Race says that dialogue in the Church is subject to the controls of a theology of religions, which believes Christianity to be the final truth. This is made clear in the document *Dialogue and Proclamation*: "Inter-religious Dialogue is an integral element of the Church's evangelising mission."[54] Further, acknowledging the implications of dialogue, the International Theological Commission of the Vatican said: "How can one enter into an Inter-religious dialogue, respecting all religions and not considering them in advance as imperfect and inferior, if we recognize in Jesus Christ and only in him the unique and universal Saviour of mankind?"[55]

Thus, it is amply clear that Christological concerns centred on uniqueness of Christ have dominated the discussions regarding the theology of religions. Therefore, the question that one needs to tackle is how to understand the concept of uniqueness. The pluralist thinkers, of course, view that the concept of uniqueness is not necessarily the only term available for comprehending Jesus and his religious impact. Before undertaking a detailed study on the concept of uniqueness, it must be borne in mind at the outset that the foundation for the claim of uniqueness among religions is that religion is seen as the quest for the Supreme Being. "Because of this quest for ultimate reality, religions seem to have an inherent drive to claims of uniqueness and universality."[56] But the very fact that it is expressed shows that it is conditioned.

Uniqueness of Christ

Gandhi recognized the uniqueness of Christian religion and wanted the Christians to be proud of it. On his part also, he was clearly proud of certain unique features of Hinduism. Without any pretention or inhibition he said that "cow-protection was a unique gift of Hinduism to the world" and that "it was a wonderful phenomenon in human evolution."[57]

However, he raised an objection to the way the Christian missionaries understood and proclaimed the uniqueness of Christ. They not only held themselves to be superior to other believers on account of it but even denigrated other religions as superstitions. Already as a young man, Gandhi had certain difficulties with Christianity. "He could not believe that Jesus was the only incarnate Son of God, and that only he who believed in Him, would have everlasting life. If God could have sons, all of us were his sons. If Jesus was like God, or God Himself, then all men were like God and could be God Himself."[58] Gandhi was not ready to believe literally that Jesus by his death and by his blood redeemed the sins of the world. Metaphorically there might be some truth in it, he said.

Again, according to Christianity, only human beings had souls, not other living beings, for whom death meant complete extinction; while Gandhi held belief contrary to it. He could accept Jesus as a martyr, an embodiment of sacrifice, and a divine teacher and not as the most perfect man ever born. His death on the cross was a great example to the world. Philosophically there was nothing extraordinary in Christian principles. From the point of view of sacrifice, for Gandhi, the Hindus greatly surpassed the Christians. Hence it was impossible for Gandhi to regard Christianity as a perfect religion or the greatest of all religions.

In shaping his view on uniqueness of Christ, Gandhi was also influenced by the writings of Leo Tolstoy. According to Tolstoy, Jesus held no monopoly of truth. The teachings of Jesus were true, not because he was the Son of God but because it coincided with the light of human conscience.

> Take away the Church, the traditions, the Bible and even Christ Himself, the ultimate fact of man's knowledge of goodness that is of God, directly through reason and conscience will be as clear and certain as ever and it will be seen that we are dealing with

truths that can never perish – truths humanity can never afford to part with.[59]

In other words, Jesus' revelation is revelation not because it was something exclusive from the rest of revelation in humankind but it was the *sine qua non* of humanity itself. This means that even without his appearance on earth humanity would have lived with some kind of principles, which Jesus himself taught. So the uniqueness of Jesus, according to Tolstoy, consisted not in the truth he revealed but in illustrating the truths of humankind. It was a unique exemplar of living the principles which ought to govern the humankind if it is to survive. In that sense, Jesus really redeemed the world. He is the saviour of the world not in the sense of being the only one who saved as if before him or without him the world was unsaved.

For Christians, the two-nature Christology of Chalcedon was the dominant understanding of the person of Jesus Christ throughout the history of the Church. The Council of Chalcedon formulated the Chalcedonian definition in 451. The Council did not wish to amend or replace the earlier Nicene Creed (of 325 formulated as a response to the question of Christ's deity raised by Arius) but simply to clarify what is meant by the affirmation that Jesus was both God and human. Thus Jesus was said to be "perfect both in deity and also in humanness; this selfsame one is also actually God and actually man ... He is of the same reality as God as far as his deity is concerned and of the same reality as we ourselves as far as humanness is concerned ... one and only Christ-Son, Lord, only begotten-in two natures."[60]

However, this does not, of course, in and of itself guarantee its correctness. The creeds are carefully formulated prescriptions to clarify the explicit and implicit teachings of Scripture and stake out the acceptable parameters within which further thinking about the person and work of Christ should take place. Although expressing universal, unchanging truth, they are formulated out of a concern to address certain issues and challenges to the biblical teaching on Christ current at the time. The contexts in which the great historic creeds were formulated are in some respects significantly different from those of today. Thus, we should not expect the historic creeds of yesterday to settle every question the Church encounters today. While the historic creeds are highly relevant to the contemporary questions posed by religious pluralism and no informed Christian response to pluralism dare ignore them, there is a critical need today for Christians to articulate in a fresh way, a genuinely biblical response to the challenges presented by other religions.[61]

Besides, the plurality of gospel-writings reveals the plurality of understanding of God's one and the same revelation. Thus each New Testament writer interprets Jesus and his impact according to the community's circumstances, expectations and available theological apparatus for receiving him, with all the richness and limitations these impose. In other words, what the New Testament displays is the re-minting of symbols, images and metaphors, drawn from the stock of available terms, and their application to Jesus as part of a process of interpreting his impact for the initial generations of the first churches. Thus for Mark, Jesus is the suffering enigmatic Son of Man, confrontational in style and eventually rejected as a 'ransom for many' (Mk 10, 45), for Paul, Jesus is the Son of God, whose death and resurrection are said to usher in the era of eschatological hope, and for John, he is the enfleshed Word or Wisdom, who reveals the truth and grace of God's self-giving love. This analysis implies that the different New Testament writers need not be pressed into a mould that became convenient for serving later purposes. That is to say, the tendency to ascribe a higher Christology to, say, John's Gospel because of its logos language than Mark's Gospel reflects a later plan, not that of the first communities for whom the Gospels were written. For the New Testament witness, Jesus is better understood as the mediator of God's power and presence, rather than as an extension of God's very being.[62] In other words, each of these understandings of Jesus is unique and hence cannot be compared with one another much less valued superior or inferior to another.

Often, the uniqueness of Jesus is expressed through the doctrine of the incarnation. But such a position, in the context of dialogue, according to Alan Race, can turn out to be either arbitrary or ambiguous. The early Barthian understanding of Christian uniqueness (that Christianity alone is revelation of God through the incarnation of Christ while all religions are merely human efforts) is arbitrary. Barth wrote: "It is because we remember and apply the Christological doctrine of the *assumptio carnis* that we speak of revelation as the abolition of religion."[63] Barth was here attacking the concept of religion, which in his eyes was synonymous with the human effort to discern the purposes of God without the help of divine grace. The sovereignty of God, Barth believed, transcended all human efforts at self-justification. Barth concludes that the reality of grace in the Christian story "differentiates our religion, the Christian, from all others as the true religion."[64]

This position is arbitrary because there is no validity in distinguishing between the merely human search and the purely divine revelation. Already in the human search the divine inspiration is of great importance and necessity. "You received the spirit of adoption, enabling us to cry out, 'Abba, Father!' The Spirit himself joins with our spirit to bear witness that we are chiidren of God." (Rom 8: 15-16). Likewise, in the so-called divine revelation there must be an active response of the human. In other words, once the role of the human imagination in all aspccts of knowing, including religious knowing, is admitted, then it is difficult to differentiate so readily between the concepts of religion and revelation.

The concept of uniqueness of Jesus, expressed through the doctrine of the incarnation, can appear ambiguous in ways that could not have been envisaged earlier in Christian history. As an example of this ambiguous interpretation of incarnation, Alan Race quotes the document of the Roman Catholic Federation of Asian Bishops' Conference of 1987: "In presenting Christ as the 'Word' mediating the mysterious reality of God's presence to the world, John is implicitly admitting the presence of God's self-revelation in other religious traditions. The fact that John presents the Christ-event as an experience which ... can be identified in the universe at large, shows that the Johannine Church was prepared to enter into dialogue with the surrounding religious traditions."[65] Thus God is so committed to the world that we should expect evidence of God's presence through other religious insights. "Yet it would be wrong to conclude from this that God's universal presence implies that the knowledge of the divine presence is evenly distributed throughout the world. On the usual interpretation of the Johannine view, Jesus as '*logos* made flesh' necessarily remains the crowning achievement of God's *logos*-presence everywhere."[66]

This ambiguity in the understanding of incarnation lies in the fact that on the one hand, there is the affirmation of Jesus' solidarity with the human race and therefore potential comparability with other revealers is maintained; on the other hand, Jesus' superiority over all others is retained, for in Him 'the way, the truth and the life' (Jn 14: 6) has been manifest as in no other. This ambiguity is the source of much confusion. For, it allows Christians to highlight one side of the ambiguity when in dialogue mode, so that the unsurpassable uniqueness of Jesus is tempered (for example, by the use of terms such as decisive) and points of comparability between Jesus and other saviours is emphasised. But in theology of religions mode, the other side of the ambiguity is emphasized, in order to preserve the eventual pre-eminence of Jesus. What is given in respect through dialogue is removed through Christian absolutism, however soft it may be, when doing theology.[67]

Thus the real problem is: whether one should compromise one's original faith position (that Jesus is the word incarnate) and proceed with interreligious dialogue and cooperation or, one should carry on with the absolute claims of uniqueness and ready to suffocate dialogue resulting in religious conflicts.

The key to the solution of this problem lies in trying to understand the concept of uniqueness – whether it is constitutive which is to be narrated with little regard for the status of other religious traditions or ontic or relational or representative or it is a metaphorical affirmation, wherein uniqueness is symbolic of life-transformation both in Jesus and in his disciples or whether we should understand it in terms of theocentrism or as a live encounter and dialogue with other religions or whether we should understand uniqueness as liberative mission. We shall discuss these positions briefly and show how they are contrary to one another since each position is validated by invalidating other positions, and so, are not able to really solve the real problem of uniqueness.

However, it is possible to re-interpret the uniqueness of Christ in such a way that without losing its metaphysical content, it can be primarily used for life-transformation here and now. It is here that we find the Gandhian concept of truth very helpful in really solving the problem of uniqueness. For him, any religious uniqueness implies truth-living. In other words, uniqueness of Christ has to be re-lived in one's life. However, this does not mean that the other positions need to be totally rejected.

Uniqueness as Constitutive

The traditional position of Christianity of which Michael L. Fitzgerald seems to be the most recent exponent claims that Christ is the one saviour of all humankind. He is the only one who is able to reveal God and lead people to God. Hence, no one can enter into communion with God except through Jesus[68]. Fitzgerald is of the opinion that the unique mediation of Christ is connected with the universal salvific will of God. Here a complete identification takes place between Christ and his universal function as saviour with a particular individual, Jesus of Nazareth.

To grasp the meaning of uniqueness, Fitzgerald says that it is necessary to understand the term 'mediator' in its precise Christian meaning. The term does not simply mean a 'wise person', a 'hero' or a 'saint' who by the quality of his existence may exercise an 'intermediatory role' between heaven and earth. On the other hand, he writes: "it [mediator] means someone in whose person is present both 'true God' and 'true man'. And this title belongs to Jesus Christ in a unique way because, on the one hand, as Son of God, he participates fully in the divine uniqueness and on the other hand, he joins the human condition as a unique individual, in a determined place and at a specific time in history."[69] This has happened only in the case of Christ and therefore, he is also universal mediator. "Since Christ is the universal mediator who carries out the saving plan of God it must be said that salvation is one and the same for all human beings. There can be no road leading to God that do not converge in the only way which is Christ (Jn 14:6)."[70] Therefore, other religious traditions cannot be parallel ways of salvation; instead, the person of Jesus Christ together with the Christ-event becomes the constitutive of salvation for the whole of humankind.

Uniqueness as Ontic

As against the traditional view of the uniqueness of Christ, Raimundo Panikkar proposes an ontic understanding of uniqueness. He holds that God as an Absolute Being cannot be expressed in the finite. Every instance of revelation, therefore, is finite because every recipient receives it according to its mode. So there is little scope of superiority or uniqueness with respect to revelation since this revelation has to undergo the inherent limitations of a receiver who is limited.[71] He further argues that the reality of pluralism and historical consciousness of "the world, that is to say, the range of human experience, subjective and objective, ... [have] radically changed since the time in which Christian doctrine was formulated."[72] In other words, when the horizon of meaning changes, the sphere of understanding too must subject itself to transformation.

Hence, Panikkar claims that Christians can and must reinterpret their traditional understanding of the uniqueness of Christ.

Therefore, Panikkar maintains that the uniqueness of Christ is to be derived primarily from his position 'as the Second Person in the Trinity' as the only ontological – temporal and eternal - link between God and world. Every being is made in and through him and thus exists and participates in the Son. In this ontic aspect, he is the only one who creates, saves and glorifies. However, one should not identify this Christ with the particular individual, Jesus of Nazareth, and a particular historico-cultural entity.[73] Thus, for Panikkar, Jesus of Nazareth in whom Christ was present is only one instance or name among many related to his ontic salvific presence from the beginning of creation. Therefore, the function or role of Christ as a saviour is more important than his spatio-temporal individuality.[74]

Uniqueness as Relational

Jacques Dupuis, still another theologian, speaks of uniqueness as relational. He explains his theory by maintaining the mainline Christian understanding of uniqueness, which is constitutive. For him, constitutive uniqueness means that "the person of Jesus Christ and the Christ-event are "constitutive" of salvation for the whole of humankind; in particular, the event of his death-resurrection opens access to God for all human beings, independently of their historical situation."[75] In other words, the humanity of Jesus Christ, God's Son made flesh, is the sacrament of God's universal will to save. However, Dupuis asserts that such uniqueness should not be understood as absolute; instead, it should be construed as relational.

The historical event of incarnation marks the deepest and most crucial engagement of God with humankind because it establishes a bond of union that can never be severed. But this event by its very nature is marked by the particularity of every historical happening. Despite the trans-historical character of the risen humanity of Jesus Christ, the event is limited by its insertion in history, without which its singular significance and density would disappear. "It is, then, at once particular in time and universal in meaning, and, as such, "singularly unique," yet related to all other divine manifestations to humankind in one history of salvation – that is, relational."[76]

This becomes unavoidable because truth and grace found elsewhere, argues Dupuis, cannot be reduced to seeds or stepping stones simply to be nurtured or used and then superseded in Christian revelation. Instead, he says that they represent additional and autonomous benefits. It also implies that more divine truth and grace are found operative in the entire history of God's dealings with humankind than are available simply in the Christian tradition.

> As the "human face" or "icon" of God, Jesus Christ gives to Christianity its specific and singular character. But, while he is constitutive of salvation for all, he neither excludes nor includes other saving figures or traditions. If he brings salvation history to a climax, it is by way not of substitution or supersession but of confirmation and accomplishment.[77]

Dupuis further claims that other recent authors also subscribe to the relational nature of the uniqueness of Christ especially those who are sensitive to the demands of an open-ended theology of religious pluralism. Thus quoting Claude Geffré, Dupuis writes: "Without compromising the absolute commitment inherent to faith, Christianity can be considered as a relative reality; not, however, in the sense in which "relative" is opposed to "absolute," but in the sense of "relational." The Truth to which Christianity witnesses is neither exclusive nor inclusive of all other truth; it is related to all that is true in other religions."[78]

Uniqueness as Representative

According to Alan Race, it is possible to solve the problem of uniqueness by using the distinction between Jesus as representative or constitutive[79] of the experience of Christian salvation – a distinction enunciated by the process theologian Schubert Ogden. Here we can speak of Representative Christology and Constitutive Christology. The symbolic or metaphorical Christology aligns with Representative Christology. "It considers Jesus to be the consolidated exemplar (embodiment, mediation) of universal salvation. Jesus *uncovers*, in the act of faith-response to his impact, the self-giving of God for the life of the world."[80] Here Jesus is comparable with other saviours. Constitutive Christology, on the other hand, means, "Jesus somehow causes or inaugurates what was non-existent previously. He becomes the *origin* of what may be known in various (inadequate) guises elsewhere but is celebrated overtly in the Church."[81] In this type, Jesus alone is the saviour. "As constitutive saviour, he stands alone."[82]

Uniqueness as Metaphorical

John Hick offers a metaphorical understanding of uniqueness by rejecting the traditional understanding of incarnation. He wrote:

> The idea of the incarnation of God in the life of Jesus, so understood, is thus not a metaphysical claim about Jesus having two natures, but a metaphorical statement of the significance of a life through which God was acting on earth. In Jesus we see a man living in a startling degree of awareness of God and of response to God's presence.[83]

There seems to be three main reasons for the rejection of the traditional position. First, Hick was clearly very much perplexed by what he saw as the implications of the orthodox doctrine: if Jesus was really the eternal creator God become human, then it becomes very difficult indeed to treat Jesus, the New Testament, and Christian faith as being on the same level as phenomena from other religious traditions. Second, Hick said that to affirm that the historical Jesus of Nazareth was also literally God "is as devoid of meaning as to say that this circle drawn with a pencil on paper is also a square."[84] Third, John Hick's treatment of Christology relied heavily upon the more radical wing of New Testament scholarship, which showed how fragmentary and ambiguous are the data available to us on Jesus of Nazareth.[85]

Now, John Hick defined a myth as "a story or statement that is not literally true but which tends to evoke an appropriate dispositional attitude to its subject matter."[86] And Hick defined true religious myths as "those that evoke in us attitude and modes of behaviour, which are appropriate to our situation in relation to the Real."[87] Elsewhere, Hick said that a true myth is "a story which is not literally true but that nevertheless tends to evoke in the hearer an appropriate dispositional attitude to the story's referent which in the case of myth always transcends the story itself."[88]

Therefore, Hick claimed that the traditional exclusive claim which depended upon a central symbol should best be understood metaphorically or mythologically rather than literally. In Hinduism this central symbol is the eternal and absolute character of the Vedas as containing all truth without exception; in Buddhism, the global completeness of the Buddha's insight, so that there can be no other aspects of reality than the *pratityasamutpada* of which he became so vividly aware in his Enlightenment; in Judaism, the absolute character of the Torah, given to God's chosen people; in Islam, the eternal and absolute character of the Qur'an as God's final Word; and in Christianity, the deity of Jesus as the Second Person of the divine Trinity living a human life, so that Christianity alone among the religions was founded by God in person.[89]

Each religious community has to find the right way to use its own mythology. It is not the task of a Christian to tell Buddhists, Muslims or Hindus how to develop their symbol and belief systems in response to their consciousness that their own faith is not the one-and-only but one-among-several. Mutual discussion and criticism are possible and helpful within a dialogue in which there is a good basis of trust. But, broadly speaking, religious traditions are changed from within rather than from without, even though the change from within is often a response to what is going on outside. The duty of the religious thinker is to think critically about his own tradition, and to support those within other traditions who are likewise thinking critically, rather than to launch external attacks upon those other traditions.[90]

In Christianity, for example, the one abiding factor is its communal memory of Jesus as the man who was so totally open to God that one could see the divine love at work in his life (including his self-giving death and his Easter appearances), and could hear through his words the divine love calling people to open themselves to God and to be channels of his loving purpose on earth. Christians have traditionally expressed his significance for them in mythological language by calling him God incarnate, Son of God, and so on. But if this symbolic language is treated as literal, then there will be unwarranted inferences from it. And now that God is introducing the Christians, in the 'one world' of today, to his other children, Christians must not be misled into inferring that they are less truly God's children than themselves, or that He has given them only inferior opportunities to know Him and only a second-class status in relation to themselves. Hick believes that Christians are not being unfaithful to the revelation of God's limitless love in Jesus when they see Him as constituting a particular disclosure of a universal reality. On the contrary, they are thereby taking the universal reality of God's love seriously.[91]

Strictly speaking, 'someone is unique' simply means that there is only one of him/her. In this sense everyone is unique. But when Church speaks of the uniqueness of Christ it means something more. It means that Jesus is the unique Son of God and is as such the sole doorway to salvation, the one and only point of saving contact between God and humans, so that sooner or later all humans must, if they are to come to God, find him and respond to him in the person of Jesus Christ[92]

But Hick argues that the language, which bestowed titles to Jesus such as Son of God and God incarnate, is poetic or mythological and it appropriately expresses loving devotion and commitment of the disciple. However,

> . . . such language is misused when it is treated as a set of literal propositions from which to draw further literal conclusions. That the imagery of incarnation lacks any non-metaphorical meaning was made clear by the history of the Christological heresies, most of which were misguided attempts to give literal content to the idea of incarnation instead of leaving it in the realm of mystery and religious myth. That Jesus is my Lord and Saviour is language like that of the lover for whom his Helen is the sweetest girl in the world. Logically, there can only be one sweetest girl in the world; but if we treat the lover's words literally and infer from them the claim that every other girl in the world is less sweet than Helen, we shall not be doing justice to the kind of language he is using. And likewise if from the confession of Jesus as Lord and Saviour we infer that men cannot respond to God except through Jesus, we misuse the language of personal commitment and turn living religion into dogmatic exclusiveness.[93]

In this way, Hick is of the opinion that it is entirely appropriate for Christians to have an absolute commitment to Jesus Christ and to regard him as their Lord and Saviour, so long as they recognize that followers of other religious traditions have their own equally legitimate objects of ultimate devotion and commitment. Jesus may be the Saviour for Christians, but he is not necessarily Lord and Saviour for all persons in all cultures.[94]

Uniqueness as Theocentric

Another theologian, Paul Knitter endeavoured to understand uniqueness by proposing a theocentric Christology. He admitted "that Jesus *is* unique, but with a uniqueness defined by its ability to relate to – that is, to include and be included by – other unique religious figures."[95] He viewed Jesus "not as exclusive or even as normative, but as *theocentric*, as a universally relevant manifestation (sacrament, incarnation) of divine revelation and salvation."[96] The statement that Jesus is theocentric meant that his mission and person were profoundly kingdom-centered or God-centered. "All his powers were to serve this God and this kingdom; all else took second place. 'Thy kingdom come; thy will be done,' was the content of his prayer and his work."[97]

However, Knitter was aware of the inevitable exclusivism that exists in such biblical texts as 1 Tim 2:5, Acts 4:12, Jn 1:14, 14:6 and Heb 9:12. He notes that it is "either dishonest or naïve to argue that the early Christians really did not mean or believe what they were saying . . . When the early Jesus-followers announced to the world that Jesus was 'one and only,' they meant it."[98] Thus the Christian communities under the various Jewish and Gentile influences came to identify Jesus with the Logos or with Wisdom.[99] In spite of this awareness, Knitter held that the various interpretations or images of Jesus in the New Testament must not be taken literally. They should be understood more as "impressionistic paintings than as photographs."[100] Christological language is mythical or figurative, not literal.

Thus, according to Knitter when Peter stated that salvation is found in no one else,

> for there is no other name ... by which we must be saved" (Acts 4:12) or when Jesus is called the "one mediator between God and men" (1 Tim 2:5), the intention here is not to make an all-embracing metaphysical claim, which categorically rules out the possibility of there being any other saviour. For this is not the language of "philosophy, science or dogmatics" but of "confession and testimony.[101]

In the words of Krister Stendahl, whom Knitter quotes approvingly, this is "love language, caressing language,"[102] which expressed one's absolute devotion and commitment to Jesus Christ.

Paul Knitter, further, claimed that we must make a fundamental distinction between the essential core message of the New Testament and the medium used to communicate this message. And all of the 'one and only' qualifiers to the various Christological titles must be seen as pertaining more to the medium used by the New Testament writers than to its core message. Such exclusivistic formulations did not belong to the main content of what the early church experienced and believed.[103]

Besides, Knitter also suggested that it was inevitable that the early Christians who belonged to classical culture couched their expressions in highly exclusive categories. He wrote:

> [C]lassicist culture, in distinction from contemporary *historical* culture, took it for granted that truth was one, certain, unchanging, normative. For anything to be true, to be reliable, it had to bear these qualities. Certainly the early Christians were aware that there were many truth-claims in the world around them. For the most part, however, they felt that if any one of these claims really were true, it had to either conquer or absorb the others. That is what truth did. Unavoidably, then, when they encountered the overwhelming truth of Jesus, they would *have* to describe it as the only or the final truth. Today, however, in the world of historical consciousness, coupled with a new experience of pluralism, it seems possible for Christians to feel and announce the saving truth about Jesus and his message without the requirements of classicist culture – that is, without having to insist that Jesus' truth is either exclusive or inclusive of all other truth.[104]

The early Christians, then, were captives of their classicist culture and could not help expressing their commitments in exclusive categories. Fortunately, we know better today and can avoid the pitfalls of exclusivism inherent in classicist culture.

Thus, Knitter averred that the exclusive understanding of truth operative in the New Testament was due to the classicist culture in which the New Testament was born, that the early Christians were perplexed, and that our more enlightened historical cultural today need not be bound by such primitive views.

In advocating a shift from Christocentrism to theocentrism, Paul Knitter in effect is negating the epistemological priority traditionally given to the person of Christ. In other words, Christ has to be known from what we know about God. Here there is no possibility of reading off what God is like from observing what Jesus is like. Further, it presupposes that we have significant knowledge of God - what he is like and what he expects from humankind – apart from any reference to Jesus Christ. However, for Christians the main source of knowledge about God is the person of Jesus Christ. But Knitter offers no clue as to the epistemological source of theocentric theology.[105]

In response to the criticism regarding the lack of epistemological source for theocentric theology, Paul Knitter recommended that the fundamental source from which we draw our idea of God is our personal and societal experience of our world and ourselves. More specifically, he admits two sources of knowledge of God – human experience and secondly, the person and message of Jesus. Both are "genuine sources of revelation and neither can be held up as in any way epistemologically determinative over the other."[106]

Paul F. Knitter in recent times effected a change in his understanding of uniqueness. He held that uniqueness of Jesus should be understood as "the way he announced a *God who loves and takes the side of victims* and the way he emptied himself in incarnating and living this God's life for others."[107]

Uniqueness as Live Encounter

The Indian Theological Commission[108] favours an understanding of uniqueness in terms of live encounter and dialogue with other religious traditions. In its statement, it points out the limitations of the categories currently used in comprehending uniqueness and holds that these betray theoretical approaches to the faith of other people. The claims to uniqueness, according to the statement, stem merely from a monocultural, speculative and academic point of view. The Indian Theologians declared that they would rather approach the issue from a different point of view, that, namely, of a live encounter and dialogue. In such an approach, they say that Christ remains *for us* constitutionally the way to the Father. However, while the theologians continue to approach the problem from their own faith perspective, they also want to understand the purpose and meaning of the wonderful religious variety around them and its role and function in the attainment of salvation.[109]

The Statement further adds:

> The religions of the world are expressions of the human openness to God. They are signs of God's presence in the world. Every religion is unique and through this uniqueness, religions enrich one another. In their specificity, they manifest different faces of the supreme Mystery which is never exhausted. In their diversity, they enable us to experience the richness of the One more profoundly. When religions encounter one another in dialogue, they build up a community in which differences become complementarities and divergences are changed into pointers to communion.[110]

Uniqueness as Liberative

Orlando E. Costas, a leading liberation theologian from Latin America, attempts to explain uniqueness as the liberating mission of Christ by examining the historicity of Jesus of Nazareth – the life and ministry of Jesus in a particular socio-historical context, and, death and resurrection of Jesus. From an analysis of these events, he concludes that Jesus is a unique Lord because he is the crucified Lord who identified himself forever with suffering humanity and revealed God's righteousness in history by taking upon himself the unrighteousness of the world. Since this unique experience was given universal validity in the resurrection, Jesus is also the universal Lord. The resurrection is the confirmation of the fact that the way of the cross is neither intellectual 'foolishness' nor a religious 'scandal' but obedience to the God who is greater than science. Such an understanding of the Lordship of Christ does not lead to denigration of other lords of other religions; instead, it challenges the Christian to a life of commitment and engagement in the liberating mission of the crucified and risen Lord among the marginalized and the disfranchised of society.[111]

Uniqueness as Truth-living

From the above discussion on the understanding of the uniqueness of Christ (from the standpoint of Christian scholars), it is clear that an agreement seems to elude them as to the exact nature of uniqueness. The very disagreement among the various positions reveals the inadequacy of their respective positions. Besides, many of their speculations regarding uniqueness implied a claim to the superiority of Christianity over other faiths, which obviously, will not be acceptable to the believers of other religions as they too claim uniqueness for their respective religions. Further, the issue of uniqueness considered by most of these theologians betrays a Western problematic. Felix Wilfred is of the opinion that the language of uniqueness "has its presuppositions and epistemological background, and it is not clear that [it] could be extrapolated to other cultural areas . . . Seen from the Indian perspective, tradition and frame of reference, the need to use the language of uniqueness does not arise."[112] It is at this juncture that Gandhi's position seems to assert itself as a viable alternative to the existing set of inadequate positions.

'Satyo-centrism' Applied to Christological Pluralism

Gandhi believed that the followers of different religions must live the unique features of their religions and not merely keep on narrating them to their advantage. Gandhi did examine the Christian claims of uniqueness attributed to Jesus using such words as 'begotten', 'son of God' and the like. It is after a careful and prayerful examination of such claims that he concluded that it is pompous to speak about them as indicating the greatness of Christianity. He wrote:

> We may each of us be putting our own interpretation on the word God – God who embraces not only this tiny globe of ours, but millions and billions of such globes. How can we, little crawling creatures, so utterly helpless as He has made us, how could we possibly measure His greatness, His boundless love, His infinite compassion, such that He allows man insolently to deny Him, wrangle about Him, and cut the throat of his fellowman?[113]

The very concept of incarnation and death on the cross implies limitation. "He, of His own accord limits Himself. He died on the cross because He was limited by the flesh."[114] Again he argues: "God has the whole humanity as his children. How can I limit God's grace by my little mind and say that this is the only way?"[115] Further, the words 'begotten' and 'son of God' ascribed to Jesus, according to Gandhi means that Jesus was nearer and the most experienced of God. Gandhi wrote: "To me, it (the word 'begotten') implies a spiritual birth. My interpretation, in other words, is that in Jesus' own *life* is the key of his nearness to God; that he expressed, as no other could, the spirit and will of God. It is in this sense that I see him and recognize him as the son of God."[116] Elsewhere Gandhi said:

> I regard Jesus as a great teacher of humanity, but I do not regard him as the only begotten son of God. That epithet, in its material interpretation, is quite unacceptable. Metaphorically, we are all begotten sons of God, but for each of us there may be different begotten sons of God in a special sense. Thus, for me, Chaitanya may be the only begotten son of God.[117]

Moreover, Gandhi argued that the literal meaning of the word 'begotten son of God' goes against reason. For, he said,

> God can't marry and beget children. The word 'son' there can only be used in a figurative sense (in a spiritual sense). In that sense

> everyone, who stands in the position of Jesus, is a begotten son of God. If a man is spiritually miles ahead of us, we may say that he is in a special sense, the son of God, though we are all children of God. We repudiate the relationship on our lives, whereas his life is a witness to that relationship.[118]

In this way, Gandhi refused to accept a literal meaning to the term 'begotten'. "The adjective 'begotten' has for me a deeper and possibly a grander meaning than its literal meaning. For me it implies spiritual birth. In his own times he was the nearest to God."[119]

Regarding the doctrine of atonement of Christ, Gandhi showed that the redemption by Christ is meaningless to an individual unless he/she decides to change his/her sinful life. This attitude is well brought about in his conversation with one of the Plymouth Brothers in South Africa. Looking at Gandhi's scrupulous way of life, the Plymouth Brother once told Gandhi that he could never have peace. The perfection of his belief, according to the Plymouth Brother, is that as he believes in the atonement of Jesus, his own sins do not bind him. He says: "Sin we must. It is impossible to live in this world sinless. And therefore Jesus suffered and atoned for all the sins of mankind. Only he who accepts His great redemption can have eternal peace. Think what a life of restlessness is yours and what a promise of peace we have."[120]

However, Gandhi was not convinced by the arguments given by the Plymouth Brother regarding the uniqueness of Christianity in respect of the atonement theory. Gandhi said that he did not seek redemption from the consequence of his sin. Rather he sought to be redeemed from sin itself, or rather from the very thought of sin. "Until I have attained that end," says Gandhi, "I shall be content to be restless."[121] This does not mean that Gandhi disbelieved in the redemption wrought by Christ. He maintained that Jesus atoned for the sins of those who accepted his teachings by being an infallible example to them. But "the example was worth nothing to those who never troubled to change their lives."[122]

Therefore, Gandhi held that the *raison d'etre* of Christianity is to make the possibility of life, death and resurrection of Jesus a reality in the life of Christians and in the social structures that surround them and not merely to repeat that historical event. What is more important, according to Gandhi, is not to preach Christ as a historical truth but to show how he affects one's life here and now. ". . . God did not bear the Cross only 1900 years ago, but He bears it today. It would be poor comfort to the world if it had to depend upon a historical God who died 2000 years ago. Do not then preach the God of history, but show Him as He lives today through you."[123] Elsewhere, Gandhi says; "Living Christ means a living Cross; without it, life is living death."[124]

Again, Gandhi held that different religions could never be based purely on historical figures and personalities. If religion were to be based on history, "faith would be undermined."[125] "Divine knowledge is not something, which can be borrowed from historical books. Rather it has to be realised in oneself. Books are at best an aid, often even a hindrance."[126] Instead, Gandhi's emphasis was on that aspect of living out one's Truth.[127]

This does not mean that for Gandhi, truth-living is to be simply taken as a life-oriented message. He did give due importance to theorization/theologization of the message. The truth-living should also pursue a doctrinal framework, which will explain and confine the life-orientation in one's life. In his understanding, each doctrinal framework, or for that matter each religious framework, is a relative truth. Referring it to the Absolute Truth, we can validate each one of them. Gandhi not only spoke of truth in its absolute sense, but also believed that every religion contains Absolute Truth. For Gandhi held, "Truth or Revelation is present in every religion because they all are based on common fundamentals, they have produced great saints."[128] It implies that "Revelation (Truth) is the exclusive property of no nation, no tribe."[129] In this way, Gandhi argued that recognition of uniqueness in every religion means acceptance of the presence of Absolute Truth in every religion. He gives paramount importance to the core of religions, namely, living the claims in actual life-context. In so far as any theory contributes to life-Attainment/Perfection/Transcendence, it is 'validatable' because the actual living of the truth vindicates the claim of truth.

Applying this epistemological criterion to the variety of the Christological theories, we can say that each of them will be a relative truth. Any theological position regarding the uniqueness of Christ can be valid provided that it re-enacts the Christ-event (birth, death and resurrection of Christ) everyday in our actual life-context. In other words, Gandhi's position seems to provide us with a criterion to gauge the variety of responses to the Christological concerns and establish the validity of each one of them. In so far as the varied Christological typologies help their respective adherents to approximate their life to the Absolute Truth, they can be validated and hence need not be rejected. This approximation to the Absolute Truth means whether these typologies can effect life-transformation in the lives of the proponents whereby giving them the opportunities to become saints. After all, the harvest of saints found in each religion is the sure sign of the presence of Absolute Truth. Hence every position is judged not so much from the perspective of speculation or logic as from the fact of saints.

Such an understanding of truth is possible because, for Gandhi, truth has not only epistemological bearings but also has metaphysical ramifications as discussed in the second chapter. His concept of *satya,* which is derived from S*at* meaning the existent or Reality, is not only truth-affirmation but also Truth in itself. In other words, it is a reality to be lived as well as a reality in itself. This position of Gandhi differs from Michael Amaladoss, who understood truth only as truth-affirmation. For Amaladoss, reality and truth "are not the same, though they are related. We normally characterize affirmations as true. An affirmation is considered true when what it says corresponds to what is in reality."[130]. Hence he claimed that truth can be many. "We predict truth, not about reality-in-itself, but about affirmation concerning it."[131] However, he agrees that every truth need not be plural. "There need not be a pluralism in affirmations of simple facts. As soon as reality is in some way related to the human then there are reasons for possible pluralism."[132] In making this distinction between reality and truth, Amaladoss runs into the danger of making reality to be misunderstood and misrepresented. It can mean either noumenon or phenomenon, and if it is noumenon, it cannot be known at all. Further, he reduced the connotation of truth, by understanding it only in the epistemological sense[133]. But for Gandhi, it is truth (transformed life) that validates reality (the Absolute Truth). Likewise, any theory (truth-affirmation) can be validated provided it is oriented to the Absolute Truth (the Reality). In other words, it is through 'satyo-centrism' that we are able to appreciate various Christological typologies concerning the uniqueness of Christ.

'Satyo-centrism' Applied to Religious Pluralism

All that we have discussed in the preceding section about the theological pluralism of Christological concerns is just an illustration. If we apply Gandhi's position of truth to religious pluralism, we can justifiably say that each one of the varied religions is 'validatable' provided that it enables its respective believers to approximate the

Absolute Truth in their own life-contexts – cultural, historical, societal and national. In fact, Gandhi argues that all religions are valid since all of them have produced great saints.

It then follows that, the variety of religions are the varied relative truths, in so far as they all relate themselves to Absolute Truth and concretise It in the variety of life-situations and hence valid. If this is right then no religion (relative truth) can claim superiority over any other religion (another relative truth) merely on the basis of its acclaimed uniqueness. Hence, Gandhi pleaded with the Christian missionaries not to blindly assert the uniqueness of Christianity but rather adopt an open-minded and humble approach to the problem of religious pluralism. What was said by Gandhi to the missionaries of the past may be applicable to today's Christian theologians as well. He wrote:

> Do not flatter yourselves with the belief that a mere recital of that celebrated verse in St. John[134] makes a man a Christian. If I have read the Bible correctly, I know many men who have never heard the name of Jesus Christ or have even rejected the official interpretation of Christianity, will, probably, if Jesus came in our midst today in the flesh, be owned by him more than many of us. I, therefore, ask you to approach the problem before you with open-mindedness and humility.[135]

Gandhi also held that there is no point in proving the uniqueness of the fact of Christ by comparing it with that of the founders of other religions.

> The simple reason is that we have no data. Historically, we have more data about Mohammed than anyone else because he was more recent in time. For Jesus, there is less data and still less for Buddha, Rama and Krishna; and when we know so little about them, is it not preposterous to say that one of them was more divine than another? In fact, even if there were a great data available, no judge should shoulder the burden of sifting all the evidence, if only for this reason that it requires a highly spiritual person to gauge the degree of divinity of the subjects he examines. To say that Jesus was 99 percent divine, and Mohammed 50 percent, and Krishna 10 percent, is to arrogate to oneself a function, which really does not belong to me.[136]

Hence, uniqueness of Jesus is to be re-lived in the life of the followers and not to be compared. Comparisons are unnecessary for comprehending the person of Jesus and his impact. A mother occasionally may make a claim that she has sacrificed all her health for her children's sake. Sometimes, it is a claim of unique love too. Does this mean that the children must compare her claim with the claims of other mothers in order to see her impact on them? So also the unique claim of Jesus is made to evoke one's utter commitment to Him. If one realises these claims in their proper context, one would all the more be challenged to live a more dedicated and committed life of utter discipleship to this master. Without realising this, if believers were trying to compare these claims of the master with the claims of other masters or speculate about them, one would be not only missing the point but also making an unwarranted exercise. Similarly, every religious tradition must re-live its unique features instead of comparing them with unique the features of other religions.

After all, diversity of faiths is a necessity. "Though all soils have the same predominant characteristics, we know that the same seeds do not fare equally well in all soils."[137] Faith, according to Gandhi, must be tested according to the diverse conditions and not imposed simply.

> Surely it is a dangerous thing to present it to those who have been brought up in a different belief. And it would appear to me to be impertinent on my part to present my untested belief to the professor of another which, for ought I know, may be as true as mine. It is highly likely that mine may be good for me and his for him. A thick woollen coat would be the best thing for one living in the cold regions of the earth, just as a piece of loincloth for another living near the equatorial regions.[138]

Further, the revealed truth must share the imperfection of the medium through which it is revealed. "The divine Light having been vouchsafed to all religions through an imperfect medium of flesh, they must share in more or less degree the imperfection of the vehicles."[139] Besides, for an infinite God, only one way is impossible. "Because you adore your mother, you cannot wish that all the rest were your mother's children. Just as that is a physical impossibility this one is a spiritual impossibility. God has the whole humanity as His children. How can I limit God's grace by my little mind and say this is the only way?"[140] Each religion has its own attractions to its votaries. Thus, Gandhi said: "Hinduism, with its message of Ahimsa is to me the most glorious religion in the world – as my wife to me is the most beautiful woman in the world – but others may feel the same about their own religion."[141]

Therefore, Gandhi was of the opinion that what is important is not the speculative claim about Christ's uniqueness, but doing God's will as uniquely as Jesus Christ did. Gandhi says: "If Jesus came to earth again, he would disown many things that are being done in the name of Christianity. It is not he who says 'Lord, Lord' that is a Christian, but 'He that doeth the will of the Lord' that is a true Christian. And cannot he who has not heard the name of Christ Jesus do the will of the Lord?"[142]

Again quoting Matthew 7:21, Gandhi told a Christian friend who wanted to convert him:

> "It not he who says to me, 'Lord, Lord,' ... who enters the Kingdom of Heaven, but he that doeth His will." I reminded him: "I am conscious of my weaknesses and try to fight them, - not in my own strength but in the strength of God. Is that enough or do you wish me to repeat parrot-like that Jesus had cleansed me from all sin?"[143]

In fact, this is the crux of being a Christian. But this can be practised even by a non-Christian, and hence, all religions are fundamentally the same.

In doing the will of God, which for Gandhi is nothing but truth-living, one can give real witness to his/her God, which is Truth, and to His teachings. "Spiritual life has greater potency than Marconi waves. When there is no medium between me and my Lord and I simply become a willing vessel for His influence to flow into it, then I overflow as the water of the Ganges at its source. There is no desire to speak when one lives the Truth. Truth is most economical of words. There is thus no truer or other evangelism than life."[144]

Gandhi also lamented the exclusive attitude of Christians towards other religious traditions. He wrote: "Today they tell people that there is no salvation for them except through the Bible and through Christianity. It is customary to decry other religions and to offer their own as the only one that can bring deliverance. This attitude must be radically changed."[145] He called for a more sympathetic and broader outlook on the part of Christian missionaries while relating to people of other religious traditions accepting them as fellow pilgrims in their journey towards the divine abode.

To wipe out exclusivistic attitude among religions, Gandhi rejected any literal interpretation given to scriptures. He held that literal interpretation given to select passages of the scriptures could generate a claim of superiority of one religion over another. He, therefore, said that it is wrong to give literal meaning to some texts of the Bible, for example, in spite of its own clear statement that "the letter killeth, the spirit giveth life."[146] In rejecting the literal interpretation of scriptures, Gandhi did not imply that the writers of scriptures were untruthful persons. "They wrote in a mood of exaltation ... I learnt the art of estimating the value of scriptures on the basis of their ethical teaching."[147] Therefore, Gandhi is of the opinion that one must follow the criteria of truth and non-violence in interpreting the scriptures. He wrote: "I apply the test of Truth and Ahimsa laid down by these very scriptures for interpretation. I reject what is inconsistent with that test, and I appropriate all that is consistent with it."[148] He also promoted other criteria for interpreting the scriptures like reason and morality. Gandhi said: "I would reject all scriptural authority if it is in conflict with sober reason or the dictates of the heart."[149] Regarding the morality criterion, Gandhi wrote: "That which is opposed to the fundamental maxims of morality, that which is opposed to trained reason, cannot be claimed as Shastra no matter how ancient it may be."[150] Finally, when there are subjects where reason cannot take one far, one has to accept things in faith. "Faith then does not contradict reason but transcends it."[151]

In this way, Gandhi held that it is obligatory for believers, Christians for example, to live the unique claims of Christianity through the re-enactment and re-living of Christ's life, death and resurrection in their concrete life-situations. To put it broadly, truth-living of a Christian amounts to doing God's will with utmost commitment even to the total debasement of self. This view of Gandhi appears to be corroborated by Dr. Israel Selvanayagam, who remarked, "When Jesus claimed that he was the way and no one could come to the Father except by him, what he meant was not a spatial or geographical passage but a window to understand the will of God the Father at a time of crisis and confusion"[152] for the disciples. Otherwise, he argues, millions of people before and after Christ who in some way had an experience of God will be excluded. It also affirms that God is not only the Father of Jesus but also the Father of all.[153]

Such a possibility is available to believers of every religion. This implies that what is important is not which religion one belongs to, but rather how one lives one's religion. In other words, a constant growth towards holiness irrespective of one's religious tradition is of utmost value to Gandhi. "My constant prayer ... is for a Christian or a Mussalman to be a better Christian and a better Mohammedan. I am convinced, I know, that God will ask, asks us now, not what we label ourselves, but what we are, i.e., what we do. With Him *deed* is everything; *belief* without deed is nothing. With Him, doing is believing."[154] Hence Gandhi criticized the Christian scholars for unduly defending themselves upon their unique claims.

Truth-living also implies that life witness is proclamation and not vice versa. Proclamation of one's religious uniqueness must be patterned after the "Gospel of the Rose,"[155] that is, live the truth that one professes to establish the fragrance of uniqueness in one's life and then, the fragrance will spread itself spontaneously and naturally. Hence Gandhi writes:

> To live the gospel is the most effective way – most effective in the beginning, in the middle and in the end. Preaching jars on me and makes no appeal to me, and I get suspicious of missionaries who preach. But I love those who never preach but live the life according to their lights. Their lives are silent, yet most effective, testimonies. Therefore I cannot say what to preach, but I can say that a life of service and uttermost simplicity is the best preaching.[156]

Another implication of truth-living is that there is a need to transcend theology in order to bring about real transformation of one's life. To put it in the words of Gandhi:

> All I can say is that there should be less theology and more of truth in all that you say and do.... Amongst agents of the many untruths that are propounded in the world one of the foremost is theology. I do not say that there is no demand for it. There is a demand in the world for many a questionable thing. But even those who have to do with theology as part of their work have to survive their theology.[157]

Hence Gandhi's emphasis is not so much on theology as on the living of the tenets of religion. This is because Gandhi held that theology is not spirituality. "We often confuse spiritual knowledge with spiritual attainment. Spirituality is not a matter of knowing scriptures and engaging in philosophical discussions. It is a matter of heart culture, of immeasurable strength."[158]

In this way, by appealing to the essence of religion, namely, living a life approximating the Absolute Truth, Gandhi was able to point out the futility of different religions' claims to superiority over others. This Absolute Truth is found in all the religions as they all have produced saints. Hence all religions are equal. Therefore, what is important for the believers is that they should live the acclaimed unique features of their religions that they subscribe to rather than narrate them. This is because even these features are validated by approximating to the Absolute Truth, and validation means effecting a life-transformation.

Similarly, since truth is a reality to be lived as well as Reality in itself, for Gandhi, metaphysically it is truth (transformed life) that validates reality (the Absolute Truth)[159]. Hence, any religion (truth-affirmation) can be validated provided it is oriented to the Absolute Truth (the Reality). And this can be proved from the fact that religions provide contexts for life-transformation to their believers. In other words, it is through 'satyo-centrism' that we are able to affirm the worth of each religion, thereby appreciating and legitimising religious pluralism.

In fine, Gandhian position of 'satyo-centrism' is indeed an epistemological and a metaphysical foundation for the theology of religions.

'Satyo-centrism' Through Meta-religion

The Gandhian foundation for the theology of religions that we have arrived at in the foregoing section will be better appreciated if we examine the concept of meta-religion or Religion understood as the Absolute Truth in its fullness. To comprehend this, we need to consider the trans-religious experience of God that Gandhi lived in his own person and inculcated among the people with whom he came in contact. It was through his experiences of God in different religions that Gandhi was able to arrive at the realm of meta-religion.

Being rooted in his own tradition and exposed to other religious traditions already as a boy, Gandhi was able to appreciate the worth of other religions. The contact with people of diverse religions, people who belonged to no-religion, and people who positively denied God, helped Gandhi to bring out a unique formulation of a trans-religious understanding of God so that he can include all his fellow-seekers, even the so-called atheists. He centred his trans-religious experience of God on Truth. It is expressed not only in his continuous and relentless search after Truth, but also in his subsequent identification of Truth with God and the final shift to 'Truth is God.' This enabled Gandhi to experience a trans-religious faith, which in turn, helped him to establish a total communion with the followers of other religions. C.F. Andrews, commenting on it, writes: "In all my many intimate talks on religion with Mahatma Gandhi, amid many divergences and shades of contrast, I have never felt that there was any difference between us with regard to this ultimate belief (in God)."[160]

Although, one can notice significant differences among religions with regard to rituals, beliefs, doctrines and practices, these are only due to cultural and historical differences. But when one gets beneath these external cultural and historical trappings and reaches the realm of trans-religion, it is clear that the teachings of religious founders are basically the same thing. "Each expressed the Truth in terms appropriate to his own time and culture, and thus we have the many external, and really quite insignificant, differences between the religions today."[161] Besides, the attainment of the fundamental goal of human life is the same for all the religions. This is evident not only from the fact that saints have emerged in all religions, but also from the fact that saints' lives are both similar in nature and parallel to each other.

All these factors enabled Gandhi to rise above the existing religions to recognize the Religion, which he prized above all other religions. This religion is not formal or customary religion, but that religion which underlies all religions, "which brings us face to face with our Maker."[162] It is not Hinduism either, but

> the religion which transcends Hinduism, which changes one's very nature, which binds one indissolubly to the truth within and which ever purifies. It is the permanent element in human nature which counts no cost too great in order to find full expression and which leaves the soul utterly restless until it has found itself, known its Maker and appreciated the true correspondence between the Maker and itself.[163]

In other words, it is the Religion or the essence of religions "which changes one's very nature, which binds one indissolubly to the truth within and which ever purifies."[164]

C.F. Andrews in his *Mahatma Gandhi's Ideas* compared Gandhian understanding of meta-religion with that of Radhakrishnan, who defined religion as "not the Religion you will get after reading all the scriptures of the world. Religion is not really that is grasped by the brain, but a heart grasp."[165] Thus true religion must transcend not only the religions of the world but also rational outlook. It is this meta-religion that Gandhi emphasized in his life. He called it the religion of truth.

When Dr. S. Radhakrishnan asked Gandhi how he is led to religion, Gandhi replied:

> "I take that the present tense (in the question) has been purposely used instead of the past. I am being led to my religion through Truth and non-violence, i.e., love in the broadest sense. I often describe my religion as religion of Truth. Of late, instead of saying God is Truth I have been saying Truth is God, in order more fully to define my Religion."[166]

The distinction between Faith and belief made by Panikkar explains the concept of meta-religion. Faith is a primal anthropological act; its very function is to open people to transcendence, salvation or liberation. It is a fundamental constitutive element of the human person. Belief, on the other hand, is the concretisation of this primordial human act in a particular, emotional, intellectual and cultural way. Faith is more than belief and, therefore, one should not identify Faith with belief. Such an identification will corrupt belief and lead it into exclusivism. Faith as a personal act is common and is at work in all authentic religions.[167]

However, Gandhi's concept of meta-religion surpasses Panikkar's view because he relates it with both morality and truth. To understand how he relates religion with morality it is important to keep in mind that one of the firm beliefs of Gandhi is that there is an ordered moral government present in the universe.[168] Rooted in this belief, Gandhi argued that the ordered moral government of the universe, which is not less real because it is unseen, should evidently bind humankind too, in so far as they form part of the universe. It is this indeed which forms the basis of human's morality. For him, "true morality consists not in following the beaten tracks, but in finding out the true path for ourselves and in fearlessly following it."[169]

Gandhi gives a simple but decisive criterion to discern the true path. "Our desires and motives may be divided into two classes – selfish and unselfish. All selfish desires are immoral while the desires to improve ourselves for the sake of doing good to others are truly moral. The highest moral law is that we should unremittingly work for the good of mankind."[170] It is through the "incessant toil in the service of ... [the] country and therethrough of humanity,"[171] that Gandhi realised the good of humankind. He had a predilection for the poor. "I have always had a love for the poor all my life and in abundance ... I have never felt that there was any difference between the poor and me. I have always felt toward them as my own kith and kin."[172] Speaking about his work among them, Gandhi says: "I see in the fellowship with them [the masses] the God I adore. I derive from that fellowship all my consolation, all my hope and all the sustaining power I possess."[173] In the light of this analysis, then, it is no wonder that Gandhi combines both truth and morality on the one hand, and truth and religion on the other. "There is no religion higher than Truth and Righteousness."[174]

Through an examination of the original meaning of the term used to refer to religion, Gandhi further establishes his point. In the Western tradition, the word religion comes from the Latin word '*religio*' which means 'that which binds' and in the Indian tradition, the word religion comes from the Sanskrit word '*dharma*' which means 'that which holds'. To quote Gandhi: "The root of religion is 'that which binds.' The root meaning of its Sanskrit equivalent *Dharma* is 'that which holds'. It sustains a person as nothing else does. It is the basis of fundamental morality. When morality incarnates itself in a living man it becomes religion, because it binds, it sustains him in the hour of trial."[175] Gandhi, in this way, lays emphasis on morality, which is the core of religion. He says: "As soon as we lose the moral basis, we cease to be religious. There is no such thing as religion overriding morality. Man, for instance, cannot be untruthful, cruel and incontinent and claim to have God on his side."[176]

Thus, in this meta-religion, Gandhi worshipped Truth as God and faith became the only means of accepting His existence. "Reason is powerless to know Him. He is beyond the reach or grasp of reason. But I need not labour the point. Faith is essential in this matter."[177] When reason fails, faith takes over. "Faith then does not contradict Reason, but transcends it. Faith is a kind of sixth sense which works in cases which are without the purview of Reason."[178] Thus Gandhi says that an immovable faith is a pre-requisite for Truth realization. For, faith rejects all that is contrary to truth and love and accepts the moral governance of the world.

His faith in Truth was so dynamic that Gandhi could see newer light of truth every day and read in them new meanings. This faith was more vital than air and water so that a collapse in faith in God implied sure death. This faith enabled Gandhi to undergo strenuous strain and stress without ever breaking down. "They that wait upon the Lord shall renew their strength: They shall ... not be weary; and they shall ... not faint."[179] Lack of faith is often due to over-attachment to ever-perishing and perishable body. "The greater the faith, the greater is the strength."[180] This faith must be lived so that it can spread its aroma like the rose its scent. For, "faith does not admit of telling. It has to be lived and then it becomes self-propagating."[181] In this way, for Gandhi faith in God became an all-embracing living force.

Although Gandhi spoke of meta-religion wherein all the religions of the world will meet and from where every religion can draw its sustenance, he was aware of the fact that different people were at different stages in the ladder of God-realization. Hence there is a need to understand the varied levels of faith among the people and to accept the variety of worships. Therefore, "people may worship Rama as the husband of Sita or as the son of Dasharatha."[182] Thus Gandhi believed in the dictum: "To each man according to his faith."[183] But since all religions are one at source, Gandhi believed that at the end of their spiritual journey, all will reach the same Cosmic Being, Truth. Therefore, Gandhi advocated an appreciation of different faiths of the people and inculcated devotion towards faith exemplars of various religious traditions.

Thus, for the theology of religions, 'satyo-centrism' becomes the most viable position. It is the most feasible theory because whereas in other theories, scholars seem to validate their positions by invalidating other theories, Gandhi validates his position by validating every other position because each position is a relative truth needing validation by approximating to the Absolute Truth. Further, so long as *satya* is understood with reference to Reality it becomes the metaphysical foundation for the theology of religions and when it is understood with reference to validation of truth-affirmation, it becomes the epistemological foundation for the theology of religions. It is also possible to resolve every other conflict that arises in the theology of religions by appealing to this criterion.

CONCLUSION

To conclude this chapter, it can be said that truth was the overriding concern of Gandhi not only in his every field of activity as it was shown in second chapter but also in his understanding of religion and in solving the issues arising out of religious plurality. Seeing every aspect of religion from the light of truth helped Gandhi to be devoted to his religion while appreciating and accepting whatever good in other religions without ever condemning them and considering them as inferior. Such an approach enabled Gandhi to notice the various accretions in his religion and strenuously worked for their removal. It also helped him to detect defects in other religions and as an honest seeker after truth, Gandhi humbly pointed them out to their followers in the hope that they may be removed. In so doing his only aim was to purify every religion of its accretions so that it can become a torch bearer to its followers in their quest for the divine.

Gandhi firmly believed that what is more important is to underscore the common features found in different religions and not so much to highlight the differences or aberrations, which he felt should be cleansed by the followers themselves. Thus every religion provides a comprehensive view of reality and a context for what Alan Race says "transcendent vision and human transformation."[184] For John Hick, the common feature shared by all religions is "common ethical ideal or a common soteriological structure."[185] These may be distinctly expressed in different religions: *Moksha* in Hinduism, *Nirvana* in Buddhism, salvation in Christianity and *Kevala* in Jainism. Yet, at a deeper level they are meant to raise people towards the Transcendent Being by enabling them to obtain Perfection/Attainment/Realization. After all, "each religion is the living expression of the souls of the vast groups of people,"[186] carrying within it the echo of thousands of years of searching for God and taught generations of people how to pray.

Religion is primarily meant for living and not so much for preaching or teaching, much less, for speculating. While theorizing it, one may formulate universal principles. But when it comes to living, it is very difficult to form such principles as they pertain to the climes, time and culture of persons and races. Therefore, any criterion suggested by the followers of a religion is mainly intended for themselves and not for others. Hence what is important is not so much what religion one belongs to, or what one happens to believe but how sincere one is with regard to one's moral and ethical life, contributing at the same time to the welfare of society at large. If at all, a religion is to be evaluated, one should not grade it in relation to other religions – their doctrines, rituals, unique features or theologies - but should identify whether that tradition is a salvific human response to the Real, and for this, one must look at the spiritual and moral fruits it produces. In the light of this criterion, it can be easily concluded that every religion constitutes a context for salvation or liberation, for each has produced its own harvest of saints. This is precisely what is summed up by 'satyo-centrism.'

NOTES

1. M.K. Gandhi, *Hindu Dharma* (New Delhi: Orient Paperbacks, 1995), pp. 18-19. Henceforth, Gandhi, Hindu Dharma.
2. Cf. *Harijan*, 13-3-1937, p. 37 at p. 39; as cited by Gandhi, In Search of the Supreme, vol. 1, pp. 27-28.
3. *Harijan*, 5-12-1936, p. 337 at p. 339; as cited by Gandhi, In Search of the Supreme, vol. 1, p. 210.
4. Gandhi, Autobiography, p. 221.
5. *Collected Works of Mahatma Gandhi*, vol. 29, pp. 443-444; as cited by Nayar, Salt Satyagraha, p. 24.
6. Cf. Louis Fischer, *The Life of the Mahatma Gandhi*, pp. 79-80; as cited by Nayar, Satyagraha at Work, p. 188.
7. Cf. Pyarelal, Early Phase, p. 198.
8. In fact, Gandhi declined to join the theosophist society on the plea that his knowledge of his own religion was very meagre. However, it was Madame Blavatsky's Key to Theosophy that led him to read books on Hinduism, which freed him of his prejudice against Hinduism fostered by the Christian missionaries.
9. Gandhi, Autobiography, pp. 57-59.
10. Pyarelal, Early Phase, p. 327.
11. Cf. Pyarelal, Early Phase, p. 546.
12. Dr. A. Pushparajan, "Resolution of an Inter-Personal Conflict in a Multi-religious Context" (Madurai: Unpublished article), p. 7.
13. In the second chapter there is brief description of Raychandbhai. However, for a detailed depiction of him, cf. Gandhi, Autobiography, reprint 1976, pp. 64-65.
14. *Young India*, 6-2-1925, p. 273.
15. Gandhi himself narrates this conflict in his Autobiography. Cf. Gandhi, Autobiography, reprint, 1976, pp. 100-102.

16. Cf. Pyarelal, The Last Phase, book 2, p. 71. The prayer meeting took place on 10 December 1946.
17. Cf. *Young India*, 6-12-1928; as cited by Gandhi, All Religions are True, p. 22.
18. *Harijan*, 30-1-1937, p. 407; as cited by Gandhi, My God, p. 36.
19. *Young India*, 4-6-1931, p. 129; as cited by Gandhi, In Search of the Supreme, vol. 3, p. 143.
20. *Harijan*, 26-5-1946; as cited by Gandhi, All Religions are True, p. 8.
21. *Harijan*, 13-3-1937, p. 38; as cited by Gandhi, My God, p. 36.
22. Gandhi, From Yeravda Mandir, p. 26.
23. *Young India*, 25-5-1921, pp. 161-162; as cited by Gandhi, My God, p. 49.
24. Gandhi, All Religions are True, p. 65.
25. *Collected Works of Mahatma Gandhi*, vol. 12, p. 84; as cited by Narayan, Selected Letters, p. 358.
26. Prayer Speech, 20-2-1947; as cited by Pyarelal, The Last Phase, book 2, p. 198.
27. *Harijan*, 2-2-1934, p. 8; Gandhi, My God, p. 36.
28. The Diary of Mahadev Desai, vol. 1, p. 120; as cited by Narayan, Selected Letters, pp. 382-383.
29. *Harijan*, 18-8-1946, p. 267; as cited by Gandhi, In Search of the Supreme, vol. 1, p. 18.
30. Pyarelal, Early Phase, p. 277.
31. *Young India*, 20-8-1925; as cited by M.K. Gandhi, *Christian Missions: Their Place in India*, ed. Bharatan Kumarappa, reprint 1960 (Ahmedabad: Navajivan Publishing House, 1941), p. 70. Henceforth, Gandhi, Christian Missions.
32. *Young India*, 23-9-1926, p. 333; as cited by Gandhi, In Search of the Supreme, vol. 3, p. 40.
33. Gandhiji's letter dated November 26, 1894, to the Natal Mercury, December 12, 1894; as cited by Pyarelal, Early Phase, p. 325.
34. *Collected Works of Mahatma Gandhi*, vol. 4, p. 409, Indian Opinion, April 15, 1905; as cited by Pyarelal, *Mahatma Gandhi – The Birth of Satyagraha – From Petitioning to Passive Resistance*, vol. 3 (Ahmedabad: Navajivan Publishing House, 1986), p. 356. Henceforth, Pyarelal, The Birth of Satyagraha.
35. *Young India*, 23-9-1926, p. 333; as cited by Gandhi, In Search of the Supreme, vol. 3, p. 39.

36. *Young India*, 26-2-1925, p. 74; as cited Gandhi, In Search of the Supreme, vol. 2, p. 24.
37. *Harijan*, 28-11-1936, p. 330; as cited by Gandhi, My God , p. 38.
38. Gandhi founded the Tolstoy Farm in 4 June 1910 to lodge the families of the satyagrahis in South Africa. The Farm which consisted of 1100 acres belonged to Mr. Kallenbach, a German who was sympathetic to the cause of the Indians.
39. Gandhi, Autobiography, p. 277.
40. Pyarelal, The Last Phase, book 1, p.101.
41. Cf. Pyarelal, The Last Phase, book 2, p. 69.
42. *Harijan*, 3-3-1946, p. 26; as cited by Pyarelal, The Last Phase, book 2, p. 69.
43. Cf. Pyarelal, The Last Phase, book 2, p. 69.
44. *Harijan*, 17-8-1947, p.281; as cited by Gandhi, In Search of the Supreme, vol. 1, pp. 200-201.
45. Cf. *Ashram Observances in Action*, (1959 Edn), chapter III; as cited by Gandhi, In Search of the Supreme, vol. 1, p. 193.
46. Cf. Pyarelal, The Last Phase, book 2, p. 164.
47. *Ashram Observances in Action*, (1959 Edn), Chapter. II; as cited by Gandhi, In Search of the Supreme, vol. 1, p. 192.
48. This is because, as already discussed in chapter two, Gandhian understanding of relative truth does not suffer from relativism. Cf. pp. 135-140.
49. Harvey Cox, *Many Mansions: A Christian's Encounter with Other Faiths* (Boston: Beacon Press, 1988), pp. 7-8. Henceforth, Cox, Many Mansions.
50. Cox, *Many Mansions*, Pp. 8-9.
51. Jaroslav Pelikan, *Jesus Through the Centuries: His Place in the History of Culture* (New Haven: Yale University Press, 1985), p. 1.
52. Wolfhart Pannenberg, "Religious Pluralism and Conflicting Truth-Claims," *The Myth of Christian Uniqueness Reconsidered: the Myth of a Pluralistic Theology of Religions*, ed. Gavin D'Costa (Maryknoll: Orbis Press and London SCM Press, 1987), p. 100.
53. Stanley J. Samartha, *Between Two Cultures: Ecumenical Ministry in a Pluralist World* (Geneva: World Council of Churches Publications, 1996), p. 127; Emphasis in the original.
54. James A. Scherer and Stephen B. Bevans, eds., *New Directions in Mission and Evangelization* 1, Basic Statements 1974-1991, chapter 14; as cited by Race, Interfaith Encounter, p. 107.

55. International Theological Commission, *Christianity and the World Religions* (Vatican: 1997), p. 15; as cited by Race, Interfaith Encounter, p. 105.
56. Richard, What are they Saying, p.1.
57. Bharatan Kumarappa, ed., *How to Serve the Cow* (Ahmedabad: Navajivan Press, 1954, reprint 1959), pp. 3-4.
58. Gandhi, Autobiography, p. 113.
59. Kalidas Nag, *Tolstoy and Gandhi* (Patna: Pustak Bhandar, 1950), p. 32.
60. John H. Leith, ed., *Creeds of the Churches*, 3rd ed. (Atlanta: John Knox Press, 1982), pp. 35-36.
61. Cf. Netland, Dissonant Voices, PP. 239-240.
62. Cf. Race, Interfaith Encounter, pp. 66-67.
63. Karl Barth, *Church Dogmatics*, vols. 1, 2 (Edinburgh: T & T. Clark, 1956), p. 297. Henceforth, Barth, Church Dogmatics.
64. Barth, Church Dogmatics, p. 327.
65. Theological Advisory Commission of the Federation of Catholic Asian Bishops' Conferences, "Seven Theses on Inter-religious Dialogue: An Essay in Pastoral Theological Reflection," reprinted in *International Bulletin of Missionary Research* 13, No. 3, July1989; as cited by Race, Interfaith Encounter, p. 72.
66. Race, Interfaith Encounter, p. 72; Emphasis in the original.
67. Cf. Race, Interfaith Encounter, pp. 72-73.
68. Cf. RM, Para. 5.
69. Fitzgerald, "Emerging Christian Theology of Religions," p. 323. This is also the official position of the Catholic Church and the Catholics subscribe to it. The only problem here is that it may not be acceptable to believers of other religious traditions as it undermines the basic equality of religions. According to Paul F. Knitter, what animated the Catholic Church to hold this view is that to lose or dilute the uniqueness of Jesus is to lose or dilute the Church's missionary identity. But it is possible to uphold uniqueness of Christ without jeopardizing both the missionary commitment of the Church and interreligious harmony. Cf. Paul F. Knitter, "The Abiding Task of the Church in Mission to Proclaim the Uniqueness of Jesus," *The Church in Mission: Universal Mandate and Local Concerns*, eds. Thomas Malipurathu and L. Stanislaus (Anand: Gujarat Sahitya Prakash, 2002), pp. 119-120. This Paper was presented at an International colloquium entitled "The Church in Mission: Universal Mandate and Local Concerns" held at Ishvani Kendra, Pune from the 24th to the 27th October 2001. Henceforth,

Knitter, "The Abiding Task of the Church in Mission."

70. Fitzgerald, "Emerging Christian Theology of Religions," p. 323.

71. Cf. Karokaran, "Raymond Panikkar's Theology of Religions," p. 664.

72. Cf. Raimundo Panikkar, *Salvation in Christ: Concreteness and Universality, The Super Name* (Santa Barbara: 1972), privately published. The main portion of these privately published lectures was reprinted as "The Meaning of Christ's Name in the Universal Economy of Salvation," *Evangelization, Dialogue and Development*, ed. Mariasusai Dhavamony (Rome, Gregorian University Press, 1972), pp. 195-218.

73. Cf. Raimundo Panikkar, *Trinity and the Religious Experience of Man* (Maryknoll: Orbis Press, 1975), pp. 53-55.

74. Cf. Raimundo Panikkar, *The Intrareligious Dialogue* (New York: Paulist Press, 1978), p. 36.

75. Dupuis, Towards a Christian Theology of Religious Pluralism, p. 387.

76. Dupuis, Towards a Christian Theology of Religious Pluralism, p. 388.

77. Dupuis, Towards a Christian Theology of Religious Pluralism, p. 388.

78. Dupuis, Towards a Christian Theology of Religious Pluralism, p. 388.

79. Depending on the models – exclusivism, inclusivism or pluralism – that the Christian theologians take in relating to other religious traditions, we can speak of different types of Christologies such as Constitutive Christology, Normative Christology, Representative Christology, etc. In the inclusive model, theologians held that the possible presences in other religions of faith, grace and salvation are brought by Christ, who is the constitutive source of salvation available both within and outside Christianity. This model envisages a Christocentric universe and a Christ who is the constitutive mediator of salvation. On the other hand, in the normative model, instead of being the constitutive mediator of salvation, Christ is the normative mediator who by the exemplary nature and fullness of the same Christ-event corrects and fulfils the other media of salvation, which remain intrinsically salvific. Therefore, he also becomes the representative mediator of salvation for other religious traditions. For further readings, cf. P. Rossano, "Christ's Lordship and Religious Pluralism," *Christ's Lordship and Religious Pluralism*, eds. G. Anderson and T. Stransky (Maryknoll, New York: 1981), pp. 96-110; A. Dulles, *Models of Revelation* (Dublin: Gill & McMillan Ltd., 1983); H. Küng, *On Being a Christian* (London: Collins, 1977); W. Bülmann, *God's Chosen Peoples* (Maryknoll, New York: 1983).

80. Race, Interfaith Encounter, p. 76; Emphasis in the original.

81. Race, Interfaith Encounter, p. 76; Emphasis in the original.

82. Paul Knitter, "Catholics and Other Religions: Bridging the Gap Between Dialogue and theology," *Louvain Studies*, 24 (1999), pp. 319-54; as cited by Race, Interfaith Encounter, p. 76.
83. John Hick, *The Metaphor of God Incarnate* (London: SCM Press, 1993), p. 106.
84. John Hick, *The Center of Christianity* (New York: Harper & Row, 1978), p. 31.
85. Cf. John Hick, "Jesus and the World Religions", *The Myth of God Incarnate*, ed. John Hick (London: SCM Press, 1977), pp. 167-178.
86. Hick, An Interpretation of Religion, p. 248.
87. Hick, An Interpretation of Religion, p. 248.
88. Hick, The Rainbow of Faiths, p. 101.
89. Cf. Hick, The Second Christianity, p. 91.
90. Cf. Hick, The Second Christianity, p. 91.
91. Cf. Hick, The Second Christianity, pp. 91-92.
92. Cf. Hick, The Second Christianity, p. 26.
93. Hick, The Second Christianity, p. 32.
94. Cf. Netland, Dissonant Voices, p. 242.
95. Knitter, No Other Name, pp. 171-172; Emphasis in the original.
96. Knitter, No Other Name, pp. 171-172; Emphasis in the original.
97. Knitter, No Other Name, p. 173.
98. Knitter, No Other Name, pp. 182.
99. Cf. Netland, Dissonant Voices, p. 250.
100. Netland, Dissonant Voices, p. 180.
101. Netland, Dissonant Voices, p. 185.
102. Krister Stendahl, "Notes for Three Bible Studies," *Christ's Lordship and Religious Pluralism*, eds. Gerald H. Anderson and Thomas F. Stranskey (Maryknoll, New York: Orbis, 1981), p. 14.
103. Knitter, No Other Name, P. 182.
104. Knitter, No Other Name, p. 183; Emphasis in the original.
105. Cf. Knitter, No Other Name, p. 255.
106. Paul F. Knitter, "Theocentric Christology: Defended and Transcended," *Journal of Ecumenical Studies* 24 (Winter 1987), p. 43.
107. Knitter, "The Abiding Task of the Church in Mission," p. 123. Emphasis in the original.

108. The Indian Theological Commission held its thirteenth annual meeting from 28-31 December 1989. Its statement was issued under the title *Towards an Indian Christian Theology of Religious Pluralism*. For the text of the statement, cf. K. Pathil, Religious Pluralism, pp. 338-349.

109. Cf. *Towards an Indian Christian Theology of Religious Pluralism*; as cited by K. Pathil, Religious Pluralism, pp. 342-346.

110. *Towards an Indian Christian Theology of Religious Pluralism*, para, 32; as cited by K. Pathil, Religious Pluralism, pp. 347-348.

111. Cf. Orlando E. Costas, "A Radical Evangelical Contribution from Latin America," *Christ's Lordship & Religious Pluralism*, eds. Gerald H. Anderson and Thomas F. Stranksy (New York, Maryknoll: Orbis Books, 1981), pp. 133-156

112. Felix Wilfred, "Some Tentative Reflections on the Language of Christian Uniqueness: An Indian Perspective," *Pro Dialogo Bulletin* 85-86 (1994) 1, p. 57.

113. *Young India*, 8-12-1927, p. 413; as cited by Gandhi, In Search of the Supreme, vol. 3, p. 336.

114. *Harijan*, 17-4-1937; as cited by Gandhi, All Religions are True, p. 49.

115. *Harijan*, 18-7-1936, p. 177 at p. 178; as cited by Gandhi, In Search of the Supreme, vol. 3, p. 24.

116. Gandhi, All Religions are True, p. 66; Emphasis added.

117. *Harijan*, 17-4-1937; as cited by Gandhi, All Religions are True, p. 49.

118. *Harijan*, 6-3-1937; as cited by Gandhi, All Religions are True, p. 47.

119. *Harijan*, 18-4-1936, p. 76; as cited by Gandhi, In Search of the Supreme, vol. 3, p. 332.

120. Gandhi, Autobiography, pp.103-104.

121. Gandhi, Autobiography, p.104.

122. *Harijan*, 18-4-1936, p. 76; as cited by Gandhi, In Search of the Supreme, vol. 3, p. 333.

123. Gandhi, Christian Missions, p. 103.

124. *Young India*, 31-12-1931; as cited by Gandhi, All Religions are True, p. 58.

125. Gandhi, All Religions are True, p. 52.

126. K. Kripalani, ed., *All Men are Brothers* (Ahmedabad: Navajivan Publishing House, 1960), p. 79. Henceforth, Kripalani, All Men are Brothers.

127. Cf. *Young India*, 26-2-1925; as cited by M. K. Gandhi, *The Teachings of the Gita*, ed. Anand T. Hingorani (Bombay: Bharatiya Vidya Bhavan, 1971), p. 35.

128. *Young India*, 22-12-1927; as cited by Gandhi, All Religions are True, p. 2.

129. *Young India*, 25-8-1924; as cited by Gandhi, All Religions are True, p. 25.

130. Amaladoss, Making Harmony, p. 92.

131. Amaladoss, Making Harmony, p. 116.

132. Amaladoss, Making Harmony, p. 116.

133. For Amaladoss defined truth as a correspondence between reality and affirmation obtained through perception, inference, testimony, etc. Cf. Amaladoss, Making Harmony, p. 116, pp. 93-94. One reason for this narrow understanding of the term truth is that Amaladoss does not consider the term truth in its Sanskrit equivalent satya nor does he attempt to derive the root meaning of the term truth from the Sanskrit root sat. Hence Gandhian understanding of truth seems to be superior.

134. The celebrated verse in St. John is 3:16. For Gandhi writes elsewhere about missionary activities: "If therefore, you go on serving people and ask them also to serve, they would understand. But you quote instead John 3:16 and ask them to believe it. That has no appeal to me, and I am sure people will not understand it." Gandhi, All Religions are True, p. 89; *Harijan*, 18-9-1936.

135. *Young India*, 6-8-1925, p. 273; Gandhi, All Religions are True, p. 76; Gandhi, In Search of the Supreme, vol. 3, pp. 327-328.

136. *Harijan*, 17-4-1937; as cited by Gandhi, All Religions are True, p. 48.

137. *Harijan*, 13-3-1937; as cited by Gandhi, All Religions are True, p. 113.

138. *Harijan*, 28-9-1935, p. 260; as cited by Gandhi, In Search of the Supreme, vol. 3, p. 65.

139. *Young India*, 21-3-1929; as cited by Gandhi, All Religions are True, p. 88.

140. *Harijan*, 18-7-1936; as cited by Gandhi, All Religions are True, p. 93.

141. *Young India*, 19-1-1928; as cited by Gandhi, All Religions are True, p. 84.

142. *Harijan*, 11-5-1935; as cited by Gandhi, Christian Missions, p. 107.

143. *Young India*, 18-6-1925; as cited by Gandhi, All Religions are True,

p. 79.

144. *Harijan*, 12-12-1936; as cited by Gandhi, All Religions are True, pp. 98-99.

145. *Harijan*, 14-7-1947; as cited by Gandhi, All Religions are True, p. 101.

146. *Harijan*, 18-4-1936, p. 76; as cited by Gandhi, In Search of the Supreme, vol. 3, p. 332. In fact, Gandhi here quotes from the New Testament, 2 Cor 3: 6.

147. *Harijan* 18-4-1936; as cited by Gandhi, All Religions are True, p. 19.

148. Gandhi, Hindu Dharma, p. 39.

149. *Young India*, 8-12-1920, p. 3; as cited by Gandhi, In Search of the Supreme, vol. 1, p. 112.

150. *Young India*, 20-10-1927, p. 352; as cited by Gandhi, In Search of the Supreme, vol. 1, p. 113.

151. *Harijan*, 6-3-1937, p. 25; as cited by Gandhi, In Search of the Supreme, vol. 3, p. 18.

152. Israel Selvanayagam, "Re-reading John 14:6 in the Context of Two Recent Events in the United Kingdom," *Current Dialogue*, 40 (December 2002), p. 48. Henceforth, Selvanayagam.

153. Cf. Selvanayagam, p. 48.

154. *Young India*, 4-9-1924; as cited Gandhi, All Religions are True, p. 59; Emphasis in the original.

155. By "Gospel of the Rose," Gandhi meant the following: " . . . let your life speak to us, even as the rose needs no speech but simply spreads its perfume. Even the blind . . . do not see the rose . . . But the Gospel that Jesus preached is more subtle and fragrant than the Gospel of the Rose. If the rose needs no agent, much less does the Gospel of Christ need any agent." *Harijan*, 17-4-1937; as cited by Gandhi, All Religions are True, p. 119.

156. *Harijan*, 29-3-1935; as cited by Gandhi, Christian Missions, p. 165.

157. *Harijan*, 23-3-1940, p. 54; as cited by Gandhi, In Search of the Supreme, vol. 3, p. 334. Gandhi made these comments when a group of Christian leaders visited him at Sevagram and requested his guidance as leaders of Christian thought.

158. Kripalani, All Men are Brothers, p. 102.

159. Repetition is necessary here.

160. *Mahatma Gandhi's Ideas*, London, 3rd Impression, 1949; as cited by J. Thekkinedatu, *Love of Neighbour in Mahatma Gandhi* (Alwaye: Pontifical Institute of Theology and Philosophy, 1973), p. 37. For

further readings on Gandhian understanding of trans-religious God, cf. A. Pushparajan, "Gandhi's Contributions to a Trans-religious Understanding of God", *Shepherd's Voice*, 1 (October-December, 2002), 4, 344-366.

161. Netland, Dissonant Voices, p. 3.

162. Bharatan Kumarappa, *My Religion* (Ahmedabad; Navajivan Publishing House, 1955, reprint 1976), p. 3. Henceforth, Kumarappa, My Religion.

163. *Young India*, 12-5-1920, p. 2; as cited by Gandhi, In Search of the Supreme, vol. 2, p. 242.

164. *Young India*, 12-5-1920; as cited by Kumarappa, My Religion, p. 3.

165. C.F. Andrews, *Mahatma Gandhi's Ideas* (London: George Allen and Unwin Ltd., 1930), p. 110.

166. *Fellowship of Faiths and Unity of Religions*, by M.K. Gandhi, edited by Prof. Abdul Majid Khan, p. 52; as cited by Gandhi, In Search of the Supreme, vol. 2, p. 265.

167. Cf. Karokaran, "Raymond Panikkar's Theology of Religions," pp. 664-665.

168. Cf. A. Pushparajan, "A Gandhian Blueprint for Interreligious Cooperation in India," *Kristu Jyoti*, 6 (March 1990) 1, pp.25-26.

169. M.K. Gandhi, *Ethical Religion* (Madras: S. Ganesan and Co., 1938), p. 38. Henceforth, Gandhi, Ethical Religion.

170. Gandhi, Ethical Religion, p. 36.

171. *Young India*, 3-4-1924, p. 113; as cited by Gandhi, In Search of the Supreme, vol. 2, p. 260.

172. *Harijan*, 11-5-1935, p. 97 at p. 99; as cited by Gandhi, In Search of the Supreme, vol. 2. p. 274.

173. *Young India*, 7-1-1926, p. 274; as cited by Gandhi, In Search of the Supreme, vol. 2, p. 274.

174. Gandhi, Ethical Religion, p. 49.

175. *Harijan*, 26-1-1934, p. 7.

176. *Young India*, 24-11-1921, p. 385.

177. *Young India*, 21-1-1926; as cited by Gandhi, Truth is God, p. 12.

178. *Harijan*, 6-6-1937; as cited by Gandhi, All Religions are True, p. 47.

179. *Young India*, 20-12-1928, p. 420; as cited by Pyarelal, The Last Phase, book 2, p. 113.

180. Pyarelal Papers: *Gandhiji's Letters to Kallenbach*; as cited by Nayar, Satyagraha at Work, p. 436.

181. *Young India*, 20-10-1927, p. 352; as cited by Gandhi, In Search of the Supreme, vol. 1, p.112.
182. *Harijan*, 22-9-1946, p. 323; as cited by Gandhi, In Search of the Supreme, vol. 1, p. 215.
183. *Harijan*, 22-9-1946, p. 323; as cited by Gandhi, In Search of the Supreme, vol. 1, p. 215.
184. Race, Interfaith Encounter, p.3.
185. John Hick, "On Grading Religions," *Religious Studies*, 17 (1981) pp. 464-65.
186. Jose Thachil, "Theology of Religions and Sacrifice," Journal of Dharma, 14 (October – December 1989) 3, pp. 329-330.

4

CONCLUDING REMARKS

Gandhi's relentless search after Truth, the Absolute, his understanding of Truth as Relative, his formulation of 'Truth is God' instead of 'God is Truth' and his application of it in every aspect of his life made the concept of truth a powerful instrument for tackling the problems of religious pluralism.

It is by analysing this concept in all its ramifications that the notion of truth is proposed as both epistemological and metaphysical foundation for the theology of religions. By this it is possible to defuse the varied issues raised in interreligious encounters not only because truth is acceptable to all, but also because it serves as a common base for both epistemology and metaphysics of religions.

John Hick posited a Copernican revolution in epistemology of religions. But, Gandhi went beyond it and embraced a truth-centred world-view of religions, which serves as an axis and a pivot for the theology of religions. It avoids the pitfalls of the different theories such as theocentric model, which in essence is very restricted in its perspective in as much as it caters mainly to the monotheistic traditions and the Reality-centred model, which is less explicable.

'Satyo-centrism,' while rejecting the absolutist tendency of exclusivism, respects every religious tradition without stipulating any special revelatory advantage to any of the religions as held by inclusivism. On the contrary, the concept of truth raises religions from their narrow parochial moorings to a more universal and a real catholic outlook wherein each religion is in a position to understand, learn and be enriched by other religions, while at the same time safeguarding its own individuality and identity. *Satya*, understood as a criterion of validation of truth-affirmations of all the religions, is a credible epistemological foundation for the theology of religions.

Ontologically, Gandhi's *satya* is also the absolute. In granting a metaphysical status to the one, universal Truth, Gandhi discarded the usual exclusive garb that pervades Western understanding of truth, which is often epistemological in nature. In its absolute sense, Gandhi equated Truth with God and made it as the only reality that exists in itself and by itself. In doing so, his understanding of the absolute became more intelligible than the existing metaphysics of religions, which is at best Aristotelian by origin and Christian by adoption. Besides, being unacceptable to other religious traditions, the Western systems are based on the logic of 'either-or,' which by its very nature is exclusive. It not only differs from the Eastern logic of 'and-and' but also overlooks the religious traditions that are non-Semitic and so-called non-monotheistic. Further, the ontological status of the absolute in every religion is debatable and is often acceptable only to the members of that particular religion. However, Truth in its absolute sense with its identification with God provides a better acceptability and ambience for interreligious fellowship. In other words, *satya* understood with reference to Reality, serves as the metaphysical foundation for the theology of religions.

The distinctive feature of this new category of 'satyo-centrism' proposed in this book is that, it does not exclude the existing ones, as if these are inferior and totally to be rejected. The new category is not hierarchically superior to any of the earlier ones. Instead, it percolates into all other models and removes the exclusive tendencies found in them so that it is possible to accept and appreciate religious variety and to live in religious harmony and fellowship. This is because every category becomes a relative truth needing approximation with the Absolute Truth.

Thus, it is possible for millions of devotees of Krishna and Rama to have their lives transformed through their contemplation of God by these names, through the different types of *puja* and through the moral codes connected with the different traditions. How this phenomenon happens one does not know. It is a mystery. One need not attempt to prove it. But the very fact of saints in every religious tradition proves the validity of that tradition. This also implies that genuine and sincere seekers must be allowed and encouraged to pursue the path that is manifest to them so that the fruits of their search will be made available to the wide following of Truth in the globe.

Likewise, one who accepts the Christocentric model can identify oneself with 'satyo-centrism' without ever giving up one's faith in Christ as the Saviour but shedding away the exclusivistic tendency. This is because truth-oriented life is boundless and is ever widening. Christ is to be seen as Truth not in the narrow or dogmatic sense or in the limited propositional form but in a more comprehensive sense, with all its implications for transforming one's personal life as well as societal structures as Gandhi understood and lived the concept of truth. Besides, the identification of God as Truth does not nullify the use of God as Christ by Christians.

Similarly, Christians need not give up the model of Church-centredness but in the new light of 'satyo-centric' approach, the Church must be open to accept other ways of salvation and legitimately uphold its own way of salvation and its mission. In this way, every condemnatory or exclusive approach or even the fulfilment approaches will have to be changed in the light of truth as evolved by Gandhi.

'Satyo-centrism,' if adopted by believers, will have serious repercussion in the understanding of theology itself. Till now, theology has been construed as faith seeking understanding of God, as manifest in one's own tradition. But now, theology has to be faith-seeking understanding of God who is present in the plurality of religious traditions. Theology, therefore, can no longer afford to ignore the Truth-manifestations of others religious traditions. Instead it has to study how best the different seekers can share their sacred legacy mutually and to cooperate with one another in making this world a better place to live in. In fact, every religious tradition is unique and every believer will have to accept that it has something to contribute by way of insights and values to the totality of spiritual heritage of human species.

Further, the prevalent practice of theologians has been to argue for one or other typology by giving innumerable reasons for supporting the particular typology. Gavin D'Costa, for example, is of the opinion that the inclusivistic position alone is capable of holding together and harmonizing the two traditional axioms of Christian faith that remain obligatory for any Christian theology of religions. On the one hand, Jesus Christ is clearly asserted to be God's decisive revelation and constitutive Saviour. On the other hand, the door is open to a sincere acknowledgement of divine manifestations in the history of humanity in various cultures and of efficacious "elements of grace" to be found in other religious traditions: elements that are salvific for their members. Revealed in a decisive manner in Jesus Christ, God (and the mystery of salvation) is nonetheless present and at work in other religious traditions. Thus the inclusivist Gavin claims to prove that pluralism and exclusivism need to be rejected. Likewise, it is possible for a pluralist theologian like John Hick by using the same weapon of argumentation to show that exclusivism and inclusivism are equally to be rejected, for inclusivism, the pluralist argues, excludes the independent existence of other religions and exclusivism accepts Christianity as the only valid religion.

This kind of play by reason only establishes the fact that reason is indeed a poor tool of analysis in matters of religion and faith. In fact, reason is not the basis for faith. Faith is something primordial and is given to people 'from above' as gratuitous gift and not something to be acquired by effort. Millions of people live their religious commitment not because they read theological treatises nor because they are taught theology but simply because of a deep inner conviction that their commitment is to their advantage and that, as far as their experiences go, they were never let down because of this faith in the divine. Their faith is not born out of any reason. It is similar to what happens in friendship and love, wherein the fidelity of the beloved is not based on things or gestures or reasons given, but on a belief that the beloved is someone precious and unique who can love and be loved. This is because even if things or gestures are withdrawn, the friendship still continues. In other words, friendship is above reason and understanding. Much more, is so, in matters of religion. People may perform the religious rites because their priests have asked them to do so. They may not even question him or his authenticity; instead they may believe that their priest does everything for their good and ask them to do only those things, which will bring upon them the blessings of the divine. Reason may not help the blind faith of the people. No kind of a doctrinal system is necessary for these people who simply accept a particular way of life on the complete faith in the veracity of the guru.

However, reason has a role in faith. When one gets doubts regarding one's faith or in matters of rituals, one needs to look for reasons for sustaining one's faith. Again, when someone's faith is destabilized, then one needs a rational basis to revitalize that shattered faith. The reason for this is that faith that is in doubt is no more faith. Now, there can also be different levels of doubts depending on the nature of the people. To remove these levels of doubts, we also need different levels of arguments and reasons. A simple kind of doctrinal system is sufficient for those who raise certain simple doubts. But a more sophisticated kind of doctrinal system can alone remove the doubts of a particular kind of people whose minds are inundated with doubts of a particular category. An entirely different kind of doctrinal system may appeal to a different category of people who had raised a completely different kind of doubts. Thus different kinds of doctrinal or theological systems are bound to arise, depending upon the different categories of doubts and the grades of sophistication with which those doubts have been cleared. This means that pluralism of theologization is bound to be present so long as there are pluralist levels of doubts and sophistications.

Further, it should be inferred from the above considerations that arguments could be of help depending on the levels of doubt that exist in people's mind. Those who have less number of doubts do not require a series of arguments to revitalize their faith while those who have more doubts will require a high level of argumentation. In other words, not everyone needs the same level of argumentation. This implies that theology is not pursued for its own sake but only when doubts arise. Hence there will be variation in the growth of theology. Therefore, we cannot speak of any superiority or inferiority of theological systems based on arguments. This in turn will imply that no system of theologization is superior to any other.

The only way to estimate a particular theological system or to judge the value of a theology is to see whether it has helped people in removing their doubts regarding faith and helped them in leading a life of truth. In other words, the 'satyo-centric' life-style is the real criterion in evaluating a theology and not the length or consistency of arguments that it generates.

Not all human beings have doubts about one and the same point. For some people, some points are taken for granted, for others they are precisely the point of contest. For still others, some points are crucial while for some others they may be trivial. According to the starting point of doubt and the gravity of the doubt the sophistication will also vary. For example, Gavin D'Costa argued for inclusivism. For, it tries to do full justice to the two most important Christian axioms: that salvation comes through God in Christ alone, and that God's salvific will is truly universal. Here, Gavin D'Costa is not raising any question about other truths regarding religions; his reasoning may not need the sophistication concerned with those truths. Instead he is very much interested in those two maxims as axiomatic of Christian faith. Hence his effort at sophistication will be centring on the question of how to safeguard them. Accordingly he will be attached only to that *ism* that explains his difficulty and in this case, it is inclusivism. For somebody else those two axioms may not seem to be the crucial points of his/her faith but something else, say, for instance, how to be a 'child of God' in order to enter into God's kingdom. This means inclusivism will not be that relevant to him/her, but rather, a different *ism* that will fulfil his/her search in a satisfactory manner.

Irrespective of the point of doubt, and level of sophistication, what is absolutely necessary in religious search is the truth-living of one's faith and attaining self-realisation, transcendence and transformation. This will be the measuring rod for judging the various theories of religions. It also implies that one can never say that a religious person who lacks a complex theoretical system is rather primitive in his/her life of religiosity as against another who has a more sophisticated system to back his/her life of faith. If at all the former is to be called primitive, he/she may be so with respect to sophistication, but this does not warrant the conclusion that his/her life of religiosity is primitive. Actually, he/she may be far more capable of tackling the fundamental predicament of human life than another person who may have a more sophisticated way of arguing in favour of his/her religious beliefs, but has not put them into practice. In other words, from the point of view of religiosity no particular system of doctrines or beliefs can be judged to be better or worse, as compared with another set of religious doctrines, although from the point of sophistication one belief-system may be superior to another.

Besides, even a paradigm shift in theology does not mean anything. At times, even the old paradigm may be useful. Thus, although today people accept that the earth is round, still the old paradigm that the earth is flat is useful. Similarly, in the religious sphere, every paradigm may be acceptable to its own respective adherents provided it helps people to lead a life of truth. Hence there is no question of superiority or inferiority of paradigms in religion. This is precisely the import of 'satyo-centrism.'

The superiority of one system or paradigm over another in terms of sophistication should never be mistaken for superiority of the religious life of one person to another's. For the doctrinal system in itself does not cause religious life, although it provides support for the thriving of religious life in the encircling gloom of doubts and queries. Hence, we may rightly conclude that it is not right to assume that only one kind of belief system can give rise to a life of religiosity. In fact, different belief systems arise not merely on account of different kinds of sophistication, but they are also the result of the life of religiosity in the sense of transcendence or attainment, which is substantially the same in the different communities of people. The different kinds of belief-systems, in turn, can give rise to eminently religious lives in the different communities. This is precisely what is implied by 'satyo-centric' approach to religions.

'Satyo-centrism,' if accepted, will also redefine the task of the theology of religions. To illustrate it again from Christianity, the disciples of Christ in the nascent Church were interested mainly in identifying Jesus of Nazareth (the particular individual who lived, preached and finally was crucified but rose from the dead on the third day) with Christ (the universal Lord, the Messiah, whom they expected to come and start a new reign). Having witnessed the resurrection event, and then recalling the various events that preceded this great experience, they began to consider him the Son of God. Obviously, their interpretation of Jesus and his impact on their communities was based on the circumstances in which they found themselves, on the expectations that they had of the Messiah and on the available theological apparatus. Needless to say, such an exercise had its own richness as well as limitations. Thus Jesus was seen as the suffering Messiah, as the Son of God, as the Word made flesh, etc. These types of elucidations demanded a greater commitment to the person of Jesus and a renunciation from the past wayward ways of living on the part of the disciples. Here there was no room for theorising; instead the disciples were busy living their lives according to the teachings of their Lord and Master, besides focusing on sharing this Good News with people of good will. In the process, the early Christian preachers came face to face with various religions, cults and cultures, but they desisted from caricaturing other faiths as false.

However, with the passage of time, several sham prophets initiated new heresies and false teachings in different quarters, which took their toll on the practical living of the Christian message. The subsequent acquisition of the status as a state religion in the Roman Empire helped Christianity to assume the role of a colonial religion. All these developments seem to have helped later Christianity to reverse the original understanding of the person of Jesus. The universal is now identified with the particular. In other words, they wanted to bracket the unknowable, ineffable, incomprehensible and all pervading reality of God in the person of Jesus of Nazareth. Jesus is not only the Lord but the Lord is to be found only in the person of Jesus negating every other instance of Lordships. But such an exercise, it seems, was unnecessary for various reasons.

This shift is merely a theoretical and rational exercise, which does not challenge the disciples to a greater commitment to their Christian living. In fact, the early Christians were not interested in such a shift as their interest was in the practical living of Christian message. Further, this new understanding of Jesus allowed the Christians to consider the worshippers of other religions as inferior or at least as anonymous Christians and they need to be brought into their Christian fold. The new trend not only added to the imperialistic designs of the Western mind but also opened the Pandora's Box on the relationships with other religious traditions. In fact, the Christian thinkers and ideologues caricatured other religions as the bastions of darkness and error. In order to save them from their ignorance, they need to be converted. As a consequence, a hostile, intolerant and confrontational relationship existed between Christians and the followers of other religious traditions.

Since the new understanding of equating the Universal Lord with the particular Jesus of Nazareth has not necessarily helped either in augmenting the personal commitment among the Christians in the person of Jesus Christ or in creating a congenial atmosphere among different religions, it is proposed that the Christians need to reverse their understanding and accept the original position, namely, that Jesus of Nazareth is the Son of God and not vice versa, as if God is represented solely in the person of Jesus of Nazareth.

This shift, of course, is in accordance with the original Christian understanding of the person of Jesus. Such a turnaround, it is hoped, will help in accepting the worth of other religions and in building up bridges of camaraderie with them. This will also help Christians in going back to the original understanding of their religion, namely, living a life of commitment to the person of Christ and to his teachings.

Besides, with the new perception of Jesus, Christians will be in a position to learn lessons in faith living found in other religious traditions. Obviously, this will result in a mutual enrichment of different religions paving the way for a complementarity of religions.

Therefore, universality of Jesus' Lordship is to be seen in missiological oneness and not merely in ontological oneness. The former identifies Jesus in his actual mission with God while the latter tries to identify the being of God with Jesus. In other words, the particular with the universal is possible and not the vice versa. Hence, as Aloysius Pieris would say, the singularity of Jesus the human being consists in the fact that he is the contradiction between Mammon and Yahweh, the defence pact between the oppressed and Yahweh. In him is revealed and embodied the contradiction which exists between God and the poor who are oppressed at the hands of the rich. Jesus thus seals God's covenant with the poor. Such a singularity is accessible to members of other religious traditions, but not the ontological oneness of the Word incarnate.

Further, it is precisely in identifying the particular with the universal that the early witnesses of Christ were able to see his uniqueness in terms of life-transformation and societal renovation. If this becomes the core of one's faith, then one can find the same point of reference in other religions as well. However, if one severs this core and shifts the question to a theoretical level by identifying the universal with this particular, then one not only misses the central element of Jesus' mission but also neglects the commonality of other religions. This is precisely here that Gandhi's 'satyo-centric' paradigm is seen as very valuable. It not only upholds specific uniqueness of Christian religion with reference to the core element of Jesus event and his mission but also provides for the possibility of mutual enrichment of religions.

In the light of 'satyo-centrism,' then, it is commendable on the part of the Christians first to get back to the original concerns of the early Christians and be satisfied with identifying the historical Jesus with the universal Lord and thereby learning from his actions of serving the poor, suffering for them, etc. and thus reliving the demands of the original experience of Christian faith. The task of theology of religions, does not consist in posing wrong questions - whether universal is particular and consequently trying to compare with other particulars. On the contrary, the task of theology of religions will be to comprehend the real core of the singularity and the real basis of early Christian confession, namely, the particular is universal (Jesus is the Lord) and apply that singularity to transformation of the individual and societal life in that context, and see how a similar confession of another 'particular is the universal' (for example, the Buddha is Lord) transforms life and the society of that context, and how these two different confessions are ultimately emphasising the chords of unity and cooperation and common responsibility between the different confessions of faith.

Thus, 'satyo-centric' theology of religions can pave the way for meaningful dialogue among religions. The interreligious dialogue, at the moment, is at crossroads. Everyone agrees that dialogue is an exchange of ideas among equals. But such equality eludes religions because each of them upholds certain unique features claiming superiority at the detriment of other religious traditions. But if 'satyo-centrism' is accepted in theology of religions, it is possible to dialogue because here each religion is a relative truth that lives in harmony with Religion, the Absolute Truth. The unique features do not show the superiority of any religion, but are meant to be lived in the lives of the followers in order to approximate to the Absolute Truth. Since the doctrines and beliefs that help religions to reach the Religion can vary, dialogue will enable religions to understand one another better. The claim of uniqueness will be understood in its proper perspective, never denigrating others for what they are and accusing them of not possessing what one claims as unique.

It is feasible for one to be rooted in the outlook of the past, and yet need not be bogged down by it, so as to suffer from historical relativism, rather one must be open to the signs of the times. While insisting upon the fundamentals of one's traditions one will never impose one formulation but rather accept and appreciate legitimate plurality of theological formulations even within one's own religious tradition.

Further, it is possible for one to make use of 'satyo-centrism' as a tool to thwart the communalistic use of religion – using religions for political, social, cultural and economic gains. According to 'satyo-centrism' the reason for the existence of religions is to effect life-transformation among their adherents. Each religious tradition should help its followers to approximate the Absolute Truth. It is not merely meant for theorizing or for gaining any sort of mileage over other groups. Gandhi himself echoed this when he humbly admitted that those who say that religion has nothing to do with politics (especially in the context of communalism) does not know the real meaning of religion. In fact, the truth-living that is proposed in different religions must sanctify every human institution including politics so that it can also become a means for humans to reach the Absolute Truth.

'Satyo-centrism' will also open up new vistas for the science of Comparative Religion. So far, Comparative Religion engaged itself in comparing doctrines, theologies, rituals, beliefs and practices of different religions. However, such comparisons can tempt the scholars to assert the superiority of one religion over another and this can cause unnecessary conflicts. Instead, if 'satyo-centric' understanding of religions is accepted then Comparative Religion will begin to compare religions on the basis of life-transformation that they can bring about among the followers and this life-transformation can be estimated from the lives of the saints that each religion produces. Hence, a new methodology will be available to the science of Comparative Religion as a result of this new theory.

Thus, in the 'satyo-centric' model, no religion can arrogate any superiority to itself and attribute an inferior status to other religions or treat others with a despairing attitude; instead, every religion will be enabled to be aware of its own imperfections in and through its contacts with other religions. By means of dialogue with them it can also learn about the other dimensions of one Religion, the various exemplars of pure and the saintly life of Attainment and Perfection. Besides, it can also incorporate all those features which can be accepted into its own tradition. Each religion will, thus, prove to be complementary to others. Thus, 'satyo-centrism' will contribute to a better understanding of interreligious relations and enhance it.

Finally, it must be borne in mind that the Gandhian perspective, in one sense, is not something new. Truth already existed as part of humanity eternally. The Gandhian contribution consisted only in grasping it and applying to every field of life in the minutest details. Gandhi himself did not claim to have originated any new principle or doctrine. He tried in his own way to apply the eternal truths to his daily life and problems. One of the main fields of his application is religious pluralism. The dissertation is precisely an attempt to grapple with that contribution and to present it systematically so as to provide the theology of religions with epistemological and metaphysical foundations.

SELECTED BIBLIOGRAPHY

Agnivesh, Swami. "The Church and Other Religions – A Hindu Perspective." *Yesu Krist Jayanti 2000: Towards a New Society.* Ed. Paul Puthanagaday. Bangalore: National Committee for Yesu Krist Jayanti 2000, 2001, 349-355.

Amaladoss, Michael. *Mission Today: Reflection From an Ignatian Perspective*. Anand: Gujarat Sahitya Prakash, 1989.

Amaladoss, Michael. *Making Harmony: Living in a Pluralist World.* Delhi: Indian Society for Promoting Christian Knowledge; Chennai: Institute of Dialogue with Cultures and Religions, 2003.

Ananthu, T.S. "Gandhi – Plus Truth and God." *Gandhi Marg.* 81 (April 1977), 100-105.

Andrew, C.F. *Mahatma Gandhi's Ideas*. London: George Allen and Unwin Ltd., 1930.

Ariarajah, S. Wesley. *Not Without My Neighbour: Issues in Interfaith Relations*. Geneva: WCC Publications, 1999.

Austin, J. L. "Truth." *Truth.* Ed. George Pitcher. New Jersey: Prentice Hall, Englewood Cliffs, 1964.

Barnes, Michael. *Religions in Conversation: Christian Identity and Religious Pluralism*. London: SPCK, 1989.

Barth, Karl. *Church Dogmatics*. Vol. 1, 2. Edinburgh: T & T. Clark, 1956.

Behn, Mira. *The Spirit's Pilgrimage*. Longmans: London, 1960.

Bloom, Allan. *The Closing of the American Mind.* New York: Simon & Schuster, 1987.

Bogliolo, Luigi. *Metaphysics*. Trans. Myroslaw A. Cizdyn. Bangalore: Theological Publications of India, 1987.

Bondurant, Joan V. *Conquest of Violence: The Gandhian Philosophy of Conflict*. Bombay: Oxford University Press, 1959.

Bosch, David. *Transforming Mission: Paradigm Shifts in theology of Mission*. Maryknoll: Orbis Books, 1991.

Bose, N.K. *My Days with Gandhi*. Calcutta: Indian Associated Publishing Company Ltd., 1953.

Bose, N.K. *Studies in Gandhism*. 2nd ed. Calcutta: Indian Associated Publishing Co., 1947.

Chander, Jag Parvesh, ed. *Teachings of Mahatma Gandhi*. Lahore: The Indian Printing Works, 1945.

Cobb, John. *Beyond Dialogue: Toward a Mutual Transformation of Christianity and Buddhism*. Philadelphia: Fortress Press, 1982.

Congar, Yves. "Christian Theology." *The Encyclopedia of Religion*. Trans. Mathew J. O'Connell. Ed. Mircea Eliade. Vol. 14. New York: Macmillan Publishing Company, 1987, 455-464.

Costas, Orlando E. "A Radical Evangelical Contribution from Latin America." *Christ's Lordship & Religious Pluralism*. Eds. Gerald H. Anderson and Thomas F. Stranksy. New York, Maryknoll: Orbis Books, 1981, 133-156.

Cox, Harvey. *Many Mansions: A Christian's Encounter with Other Faiths*. Boston: Beacon Press, 1988.

D'Costa, Gavin. *Theology and Religious Pluralism: The Challenge of Other Religions*. Oxford: Basil Blackwell, 1986.

Divarkar, Parmananda R. *The Act of Being: A Centenary Tribute to Thomas Aquinas*. Bombay: The New Man Institute, 1973.

Diwakar, R.R. "Gandhi: From 'God is Truth' to 'Truth is God.'" *Gandhi Marg* (Feb 1983), 617-626.

Diwakar, R.R. Saga *of Satyagraha*. 2nd ed. New Delhi: Gandhi Peace Foundation, 1969.

Dupuis, Jacques. *Toward a Christian Theology of Religious Pluralism*. Anand: Gujarat Sahitya Prakash, 2001.

Erikson, H. Erik. *Gandhi's Truth: On the Origins of Militant Non-violence*. New York: W.W. Norton & Co., 1969.

Fenton, John. *Finding the Way through John*. London: Cassell Mowbray, 1995.

Fitzgerald, Michael L. and Machado, Felix A. "Emerging Christian Theology of Religions." *Pro Dialogo Bulletin*. 3 (2002) 3, 313-324.

Gandhi, Arun, ed. *World Without Violence: Can Gandhi's Vision Become Reality*? New Delhi: New Age International (P) Limited, 1995.

Gandhi, M.K. *All Religions are True*. Ed. Anand T. Hingorani. Bombay: Bharatiya Vidya Bhavan, 1962.

Gandhi, M.K. *An Autobiography (The Story of my experiments with truth)*. Trans. Mahadev Desai. Reprint 1996. Ahmedabad: Navajivan Publishing House, 1927.

Gandhi, M.K. *Christian Missions: Their Place in India*. Ed. Bharatan Kumarappa. Reprint 1960. Ahmedabad: Navajivan Publishing House, 1941.

Gandhi, M.K. *Constructive Programme: Its Meaning and Place*. Ahmedabad: Navajivan Publishing House, 1945.

Gandhi, M.K. *Ethical Religion*. Madras: S. Ganesan and Co., 1938.

Gandhi, M.K. *From Yeravda Mandir: Ashram Observances*. Trans. Valji Govindji. Ahmedabad: Navajivan Publishing House, 1932.

Gandhi, M.K. *Hindu Dharma*. New Delhi: Orient Paperbacks, 1995.

Gandhi, M.K. *In Search of the supreme*. Ed. V.B. Kher. Vol. 1. Ahmedabad: Navajivan Publishing House, 1961.

Gandhi, M.K. *In Search of the Supreme*. Ed. V.B. Kher. Vol. 2. Ahmedabad: Navajivan Publishing House, 1961.

Gandhi, M.K. *In Search of the Supreme*. Ed. V.B. Kher. Vol. 3. Ahmedabad: Navajivan Publishing House, 1962.

Gandhi, M.K. *India of My Dreams*. 6th reprint. Ahmedabad: Navajivan Publishing House, 1997.

Gandhi, M.K. *My God*. Ahmedabad: Navajivan Publishing House, 1999.

Gandhi, M.K. *Nature Cure*. Ed. Bharatan Kumarappa. 10th reprint. Ahmedabad: Navajivan Publishing House, 1997.

Gandhi, M.K. *Panchayat Raj*. Ahmedabad: Navajivan Publishing House, 1959.

Gandhi, M.K. *Path Way to God*. Comp. M.S. Deshpande. Ahmedabad: Navajivan Publishing House, 1971.

Gandhi, M.K. *Ramanama*. Ahmedabad: Navajivan Publishing House, 1949.

Gandhi, M.K. *Speeches and Writings of Mahatma Gandhi*. 4th ed. Madras: Natesan, n.d.

Gandhi, M.K. *Temples and Mosques*. Bangalore: Karnataka Gandhi Smaraka Nidhi, 1993.

Gandhi, M.K. *The Message of the Gita*. Ahmedabad: Navajivan Publishing House, 1996.

Gandhi, M.K. *The Message of Jesus Christ*. Ed. Anand T. Hingorani. Bombay: Bharatiya Vidya Bhavan, 1986.

Gandhi, M.K. *The Moral Basis of Vegetarianism*. Ahmedabad: Navajivan Publishing House, 1995.

Gandhi, M.K. *The Selected Works of Mahatma Gandhi – The Voice of Truth*. Ed. Shriman Narayan. Vol. 6. 4th reprint. Ahmedabad: Navajivan publishing House, 1997.

Gandhi, M.K. *The Teachings of the Gita*. Ed. Anand T. Hingorani. Bombay: Bharatiya Vidya Bhavan, 1971.

Gandhi, M.K. *Trusteeship*. Comp. Ravindra Kelekar. Ahmedabad: Navajivan Publishing House, 1960.

Gandhi, M.K. *Truth is God (Gleanings from the writings of Mahatma Gandhi bearing on God, God-Realization and the Godly way)*. Ed. R.K. Prabhu. 11th reprint. Ahmedabad: Navajivan Publishing House, 1998.

Gilby, T. "Theology." *Encyclopedic Dictionary of Religion*. Ed. Paul Kevin Meagher. Vol. O-Z. Washington: Corpus Publication, 1979, 3497-3499.

Gispert-Sauch G. "Theology of Religions: A Review Article." *Vidyajyoti*. 49 (October 1985) 9, 465-474.

Gomes, Anastio. "Theology of Non-Christian Religions." *Indian Ecclesiastical Studies*. 12 (February 1973) 1, 3-21.

Gordis, David. "John Paul II and the Jews." *John Paul II and Interreligious Dialogue*. Eds. Byron L. Sherwin and Harold Kasimow. Maryknoll: Orbis Press, 1999.

Grelle, Bruce. "Scholarship and Citizenship: Comparative Religious Ethicists as Public Intellectuals." *Explorations in Global Ethics: Comparative Religious Ethics and Interreligious Dialogue*. Eds. Sumner B. Twiss and Bruce Grelle. Boulder, Colorado: Westview Press, 1998.

Gutierrez, Gustavo. *A Theology of Liberation*. Mary Knoll, New York: Orbis Books, 1973.

Hick, John and Paul Knitter, eds. "Towards a Liberation Theology of Religions." *The Myth of Christian Uniqueness: Towards a Pluralistic Theology of Religions*. Maryknoll, NY: Orbis Books, 1987.

Hick, John. "Jesus and the World Religions." *The Myth of God Incarnate*. Ed. John Hick. London: SCM Press, 1977.

Hick, John. "On Grading Religions." *Religious Studies*. 17 (1981), 451-67.

Hick, John. "Pluralism and the Reality of the Transcendent." *Christian Century*. 98 (1981).

Hick, John. *An Interpretation of Religion: Human Response to Transcendent*. London: Macmillan Press Ltd., 1989.

Hick, John. *God and the Universe of Faiths*. New York: St. Martin's press, 1973.

Hick, John. *God Has Many Names*. Philadelphia: Westminster, 1982.

Hick, John. *The Center of Christianity*. New York: Harper & Row, 1978.

Hick, John. *The Metaphor of God Incarnate*. London: SCM Press, 1993.

Hick, John. *The Rainbow of Faiths: Critical Dialogues on Religious Pluralism*. London: SCM Press, 1995.

Hick, John. *The Second Christianity*. London: XPress Ltd., 1994.

Hill, William J. "Theology." *The New Dictionary of Theology*. Eds. Joseph A. Kamonchak, Mary Collins and Dermot A. Lane. Bangalore: Theological Publications of India, 1994, 1011-1027.

James, William. *Pragmatism.* New York: McKay, 1907.

John Ferguson. *Religions of the Roman Empire*. Ithaca: Cornell University Press, 1970.

Justin Martyr. "The First Apology." *Writings of Saint Justin Martyr*. Trans. Thomas B. Falls. New York: Christian Heritage, Inco., 1948.

Karokaran, Anto. "Raymond Panikkar's Theology of Religions: A Critique." *Vidyajyoti.* 58 (October 1994) 10, 663-672.

Kasper, Walter. *Jesus the Christ.* London: Burns and Oates, 1976.

Kaufmann, Gordon. *God the Problem.* Cambridge, MA: Harvard University Press, 1972.

Knitter, Paul F. "Between a Rock and a Hard Place: Pluralistic Theology Faces the Ecclesial and Academic Communities." *Journal of Theology* (Summer, 1997).

Knitter, Paul F. "Catholic Theology of Religions at the Crossroads." *Christianity among World Religions. Concilium.* 183 (1986) 1, 99-107.

Knitter, Paul F. "Catholics and Other Religions: Bridging the Gap Between Dialogue and theology." *Louvain Studies.* 24 (1999), 319-54.

Knitter, Paul F. "Theocentric Christology: Defended and Transcended." *Journal of Ecumenical Studies.* 24 (Winter 1987), 41-52.

Knitter, Paul F. *No Other Name? A Critical Survey of Christian Attitudes Toward the World Religions*. London: SCM Press Ltd., 1985.

Knitter, Paul F. "New Pentecost?" *Current Dialogue.* 19 (1991), 32-41.

Knitter, Paul F. *One Earth, Many Religions: Multifaith Dialogue and Global Responsibility*. Maryknoll: Orbis Press, 1995.

Knitter, Paul F. "The Abiding Task of the Church in Mission to Proclaim the Uniqueness of Jesus." *The Church in Mission: Universal Mandate and Local Concerns.* Eds. Thomas Malipurathu and L. Stanislaus. Anand: Gujarat Sahitya Prakash, 2002, 117-146.

Kripalani, J.B. Gandhi*: His Life and Thought*. Builders of Modern Indian Series. Ed. R.R. Diwakar, Rev. ed. New Delhi: Publications Division,

Ministry of Information and Broadcasting, Government of India, 1991.

Kripalani, K., ed. *All Men are Brothers*. Ahmedabad: Navajivan Publishing House, 1960.

Kumarappa, Bharatan, ed. *How to Serve the Cow*. Ahmedabad: Navajivan Press, 1959.

Kumarappa, Bharatan, *My Religion.* Ahmedabad; Navajivan Publishing House, 1976.

Küng, Hans. *Theology for the Third Millennium: An Ecumenical View*. Trans. Peter Heinegg. New York: Doubleday, 1988.

Kuttianimattathil, Jose. "Jesus the Eminent Dialogue Partner." *Vidyajyoti*. 66 (July 2002), 7, 506-523.

Leith, John H., ed. *Creeds of the Churches*. 3rd ed. Atlanta: John Knox Press, 1982.

Lochhead, David. *The Dialogical Imperative: A Christian Reflection on Interfaith Encounter*. London: SCM Press, 1998.

Lonergan, Bernard. *Method in Theology*. London: Darton, Longman and Todd, 1975.

Maimonides, Moses. *Guide to the Perplexed* (12th century). Trans. M. Friedlander, 2nd ed. London: Routledge & Kegan Paul, 1940.

Maritain, Jacques. *Preface to Metaphysics*. London: Sheed and Ward, 1939

Martinson, Paul Varo. *A Theology of world Religions: Interpreting God, self and world in Semitic, Indian and Chinese Thought*. Minneapolis: Augsburg Publishing House, 1987.

Martinson, Paul Varo. *A Theology of world Religions: Interpreting God, self and world in Semitic, Indian and Chinese Thought.* Minneapolis: Augsburg Publishing House, 1987.

Mathews, James K. *The Matchless Weapon Satyagraha*. Bombay: Bharatiya Vidya Bhavan, 1989.

Mundadan, A.M. *Paths of Indian Theology*. Bangalore: Dharmaram Publications, 1998.

Nag, Kalidas. *Tolstoy and Gandhi*. Patna: Pustak Bhandar, 1950.

Narayan, Shriman, ed. *The Selected Works of Mahatma Gandhi: Selected Letters*. Vol. 5. Ahmedabad: Navajivan Publishing House, 1968.

Narayan, Shriman, ed. *The Selected Words of Mahatma Gandhi*. Ahmedabad: Navajivan Publishing House, 1968.

Nayar, Sushila. *Mahatma Gandhi – Satyagraha at Work*. Vol. 4. Ahmedabad: Navajivan Publishing House, 1989.

Nayar, Sushila. *Mahatma Gandhi, Final Fight for Freedom*. Vol. 8. Ahmedabad: Navajivan Publishing House, 1997.

Nayar, Sushila. *Mahatma Gandhi, India Awakened*. Vol. 5. Ahmedabad: Navajivan Publishing House, 1994.

Nayar, Sushila. *Mahatma Gandhi, Preparing for Swaraj*. Vol. 7. Ahmedabad: Navajivan Publishing House, 1996.

Nayar, Sushila. *Mahatma Gandhi, Salt Satyagraha – The Watershed*. Vol. 6. Ahmedabad: Navajivan Publishing House, 1995.

Netland, Harold A. *Dissonant Voices: Religious Pluralism and the Question of Truth*. Grand Rapids, Michigan: William B. Eerdmans Publishing Company, 1991.

Neuner, J. "The Place of World Religions in Theology." *The Clergy Monthly*. 32 (March, 1968) 3, 102-115.

Newbigin, Lesslie. *Foolishness to the Greeks: The Gospel and Western Culture*. Grand Rapids: Eerdmans, 1986.

Nicholson, R. A. *Mystics of Islam*. 1914. London and Boston: Routledge & Kegan Paul, 1963.

O'Connor, Daniel. *Relations in Religion*. Bangalore: Allied Publishers, 1994.

Ott, Heinrich. "The dialogue Between the Religions as a Contemporary Theological Responsibility." *Dialogue in Community: Essays in honour of S. J. Samartha*. Ed. C. D. Jathanna. Mangalore: Karnataka Theological Research Institute, 1982.

Painadath, Sebastian. "Theologising As Doing Mission – Inter Religious Hermeneutics in Theology." *Third Millennium: Indian Journal of Evangelisation*. 4 (October-December, 2001), 6-24.

Panikkar, Raimundo. "Have 'Religions' the Monopoly on Religion?" *Journal of Ecumenical Studies*. 11 (1974), 515-517.

Panikkar, Raimundo. "Hermeneutics of Comparative Religion: Paradigms and Models." *Journal of Dharma.* 5 (January – March 1980) 1, 38-51.

Panikkar, Raimundo. "The Meaning of Christ's Name in the Universal Economy of Salvation." *Evangelization, Dialogue, and Development.* Ed. Mariasusai Dhavamony. Rome: Gregorian University Press, 1972, 195-218.

Panikkar, Raimundo. *The Intrareligious Dialogue.* New York; Paulist Press,1978.

Panikkar, Raimundo. *The Unknown Christ of Hinduism.* Rev. ed. Maryknoll, New York: Orbis, 1981.

Panikkar, Raimundo. *Trinity and the Religious Experience of Man.* Maryknoll: Orbis Press, 1975.

Pannenberg, Wolfhart. "Religious Pluralism and Conflicting Truth-Claims." *The Myth of Christian Uniqueness Reconsidered: the Myth of a Pluralistic Theology of Religions.* Ed. Gavin D'Costa. Maryknoll: Orbis Press and London SCM Press, 1987.

Pathil, K., ed. *Religious Pluralism: An Indian Christian Perspective.* Delhi: ISPCK, 1991.

Pathrapankal, Joseph. "Making Disciples" (Mt. 28: 18-19) in the Early Church and its Contemporary Challenges." *Third Millennium.* 5 (October – December, 2002) 4, 6–25.

Pattery, George. *Gandhi – The Believer: An Indian Christian Perspective.* Delhi: ISPCK, 1996.

Pelikan, Jaroslav. *Jesus Through the Centuries: His Place in the History of Culture.* New Haven: Yale University Press, 1985.

Phan, Peter C. "The Claim of Uniqueness and Universality in Interreligious Dialogue." *Indian Theological Studies.* 31 (March 1994) 1, 44-66.

Pieris, Aloysius. "An Asian Paradigm: Interreligious Dialogue and Theology of Religions." *Month.* 26 (1993), 129-134.

Pieris, Aloysius. "Inculturation in Asia: A Theological Reflection on an Experience." *Jahrbuch für kontextuelle Theologien.* Frankfurt: Verlag fur Interkulturelle Kommunikation, 1994, 59-71.

Pieris, Aloysius. "Universality of Christianity." *Vidyajyoti.* 57 (1993), 591-595.

Pieris, Aloysius. *An Asian Theology of Liberation.* Maryknoll, New York: Orbis Books, 1988.

Plato. *The Works of Plato.* Trans. Jowet. Ed. I. Edman. New York: Modern Library, 1928.

Pushparajan, A. "A Gandhian Blueprint for Interreligious Cooperation in India." *Kristu Jyoti.* 6 (March, 1990) 1, 16-43.

Pushparajan, A. "Are Religions One?" *Journal of Gandhian Studies.* 14 (January-April 1987) 54-55, 148-163.

Pushparajan, A. "Dialogue: Crisis and Solution." *Mission Today.* 4 (July-September, 2002) 3, 177-206.

Pushparajan, A. "The Christian Encounter with Indian Culture." *Indian Missiological Review.* 9 (January 1987), 1, 8-23.

Pushparajan, A. *From Conversion to Fellowship: The Hindu-Christian Encounter in the Gandhian Perspective.* Dialogue Series No. 6. Allahabad: St. Paul's Publications, 1990.

Pushparajan, A. "Gandhi's Concept of Truth: An Epistemological Foundation For Theology of Religions." Madurai: unpublished article.

Pushparajan, A. "*Gandhi's Contributions to a Trans-religious Understanding of God.*" *Shepherd's Voice.* 1 (October – December 2002) 4, 344 – 366.

Pushparajan, A. "Resolution of an Intra-personal Conflict in a Multi-religious Context." Madurai: unpublished article.

Putti, Joseph. *Theology as Hermeneutics.* Bangalore: Kristu Jyoti Publication, 1991.

Pyarelal. *Mahatma Gandhi – Early Phase.* Vol. 1. Ahmedabad: Navajivan Publishing House, 1986.

Pyarelal. *Mahatma Gandhi – The Birth of Satyagraha – From Petitioning to Passive Resistance.* Vol. 3. Ahmedabad: Navajivan Publishing House, 1986.

Pyarelal. *Mahatma Gandhi – The Discovery of Satyagraha – On the Threshold.* Vol. 2. Ahmedabad: Navajivan Publishing House, 1997.

Pyarelal. *Mahatma Gandhi, The Last Phase*. Vol. 10. Part 2. 2nd reprint. Ahmedabad: Navajivan Publishing House, 1997.

Pyarelal. *Mahatma Gandhi, The Last Phase.* Vol. 9. Book 2. Part I. 2nd reprint. Ahmedabad: Navajivan Publishing House, 1997.

Pyarelal. *Mahatma Gandhi, The Last Phase*. Vol. 9. Book I. Part I. 2nd reprint. Ahmedabad: Navajivan Publishing House, 1997.

Race, Alan. *Christians and Religious Pluralism*. 2nd ed. London: SCM Press and Maryknoll, New York, 1994.

Race, Alan. *Interfaith Encounter: The Twin Tracks of Theology and Dialogue*. London: SCM Press, 2001.

Radhakrishnan, S. *Eastern Religions and Western Thought*. 2nd ed. London: Oxford University Press, 1940.

Radhakrishnan, S., ed. *Mahatma Gandhi: Essays and Reflections on His Life and Work*. London: Allen & Unwin Ltd., 1939.

Rahner, Karl. *Theological Investigations*. 23 vols. London: Darton, Longman & Todd, 1961-1992.

Rambachan, Anantanand. "Swami Vivekananda: A Hindu Model for Interreligious Dialogue." *Inter-Religious Dialogue: Voices from a New Frontier*. Eds. M. Darrol Bryant and Frank Flinn. New York: Paragon House, 1989.

Rao, K.L. Seshagiri. "On Truth: A Hindu Perspective." Philosophy East and West. 20 (October, 1970) 4, 377-384.

Rayan, Samuel. "Theologian As Disciple – Disciple As Theologian." *Third Millennium: Indian Journal of Evangelisation*. 4(October-December, 2001), 100-106.

Richard, Lucien. *What are they Saying about Christ and World Religions*. New York: Paulist Press, 1981.

Roberts, A. and J. Donalson, eds. *The Ante-Nicene Fathers*. Vol. 2. Grand Rapids, Michigan: Eerdmans, 1979.

Samartha, Stanley J. *Between Two Cultures: Ecumenical Ministry in a Pluralist World*. Geneva: World Council of Churches Publications, 1996.

Samartha, Stanley J. "The Lordship of Jesus and Religious Pluralism." *Christ's Lordship & Religious Pluralism*. Eds. Gerald H. Anderson and Thomas F. Stranksy. New York, Maryknoll: Orbis Books, 1981, 19-36.

Saraswati, Dayananda. 'It's Conquest, not conversion: Planting the Cross." *The New Indian Express*. 6-10-2000.

Schillebeeckx, Edward. *Church: The Human Story of God*. London: SCM Press, 1990.

Schwöbel, Christoph. "Particularity, Universality, and the Religions," *Christian Uniqueness Reconsidered: The Myth of a Pluralistic theology of Religions*. Ed. Gavin D'Costa. Maryknoll: Orbis Books, 1990.

Selvanayagam, Israel. "Re-reading John 14:6 in the Context of Two Recent Events in the United Kingdom." *Current Dialogue*. 40 (December 2002), 44-51.

Shapiro, Rabbi Rami Mark. "Moving the Fence: One Rabbi's View of Interreligious Dialogue." *Interreligious Dialogue: Voices from a New Frontier*. Eds. M. Darrol Bryant and Frank Flinn. New York: Paragon House, 1989.

Sherwin, Byron L. and Harold Kasimow, eds. *John Paul II and Interreligious Dialogue*. Maryknoll: Orbis Press, 1999.

Stendahl, Krister. "Notes for Three Bible Studies." *Christ's Lordship and Religious Pluralism*. Eds. Gerald H. Anderson and Thomas F. Stranskey. Maryknoll, New York: Orbis, 1981.

Streng, Frederick J. "Truth." *The Encyclopaedia of Religion*. Ed. Mircea Eliade. Vol. 15. New York: Macmillan Publishing Company, 1987, 63-72.

Tao Te Ching. Trans. Ch'u Ta-Kao. London and Boston: Mandala Books, 1982.

Tendulkar, D.G. *Mahatma*. Vol. 2. Bombay: Jhaveri and Tendulkar, 1952.

Thachil, Jose. "Theology of Religions and Sacrifice." *Journal of Dharma*. 14 (October – December 1989) 3, 329-342.

The Collected Works of Mahatma Gandhi. 92 vols. New Delhi: The Publications Divisions of the Government of India, 1951-7.

Thekkinedatu, J. *Love of Neighbour in Mahatma Gandhi.* Alwaye: Pontifical Institute of Theology and Philosophy, 1973.

Tillich, Paul. *Dynamics of Faith.* New York: Harper & Brothers, 1957.

Tillich, Paul. *The Courage to Be.* New Haven: Yale University Press, 1952.

Tolstoy, Leo. *The Kingdom of God is Within You.* Trans. A Delano. London: Walter Scott Ltd., 1894.

Tracy, David. *Dialogue with the Other: The Inter-Religious Dialogue.* Louvain: Peeters Press and Grand Rapids: Eerdmans, 1990.

Trigg, Roger. "Religion and the Threat of Relativism." *Religious Studies.* 19 (1983).

Troelstch, Ernest. *Christian Thought: Its History and Application.* Ed. F. Von Hugel. New York: Living Age Books, 1957.

Vineeth, V.F. "Committed to Christ & Open to all Religion: Theology as a Story of My Life." *Third Millennium: Indian Journal of Evangelisation.* 4 (October-December 2001), 22-32.

Whitson, Roberly E. *The Coming Convergence of World Religions.* New York: Newman, 1971.

Wilfred, Felix. "Some Tentative Reflections on the Language of Christian Uniqueness: An Indian Perspective." *Pro Dialogo Bulletin.* 85-86/1, 1994, 40-57.

Wittgenstein, Ludwig. *Philosophical Investigations.* 1953. Trans. G. E. M. Anscombe. Oxford: Basil Blackwell, 1963.

Wittgenstein, Ludwig. *Tractatus logico-philosophicus.* Eds. D.F. Pears and B.F. McGuinness. London: Routledge and Kegan Paul, 1961.

Zimmer, Heinrich. *Philosophies of India.* New York: Pantheon Books, 1951.

Index

A

Absolute truth, 92
Advaita, 52, 91
Advaita vedanta, 62
Advaitic, 136
Ahimsa, 113, 115, 116, 117, 118, 130, 134
Ananda, 99
Anekantavada, 91
Apara vidya, 62
Ashram, 123, 134
Ashramites, 120, 125
Ashraya, 99
Assumptio Carnis, 179
Attributes of good, 98
Aut-aut, 76
Autobiography, 26, 110

B

Beyond the present paradigms 75
Bhagavad-gita, 121
Bhakti, 104
Brahma satyam jaganmitya, 104
Brahmacharaya, 125, 127, 143
Brahman, 90, 100
Bread labour, 128
Brhadaranyka Upanishad, 93, 94
Brhaman, 100

C

Chandogya, 93
Charkha, 90, 143
Chaturmas, 88
Chit, 99
Christological concerns 173-174
Christological pluralism, 191
Civilization: Its Cause and Cure, 141
Closing of the American Mind, 45
Conditions for non-violence, 114
Context of the problem, 1
Contributing factor of pluralism, 54
Control of the palate, 127
Conversion to Fellowship, 25
Corpus, 66
Crown of Wild Olive, 121

D

Devadhideva, 165
Dharma, 94, 203
Dharmakaya, 61
Dialogue and Proclamation, 175
Discipline for Satyagraha, 130
Dvaita, 91

E

Effects of truth on Gandhi, 107
Eschatological method, 11
Exclusivism 41

Existent, 22
Existential method, 10
Extra ecclesiam nulla salus, 16

F

Fasting, 133
Fearlessness, 127

G

Gandhian perspective, 25
Gita, 128, 131, 164, 165, 166
God and the Universe of Faiths, 60
God who Loves and Takes the Side of Victims, 189
Guidelines on Dialogue, 175

H

Harijan, 26, 98, 101, 111, 140
Harijans, 140
Harishchandra, 88
Hermeneutics, 11
Hick, John, 60
Himsa, 116
Hind swaraj, 26, 141
Hindu-christian encounter, 25
Hominis redemptor, 49
Humility, 130

I

I am He, 94
Inclusivism, 46
Indian Opinion, 120, 130, 145
Influences, 87
Inner Voice, 104
Ishvara, 95, 165
Ism, 221

K

Karmayogin, 26
Kerygma, 10
Khadi, 143
Kingdom of god is within you, 121
Konfesionskunde, 9
Koran, 166

L

Liberation theology, 13
Light of Asia, 166
Linguistic analysis, 12
Logos spermatikos, 46
Logos, 179

M

Mahatma Gandhi's ideas, 202
Maya, 100
Means and ends 118
Methodology adopted in arriving at the solution 24
Moksha, 104, 112, 113
Monadology, 21
Mother India, 112

N

Nai Talim, 144
Nam, 90
Nature, 23
Navajivan, 110
Neti, neti, 93, 100
Nirguna, 61
Nirmanakaya, 61
Non-possession, 126
Non-stealing, 125
Non-violence as means to realize truth, 112

O

Objections of pluralism, 65
Organon, 7

P

Panikkar 58

Para vidya, 62

Pararthika satta, 62

Parmenides, 17

Particularity, 175

Pluralism, 50

Pneuma, 71

Possible solution to the problem 20

Pradosha, 170

Pratityasamutpada, 185

Prayer, 131

Pre-requisites for *satyagraha*, 123

Process thought, 12

Puja, 217

R

Ramanama, 94, 130, 132

Ramzan, 170

Reality with truth, 23

Relative truth, 101

Religio, 203

Religion, paradigm and model, 40

Religious pluralism 194

Religious plurality and emergence of the theology of religions, 2

Gandhian perspective, 164

Removal of untouchability, 127

Repetition of *Ramanama*, 132

Rise of other paradigms, 70

Rta, 93

Rupa, 90

S

Sacrifice, 130

Sadagraha, 120

Saguna, 61

Sambhogakaya, 61

Sarvodaya, 26, 139, 140

Sat or satya, 92, 93, 94, 96

Sat-chit-ananda, 99

Sata (the truth of Gandhi's conception), 87

Satori, 62

Satya, 92, 93, 217-225

Satyagraha, 103, 107, 120, 121, 122, 123, 124, 130, 131, 132, 133, 135, 144, 146

Satyagraha ashram, 124

Satyagrahi, 97, 117, 121, 123, 124, 127, 130, 131, 131, 133, 135, 145

Satyo-Centred theology of religions 173

Relational 182

Representative 183

Theocentric 186

Truth-living 190

uniqueness of Christ 176

– – Constitutive 180

– – Liberative 190

– – Live Encounter 189

– – Metaphorical 184

– – Ontic 181

satyo-centrism applied to christological pluralism 191

religious pluralism 194

Satyo-centrism through Meta-religion 200

Satyo-centrism, 163-215

Silence, 135

Sophist, 17

Soteria, 71

Star, 123

Statement of the problem, 13

Structure of scientific revolutions, 40
Sunyata, 62
Swadeshi, 124, 129
Swadeshism, 129
Swaraj, 138
Syadvada, 91, 169

T

Tapas, 104
Theocentric, 187
Theologia, 6, 7
Theologians on pluralism
  John Hick, 60
  Panikkar, 58
Theology and its diverse methods, 6
Theology and religious pluralism, 43, 65
Theology of religions, 39
Towards a 'satyo-centred' theology of religions, 173
Transcendental anthropology, 11
Transformative, 69
Truth, 22, 124
Truth applied to fields of action, 136
  Truth in Economics 142
  – – Education 143
  – – Journalism 144
  – – Politics 136
  – – Social Realm 139
Truth by Nature, 23
Truth in economics, 142
– – education, 143
– – journalism, 144
– – politics, 136
– – social realm, 139

U

Uncovers, 183
Unity of religions, 128
Universality, 175
Unto this Last, 122, 139

V

Vishya, 99
Vyavaharika satta, 62

W

What is truth, 92
  Absolute Truth 92
  Attributes of God 98
  Inner Voice 104
  Relative Truth 101

Y

Yeravda Mandir Gandhi and Truth, 124
Young India, 26, 119